Accolades for *My Second University*

"I have a single wish: Never again shall a generation live through what mine has. Documenting the truth is the first preventive step. Therein lies the value of *My Second University*."

—Lena Constante, author of *The Silent Escape: Three Thousand Days in Romanian Prisons*

"*My Second University* is very well written, the translation is clear and concise, and the photographs are well chosen. Dr. Stanciu Stroia's fortitude is astonishing. The interweaving of the descriptions of his arrest, trial, and imprisonment with explanatory notes in the text is effective. The information in the notes is accurate and essential for an understanding of events and their significance. *My Second University* has an important place in the prison literature published since 1989."

—Keith Hitchins, Professor of History, University of Illinois at Champaign-Urbana

"*My Second University* is an utterly impressive prison memoir. The tone is dispassionate, the analysis is rigorous, the information is uniquely important, and the notes are very useful. It is a most necessary and valuable contribution to our understanding of Romania's penitentiary universe, the state-controlled mechanisms of terror and intimidation, and the survival of human dignity under conditions of abysmal pressure."

—Vladimir Tismăneanu, Professor of Government and Politics, University of Maryland at College Park

"*My Second University* is a genuine lesson in life; a treasure of information; a testimony for future generations. Its importance is enhanced by the paucity of similar materials and the fact that if it were absent, a piece of history that should never be forgotten would be lost. Dr. Stanciu Stroia fulfilled his duties during life and as these pages attest, continues to do so after death. Not for a personal statue did he write his memories; his contemporaries have already erected one for him in their hearts."

—Ioan Ciupea, Professor of History,
National Museum of Transylvanian History

"Dr. Stanciu Stroia's Communist prison memoir is a welcomed addition to the American publishing landscape for two reasons: First, the Western world knows little about this somber chapter in Romania's history; and second, it adds another voice to a relative few. Dr. Stanciu Stroia was part of a generation that worked hard to succeed, fought during two world wars, believed in human virtues, and lived by example. The Soviet-imposed Communist regime shattered his life. Through *My Second University*, he tells us what happened, avoiding the danger posed by not knowing the truth."

—Floricel Marinescu, Professor of History and
Romanian State Chancellor (1998–2000)

"The life of a remarkable personality is entwined with that of a region. Such was the case with Dr. Stanciu Stroia and Făgăraș County. He became an unsurprising target of the Communist purge, and his story of suffering and dignity needs to be told. Publishing *My Second University* is not only a good deed, but represents a historical necessity."

—Ion Gavrilă-Ogoranu, former anti-Communist partisan and
author of *Pine Trees Break, They Do Not Bend*

"Most people learn about Communism and its horrible prisons, but few understand what it meant for the Romanian people in general and for those who opposed it in particular. It is an honorable duty to make the vicissitudes of our country known to the world, together with the virtues of its persecuted constituents. Therefore, I recommend *My Second University* wholeheartedly. The passage of time is modern man's worst enemy; anyone in possession of similarly valuable material should follow Dr. Dan Duşleag's example and publish it."

—Alexandru Ionescu, former political prisoner

"*My Second University* contains moving passages and concentrated teachings, aimed at transmitting the author's deep-reaching human experience. Dr. Stanciu Stroia's words are never bitter in spite of the injustice suffered; his moral values are clear, offering him support in adversity. The details describing life in Communist prisons and the dangers awaiting responsible citizens in the Romanian society of the late '40s and early '50s give the measure of the tragedy that struck that generation. The lists of names at the end of the book show that many others suffered in similar ways or lost their lives, caught in the social experiment that imposed the Communist dictatorship onto the democratic society of pre-World War II Romania."

—Lidia Gheorghiu Bradley, Founder,
Aspera Educational Foundation of Boston

"A distinguished medical personality, Dr. Stanciu Stroia endured with stoicism the injustices of his time. An original memoir, *My Second University* is a publishing event that restores precious files of history."

—*Tribuna* (Sibiu, Romania)

"*My Second University* is written with pain, not abhorrence, and with the serenity conferred by suffering and love. As the reader submerges himself in its pages, he becomes witness to the art of true and honest living at a time when beautiful living was not possible. Dr. Stanciu Stroia's family escaped this dark tunnel of history with the awareness that the tragic events endured should not be forgotten. The rebirth of our nation depends on this remembrance."

—*Euphorion* (Sibiu, Romania)

"*My Second University* will take readers back to another place in time, in another country, seeing life through the eyes of a courageous man and others who chose to suffer rather than give up their freedom. It brings to light a time, place, and people who were the unfortunate victims of an extreme government—a government that made every effort to sequester and silence any attempts to tell the tales of torture, discrimination, and malice inflicted on nonconforming citizens. *My Second University* is a piece of history necessary to consume, necessary to remember."

—*Times Mail* (Bedford, Indiana)

"*My Second University* is a labor of love."

—*WBIW* (Bedford, Indiana)

My Second University

My Second University

Memories from Romanian Communist Prisons

Stanciu Stroia, M.D.
1904–1987

Translation, Introduction and Notes
Dan L. Duşleag, M.D.

iUniverse, Inc.
New York Lincoln Shanghai

My Second University
Memories from Romanian Communist Prisons

Copyright © 2005 by Dan Liviu Duşleag

All rights reserved. No part of this book may be used or reproduced by any means, graphic, electronic, or mechanical, including photocopying, recording, taping or by any information storage retrieval system without the written permission of the publisher except in the case of brief quotations embodied in critical articles and reviews.

iUniverse books may be ordered through booksellers or by contacting:

iUniverse
2021 Pine Lake Road, Suite 100
Lincoln, NE 68512
www.iuniverse.com
1-800-Authors (1-800-288-4677)

ISBN-13: 978-0-595-34639-4 (pbk)
ISBN-13: 978-0-595-79385-3 (ebk)
ISBN-10: 0-595-34639-1 (pbk)
ISBN-10: 0-595-79385-1 (ebk)

Library of Congress Control Number: 2005923349
Includes bibliographical references and index

Editing: Ron Marmarelli and Alina Cîlnician
Historical Editing: Florin Constantiniu
Original Maps: Dan L. Duşleag

Front Cover Photograph: Emil Fischer
Back Cover Artwork: Mel Chin (reproduced with permission)
Cover Design: Dan L. Duşleag

Author Website: http://DDusleag.Home.Insightbb.com
Please refer any questions or comments regarding the content of this book to
My2ndUniversity@aol.com

A portion of the proceeds will be donated to charity

Printed in the United States of America

Dedicated to all the forgotten victims
Of Romania's Communist prisons
Who never had the chance
To tell their stories...

And

To my son Jonathan,
In memory of your Great-Grandfather,
A proud Romanian
And my best friend,
Until you came along...

"When justice does not succeed in being a form of memory,
Memory itself can be a form of justice."

Ana Blandiana, Romanian poet

"Vox Audita Perit, Littera Scripta Manent."
The heard word is lost, the written letter abides.

Latin maxim

CONTENTS

ACKNOWLEDGMENTS xv
INTRODUCTION 1
CHAPTER I—FAMILY 21
CHAPTER II—ARREST 31
CHAPTER III—TRIAL 50
Photographs—before prison 81
CHAPTER IV—IMPRISONMENT 99
CHAPTER V—APPEAL 152
CHAPTER VI—RELEASE 172
Photographs—after prison 197
EPILOGUE 215
LISTS OF POLITICAL DETAINEES 221
BIBLIOGRAPHY WITH EXCERPTS 241
APPENDIX 253
ABOUT THE AUTHORS 255
INDEX 259

ACKNOWLEDGMENTS

The (Sequential) Making of a Book

My Grandfather wrote this memoir between 1979 and 1986, more than twenty years after he was released from the Romanian Communist prison system. My foremost gratitude goes to him, for having had the courage to document his ordeal, despite the risk of being detained again.

My late father, Dr. Liviu Duşleag, deserves praise, because it was at his suggestion and insistence that this chronicle, the incipient version of which he reviewed before his unexpected death in 1986, came to life.

The manuscript was "deciphered" and organized by my mother, Dr. Lucia Duşleag, in Toronto, Canada, during the spring of 2000. Many thanks go to her for her efforts in getting the project off the ground and for her continuous and inexhaustible support. She was my biggest fan and loudest cheerleader, and without her assistance, the book would have remained a thought.

In the summer of 2000, graduate student Raluca Tudor from the University of Bucharest, Romania, initiated the English translation of a handful of pages under the supervision of Professor Lidia Vianu. I revised and completed the translation between December 2002 and December 2004, in Bloomington, Indiana. The result was not intended to be a verbatim rendition of the original Romanian text, but rather an honest effort at presenting the author's thoughts without altering their meaning. The subtleties of the Romanian manuscript were at times difficult to reproduce in English, which does not do the author justice.

The italic text included in brackets *{...}* constitutes addenda I have inserted to facilitate the reader's understanding of historical facts, family circumstances and medical terminology. It also contains excerpts from interviews conducted with victims of the Communist purge. The dates and descriptions of events added throughout the text are available in the public domain, and every effort has been made to ensure their accuracy.

I am honored that Florin Constantiniu, professor of history at the University of Bucharest and a member of the Romanian Academy, agreed to review the introduction and historical notes during my short visit to Bucharest in September 2004. His invaluable expertise guaranteed their correctness. Romanian historian, former State Chancellor and Presidential Advisor Floricel Marinescu provided further historical advice, for which I am also very grateful.

Professor Ioan Ciupea from the National Museum of Transylvanian History entrusted me with a list of one thousand names of political detainees, never-before-published and very pertinent to the subject of this memoir. His selfless commitment to giving these victims a voice is admirable, and represents an example for other historians of the period to follow.

Professor Keith Hitchins from the University of Illinois at Champaign-Urbana, the premier historian of Romania in the English-speaking world, kindly read the final draft. I cannot express my gratitude for his involvement in this endeavor.

Vladimir Tismăneanu, professor of government and politics and director of the Center for the Study of Post-Communist Societies at the University of Maryland, took the time to review the manuscript as well. I am thankful for his generous support.

Ron Marmarelli, a freelance editor and a member of the journalism faculty at Central Michigan University, patiently copyedited the manuscript throughout the summer, fall, and winter of 2004. My sister, Alina Cîlnician, did additional editing and proofreading. Her attention to detail, the valuable points she contributed, and her constructive criticism were well received. Dan Piekarsky's efforts in reviewing and proofreading the pre-press copy are greatly appreciated too. They all made the work fit for the publisher.

The photographs and documents included in the book were collected from family albums and archives and were selected and scanned during the summer and fall of 2004. I designed the two maps to underscore the introduction's message. The front cover photograph depicts Stanciu Stroia as a first-year medical student and was shot in 1923 by Emil Fischer, the most prestigious interwar photographer in Sibiu, Romania. I am also very indebted to American artist Mel Chin, whose photographic art titled *Jilava Prison Bed for Father Gheorghe Calciu-Dumitreasa* graces the back cover of this volume. His creation sums up the torments of Communist imprisonment better than any words. It was originally conceived for a 1982 Amnesty International exhibition that called attention to the plight of political prisoners.

Furthermore, many thanks go to Dr. David Dâmboiu and Alina and Dana Dâmboiu for being such wonderful hosts and resourceful guides during my Romanian prison-tour. Without them and Dr. Sanda Măgureanu, Lucia and Floricel Marinescu, Ștefan Andreescu, Lucia Maniu, Maria and Alexandru Ionescu, Dr. Stela Stroia, Ligia Corovei, Father Aurel Hărșan, Gabi Chelaru and Onuc Nemeș, my trip would not have been worthwhile.

Meeting ex-political detainee and author Lena Constante and being able to locate and contact Father Zosim Oancea, Dr. Constantin Diaconescu, Cornel Balaj and Ion Roșca, all former cellmates of my grandfather, was very gratifying. They were graceful in providing details about their prison nightmare.

The following people deserve a mention as well for their advice and help at various stages: Joe Dâmboiu, Dia Dumitru, Ion Gavrilă-Ogoranu, Mioara Dordea, Ovidiu Cîlnician, Terry McAdorey, Barbie Jenkins, Miles Flynn, Rachel Krupicka, Irina Eremia Bragin and Lidia Gheorghiu Bradley.

Sadly, the unexpected and premature death of Dr. Bogdan Măgureanu, a brilliant mind, a humble spirit, and a dear friend, coincided with the book's release. One of my great sources of encouragement and support, Bobi was eagerly anticipating reading this volume. An inspiration for everyone who was fortunate to know him, he will be terribly missed....

On a final note, a very special word of gratitude goes to my immediate family. My wife, Kimberly Dușleag-Schill, supplied me with smart ideas and challenging remarks, listened patiently to my constant jabbering about the book, and tolerated the distractions from my household responsibilities. Genuinely trying to grasp the importance of "your grandpa's book," my four-year-old son, Jonathan, shared in my enthusiasm.

Creating this book proved to be a task more daunting than I had ever imagined. Nevertheless, it was a rewarding learning experience. No less than twenty-six years have passed between the time my grandfather made the first entry in his note pad and I finished typing the last word of the manuscript. After years of transcribing and translating, correcting and rewriting, researching and scanning, editing and proofreading, with the emotional toll this time-consuming project took on my family and me, I have to let go of this book.

It is time for the reader to be the judge.

Dan L. Dușleag
Bloomington, Indiana, March 2005

INTRODUCTION

A Piece of Romanian (and Family) History

To better understand my grandfather's memories, one must be familiar with Romania's political situation before and during World War II and in the eventful period that followed. The next several pages do not represent an attempt at an exhaustive history lesson—numerous comprehensive textbooks written by competent individuals serve that purpose. Rather, they constitute a succinct and chronological presentation of the essential events and circumstances that shaped Romania's fate. The intention is not to overwhelm the reader with superfluous information, but to provide a framework for facilitating comprehension of the book's content.

Historical facts often differ in their packaging and labeling according to the distributor's opinions. The information selected *here* comprises well-known, rudimentary data and dates, accompanied by interpretations based on my own reading, observations, and conclusions. It is researched history supplemented by personal experience.

For the apparent redundancy of ideas, I ask the reader for forgiveness. It is aimed at underscoring necessary points. Ultimately, this introduction's ambitious proposition is to provide basic answers to timely questions: How was Communism in Romania possible? What happened to the people who opposed it? Why is it important for you, the reader, to know about it? What is the story's contemporary relevance? If the following text succeeds in delivering the intended message, the significance of knowing these answers will be evident.

On the eve of the second world conflagration, Romania was a stable monarchy with a political system balanced between the National Liberal Party and the National Peasant Party. Industrial advancement was at its peak, cultural events marked the social life, and the country reached its highest level of socioeconomic development in 1938. The architectural marvels of Bucharest, Romania's capital, earned it the affectionate appellations "The Little Paris" and "Paris of the Balkans."

Having Europe's largest petroleum reserves transformed Romania into an important factor in the world economy. It became the continent's leading crude oil producer by 1940, and its capital was the first one to be lighted by gas-powered street lamps. Vast natural resources enabled the country's economy to prosper, and Romania became an Eastern European power and the most fortunate state in the Balkans. Its foreign minister, Nicolae Titulescu, was elected Chairman of the League of Nations—the precursor of the United Nations—and Romania proved its vitality and capabilities in many other ways.

However, one careful look at the map and Romania's position at the gate of the old continent—at the crossroads of East and West, Europe and Asia, Christianity and Islam—will explain the geographical determinism under which the country has always suffered. Romania has the most disadvantageous layout of any European nation. The Western world—ordinary citizens and entire governments, alike—has frequently failed to comprehend the complexity of this delicate borderland full of contrasts, with its intricate ethnic, cultural, and political diversity. And the Western nations have offered insufficient support to the struggles of this edge of Europe, which has served as a bastion for protection of the continent's integrity and as a defense of European Christendom.

Throughout its existence, the Romanian nation had to overcome adversity in an uneven contest against empire-building powers. The indisputable truth, which is often forgotten, is that centuries of foreign aggressions and in particular four hundred years of Turkish invasions have stymied the progress of the Romanian people. The Romanians claim that they owe their backwardness to fighting waves of alien migrations, while the Westerners were busy fighting each other. The country's unstable and tumultuous past as a nation continuously hit by history's hurricanes, accounts for its current socioeconomic shortcomings. Consequently, many Romanians resent the status of second-class European citizens to which their Western counterparts have commonly relegated them. The apparent aversion and distrust toward the Romanians is seen as a result of this historical and cultural misunderstanding.

What may sound like a simplistic and fatalistic explanation proves after careful analysis to be rooted in historical reality. World War II and its profound consequences represented another tragic example of this geographically dictated destiny.

At the onset of the European hostilities, Romania was quick to declare neutrality but was unable to maintain that position. In 1939, the country was partitioned by the secret German-Soviet non-aggression pact signed by Joachim von Ribbentrop and Vyacheslav Molotov. The bleak consequence of that treaty was a radical dismemberment of Romania's territory. At first, Basarabia and Northern Bucovina were ceded to the Soviet Union. The subsequent Second Vienna Award (Vienna Dictate) led to Northern Transylvania—roughly half the region—being handed to Hungary, and following the Craiova Treaty, Southern Dobrogea was lost to Bulgaria. Romania's geographical mutilation was accomplished by its neighbors with the open backing of fascist Germany and Italy and the direct intervention of the Soviet Union.

While Romania's wealth made her the envy of the Balkans, it likewise placed her in a difficult, exploitable position. After Marshal Ion Antonescu established a military dictatorship and marginalized King Michael in 1940, the country was forced to join the Axis powers (Germany, Italy, and Japan). In return for supplying the Nazi war machine with oil—half of Germany's needs—grain, industrial products, and manpower, Romania received from Adolf Hitler a guarantee of the preservation of the integrity of its borders and the independence of its people. Since Hitler considered control of Romania an essential step before invading the Soviet Union, Romania had no other option but to yield to the German ultimatum.

In June 1941, Germany started its offensive against the Soviet Union with the support of Romanian troops. The country's commitment to the liberation of the Soviet–occupied Northern territories was in accordance with the aspiration of the entire nation. On December 12, 1941, five days after the infamous events at Pearl Harbor, Romania declared war on the

United States. This, however, was a decision "not in response to the wishes of their own people, but as instruments of Hitler," President Franklin D. Roosevelt emphasized in his message to Congress. It seemed improbable indeed that a small nation, which had no quarrel with America and where Americans were admired and respected, would be forced into this crisis. In response, the United States in June 1942 carried out the first of many aerial attacks on Romania's oil fields.

By 1943, the Red Army had won the great counteroffensive at Stalingrad, and the Romanians were obligated to retreat westward. The result was Marshal Antonescu's arrest on King Michael's orders on August 23, 1944, and the country's declaration of war on Germany the following day. Romania aligned itself with the Allied forces (the United States, Great Britain, and the Soviet Union), the Eastern German front collapsed shortly thereafter, and the war ended with the Third Reich's surrender nine months later on May 7, 1945.

Romania played a decisive role in Germany's defeat and had one of the highest casualty rates among all Allied countries. Out of more than half a million soldiers involved on the Eastern front—making Romania the fourth largest coalition force—170,000 were killed, wounded, or missing in action. Despite all of that, Romania was denied co-belligerent status at the Peace Treaty of Paris in 1947. The country was regarded as a defeated power and was required to make enormous war reparation payments to the Soviet Union. The reunification of Transylvania and most of Dobrogea with Romania was recognized, but Basarabia and Bucovina remained under Soviet jurisdiction.

When the victorious superpowers concluded their postwar plans, Joseph Stalin and Winston Churchill signed the Moscow Percentage Agreement in October 1944, delivering Romania on a platter to Bolshevik domination. The independence salvaged through its soldiers' heroism became less relevant because the nation found itself behind the Iron Curtain and in the Soviet sphere of influence. If Allied bombardment—particularly that of the Ploiești refineries in August 1943 and April-August 1944 by American B-24 Liberty planes—significantly slowed Romania's industrial growth during the war, the Soviet occupation that followed curtailed economic activity altogether. $300 million represented a colossal debt for a market that had collapsed and a workforce that was depleted, but the Soviets still undertook a methodical stripping of Romania's wealth.

The Soviet Union's imposing of its own regime on the conquered territory became the next inevitable consequence. Power landed swiftly and forcefully in the hands of the Soviet-engineered Communist Party, an impotent organization with few members and no political tradition prior to 1945. The Communists skillfully exploited the political vacuum left by the war, and King Michael was forced to abdicate and move into exile to Switzerland in December 1947. A popular republic was proclaimed to replace the monarchy, liberal political organizations were dissolved, farms came under state control (forced collectivization), and factories, banks, enterprises and estates were nationalized. Romania's foreign policy began to be solely dictated by the interests of the Soviet Union.

The West, once again, turned a blind eye to Romania's fate, as it was still doctoring its own war wounds. The country's plight all but disappeared from the Western radar and consciousness, both in the immediate postwar period and throughout the cold war.

During my childhood, I heard countless stories told by Cacova's World War II survivors about the civilized behavior of the German soldiers, who were, nevertheless, part of an occupying force at the beginning of the war, in contrast with the savagery, destruction, and looting undertaken by the "friendly" Red Army. The conduct of the Soviet troops and the subsequent exploitation and "Russification" of the occupied land were deeply resented. And the recurrent theme in the survivors' accounts was the honest belief and expectation many Romanians had in 1945 that the "Americans will come" to "rescue us from Ivan's boot." Unfortunately, they never did, nor did they ever have the intention of doing so. Despite Great Britain's early efforts at maintaining a sphere of interest in the Balkans (a 90 percent Soviet, 10 percent British partitioning of Romania was proposed by Churchill to Stalin), the 1943 Allied Tehran Conference excluded the possibility of a Balkan intervention primarily because of Dwight Eisenhower's objections. This new perceived betrayal did not surprise the naïve and fatalistic Romanians. Their *last* drop of hope vanished with the Western world's passivity in response to the 1956 Soviet invasion of neighbor Hungary (to repress an anti-Communist revolt). They understood that Communism was here to stay, and nobody would or could stop it.

The Marxism invented in Western Europe became an Eastern European property once Lenin put it into practice. The Communist utopia meant—according to German Karl Marx—the creation of a classless society, in which the community as a whole owned the property and all individuals enjoyed equal social and economic status. Revolutionary seizure of power on behalf of the proletariat was first required—per Russian Vladimir Ilyich Lenin—to overthrow the decaying capitalist system. However, such a dangerous and unrealistic ideology led in effect to a totalitarian regime, with human rights abuses like those of another misfortune of the twentieth century: fascism. Communist democracy existed only in speeches and on paper. It was a purely theoretical and philosophical notion, with the dictatorship representing its harsh equivalent in reality.

Initially, the Communist government acquired an illegal monopoly on political and police power through fraudulent elections, abuse, and intimidation. Once that was accomplished, all forms of cultural and religious expression were replaced by Communist propaganda. Information was censored, and freedom of speech and movement was restricted. The newly created society rewarded incompetence, promoted mediocrity, and eliminated virtue. It became a monstrous pyramid of persecution and suffering at the base and demagogy and corruption at its tip. The bureaucratic and inefficient economic system marched inevitably toward failure, resulting in a dismal standard of living for the average, oppressed citizen.

In a swift sequence of events, Communism managed to turn the normal world—as Romanians knew it—upside down, with complete reversal of norms and values and destruction of well-established societal structures and mechanisms. The Communist elite or "nomenklaturists" became the sole beneficiaries of this communal reorganization. Immune to the laws imposed on its own constituents, the elite made illegality legal, promoted an extreme personality cult, overt nepotism, and a convoluted network of informers in order to control all human interactions. Hunger for power,

ROMANIA, A COUNTRY AT CROSSROADS

THE ARROWS DEPICT THE AREAS WHERE WESTERN EUROPEAN, EASTERN EUROPEAN AND ISLAMIC CIVILIZATIONS CONVERGE.

GREATER ROMANIA

MAP OF ROMANIA BETWEEN WORLD WARS I AND II, CONTAINING ALL THE HISTORIC ROMANIAN PROVINCES, INCLUDING NORTHERN BUCOVINA AND BASARABIA (BOTH UNDER SOVIET OCCUPATION AFTER 1945). SINCE WWII, ROMANIA'S SURFACE HAS BEEN 237,500 SQ KM (91,699 SQ MI) - ROUGHLY ILLINOIS AND INDIANA'S SIZE COMBINED - AND IS CURRENTLY INHABITED BY 22.4 MILLION PEOPLE.

greed, self-service, ruthlessness, and illiteracy were sine qua non traits required from the leadership.

The party chief ruled like a God figure. His decision-making was absolute and uncontested. His adjutants conferred indiscriminate authority over the masses to unsophisticated subordinates, selected based on loyalty rather than aptitude. In addition to becoming mindless servants of their masters, the minions abused the power handed to them. A well-lubricated hierarchical system emerged, maintained in a status quo by all of the benefiting parties. While the select few were living the high life, the ostracized general population was sinking into poverty, driven to the brink of starvation. The inequality between the two social groups was nothing short of obscene.

Furthermore, the gap between official party slogans and reality grew increasingly wider. Life in Communism became a web of lies and an exercise in the absurd. "All animals are equal, but some animals are more equal than others," wrote George Orwell in 1944 in *Animal Farm*, a political satire about an imaginary totalitarian land. What an accurate prophecy regarding the future state of affairs in Communist countries! Although the censors banned it, I was fortunate to glance at a cartoon version of that fable, which circulated cautiously on the Romanian black market.

The "new man" that emerged from the Communist dogma was an unscrupulous opportunist with the malleability of a chameleon, conveniently switching political sides depending on personal interest and profitability. With the funds and properties stolen over decades, the privileged species turned investor-capitalist at the death of the Communist system, through an unsurprising metamorphosis.

In the Communist world, all personal liberties were infringed upon, and the state dictated by means of law and police action every meaningful daily decision. Social duties were abundant whereas individual rights were nonexistent. Reproduction control policies constituted an extreme example of state intrusion into the most intimate lives of its citizens. Seeking growth in the labor force required to build the Communist utopia, the government imposed strict pronatalism laws on the population. A total ban on contraceptive methods and a decree prohibiting any and all abortions was signed by Dictator Nicolae Ceaușescu in October 1966. To ensure compliance with the regulation, women of childbearing age were subjected to mandatory, humiliating gynecological exams. This often occurred at their places of employment and in the presence of a Securitate officer. The result was not a change in reproductive behavior, but thousands of illegal procedures leading to maternal deaths, unwanted children overpopulating dilapidated orphanages, and constant harassment of medical professionals. It was throughout those years that my father, a practicing obstetrician and fertility specialist, faced arrest if unwarranted house searches turned up *any* surgical instruments and imprisonment if he agreed to perform certain procedures, even if they were medically indicated.

The main ingredient for such an evil political order to succeed is for all of the good people to remain silent, to do nothing. But in Romania, a strong opposition to Communism did evolve and was based on national, cultural, and religious grounds. The imported ideology was in stark contrast with Romanian traditions, mentality, and psychology. It was perceived to be an alien creed and was deeply distrusted. As a result, there were numerous examples of active fighting against it, both spiritually and by means of arms, subtle or direct. And there were many victims of circumstance yielded by the process, the ones neither for nor against Communism, lacking the courage to fight it but refusing to engage in it.

"Regardless of the area inhabited, the Romanian people represented a rare example of linguistic unity and common values: belief in God and respect for the law and private property," noted historian Floricel Marinescu. "As a result, the Communist ideology failed to gain ground in Romania, which—among all Central and Eastern European states—remained the country with the least number of Communist party members, and even those were primarily of other nationalities. For a population of eighteen million people in August 1944, there were only a thousand registered Communists, a figure pointing to the movement's lack of mass support. If ideologically Romania was never at risk, the external threat remained real."

When it comes to dealing with their Communist past, some Romanians feel burdened by a sense of collective guilt—after all, the prudent majority eventually went with the political trend, looking after its own interest and adapting to the new environment. Other Romanians see the Soviet Union as the sole culprit. However, if the Soviets can be blamed for introducing this calamity by force, evidence shows it was the Romanians who adopted and perpetuated it. Countless opportunists were quick in climbing aboard the ideological bandwagon. Ultimately, those active and willing participants in the farce caused the anti-Communist resistance to falter and established the new oppressive mechanism, a faulty one destined for bankruptcy from the start and, as events proved, taking its deserved place in history's garbage can.

Throughout the 1950s, while the Romanian Communist Party leader Gheorghe Gheorghiu-Dej dictated the agenda, the country was subjected to a repressive campaign of state terror efficiently enforced by the dreaded and seemingly never sleeping Securitate, the Romanian secret police. This was executed under the directive of Joseph Stalin (self-proclaimed "Man of Steel"), the supreme ruler of the Soviet Union and a symbol of totalitarian rule and limitless personal power. In an atmosphere of general fear and distrust, with people denouncing each other, the "counterrevolutionary terrorists, bandits, conspirators, monarchists, mystical-anarchists, deviationists and imperialist spies" had to be quickly unmasked. The political spectrum became black and white without compromising gray zones, and the Communist slogan "either with us or against us" was successfully promoted. Hundreds of thousands of political arrests were made; the victims were pre-war and interwar leaders, the opponents of the new regime, clergy, small merchants, students, peasants, the educated, and the wealthy. All actual, perceived, or virtual threats to the new system were eliminated through a similar chain of events: an arrest in the middle of the night for a staged or imaginary offense, followed by a signed admission of guilt, a hasty show trial, a disproportionately long incarceration sentence, and continuous persecution of the victim's family and friends to discourage any further dissent.

Circumstances of incarceration secondary to frivolous accusations were abundant. The ease by which nonconforming spirits were excluded from society was astonishing. During my youth, I had personal knowledge of people who experienced years of confinement after publicly making an innocent political joke or following denouncement by neighbors for listening to Western radio stations (such as Radio Free Europe or Voice of America). So diffuse became the plague of Communist repression that its reflection was a motley prison population, with victims from all walks of life, socioeconomic levels, and ethnic backgrounds, having their innocence as the only common denominator. The Communist purge became a sinister slaughter of foes existing only in the executioner's mind. Artificially created problems arose concomitantly with efficient solutions from the depths of disturbed Communist thinking. The truth was the last thing that mattered to popular justice. History was rewritten and a new reality was created, in which opponents of the regime were first manufactured and then crushed, in order to justify continuation of the reprisals. A return to normal life after abusive captivity was often elusive, if not downright impossible. Countless lives were further shattered by the continuing fear engraved in the minds and souls of survivors.

Having a particular distrust of books—with the exception of their own propaganda—and highly educated citizens, the Communists felt threatened by the ability of "thinkers" to galvanize public opinion and to create groups of dissidents around them. As in other dictatorial regimes, anti-intellectualism became a fashionable policy. Prominent scholars were rounded up and jailed in hard labor camps, with some of the worst abuses of the entire Soviet bloc occurring in the notorious Aiud Penitentiary. Within these Romanian gulags, copied from the efficient Soviet model, a thorough process of humiliation and dehumanization was engineered, aimed at the psychological breakdown and physical extermination of the "enemies of the people." There are similarities of abuse perpetuated in totalitarian regimes of both political extremes, but Romania's Communist prison system stood out as an institutionalized, sophisticated "reeducation" program, seeking to correct "behavioral anomalies and thought processing deficiencies."

As General Ion Eremia, a former political convict himself, expressed it remarkably well, Communist incarceration was a "summary of four torments: hunger, cold, immobility, and solitude." "The fifth was fear," noted Dr. Constantin Diaconescu, an ex-cellmate of my grandfather's. And, emphasizing that particular order, Lena Constante, who spent eight and a half years out of twelve in solitary confinement, when asked if she had wept in prison, replied after a long pause, "I did...I cried of hunger...."

This Romanian "Stalinist period" ended in 1953 with the death of the Soviet dictator. Official denouncements of Stalin's politics were delayed for another eleven years, however, and resulted in the amnesty act of 1964, which led to the release of most political detainees. By then, the Communist system was well established, kept firmly in place by its repressive apparatus. After decades of tyranny, what threat could any individual protest pose? The game was over, the victory final, the mission accomplished. Romania had been transformed into "a nation of whisperers," as Romanian-American poet Andrei Codrescu observed, "people buried deep under a snowlike blanket of fear." The entire population was frightened into silence and passivity, effectively chained within a dysfunctional society and a well-organized police state.

Countless families suffered great injustices during that gruesome period, and ours was no exception.

My grandfather, Stanciu Stroia, was born on August 10, 1904, in the picturesque village of Cacova, within the heart of beautiful Transylvania, in Central Romania. He was a man of character, with a strong personality and a "straight vertebral column," with determination and pride but also generosity and kindness. Guided by sound moral principles, gifted with a keen sense of right and wrong and concerned with social justice, he was a great patriot and a man who stubbornly stood for his beliefs. The circumstances he lived in forced him to pay a high price for his integrity. He was a product of a democratic society and a victim of its subsequent collapse.

Son of a shepherd and fatherless when he was less than two years of age, he followed the lead of his grandfather and uncle and furthered his education through medical school. He was the president of his class and the pupil of the most illustrious Romanian internist of those times, Dr. Iuliu Hațieganu. He became the elected director of the Regional Hospital in Făgăraș, Transylvania, where he founded the internal medicine and radiology departments and built a successful practice and a well-respected name for himself. He was happily married to his high school sweetheart and the love of his life, Valeria Grama, and had two children, Lucia (my mother) and Zeno. To that point, his life had been a success story built on merit and against the odds.

In 1951, my grandfather was 47 years old and at the peak of his personal life and professional career. The turbulent times that followed are the subject of his memories. He referred to them as *a doua mea facultate*, "my second university," one that taught him many lessons, which he did not want the next generations to forget.

The 1950s were years of relative peace and prosperity in the civilized world. Yet, for the most part of that decade, my grandfather was left to rot in a desolate cell, disconnected from and forgotten by the world, punished for his uncompromising stance and his strong and noble character. Many prison incidents he describes are as captivating as they are appalling. His is not a pretty story but a disturbing one with few details spared. It does not fail to remind us of the strength and beauty of the human spirit when faced with adversity, but also of its weakness and ugliness. And it makes us wonder how one adjusts to undeserved captivity, survives, attempts to return to normalcy, and succeeds in the end. His eyewitness account is testimony to human resilience and the will to live.

Throughout his incarceration—as the reader will sense from the manuscript—my grandfather displayed a reserved optimism. He maintained a clear mind and managed somehow to salvage his weakened and diseased body. Analyzing the consequences of prison life for his health and the well-being of others with a clinician's critical eye, he helped his brothers in suffering. Despite his own anguish, he remained faithful to his Hippocratic Oath and provided medical advice, counseling, and reassurance to his fellow tormented inmates, attempting to compensate for their abandonment by the prison doctors. This element alone sets my grandfather's account apart from other prison memoirs. Some of the more disturbing events he endured or witnessed, he fails to mention, as if still trying to protect us from a period long gone. He had regrets and felt betrayed at times, but did not whimper or despair. Most significantly, he preserved his dignity and pride.

I urge the reader to pause for a minute and think intensely about how it would feel to live in continuous uncertainty and fear and to endure physical abuse and psychological humiliation, unable to move, talk, touch, interact, read or write, savor food, rest in comfort, adjust the temperature, enjoy privacy, hear news about loved ones, entertain the mind or exercise the body, even work—the multitude of God-given human rights we all take for granted, the basic needs of every living soul. Imagine enduring this ordeal for a non-existent crime, and not for hours, days, weeks, or months, but for seven long years!

Every time I went over my grandfather's notes, I could not help but wonder how *I* would have reacted if faced with similar circumstances. Would I have had the courage to stand for my convictions, the ability to keep my sanity, or the power to survive physically? As I bow with respect and humility before all of that suffering, I can only hope that I will never have to find answers to those painful questions.

Judged by our current civilized standards, the events depicted in these pages appear incomprehensible, at times so improbable that the reader could place them only in a distant and awkward land. It is impossible to grasp the magnitude of the harm inflicted upon someone's personal and family life, career and prestige, body and mind, when that individual is robbed of life's most fruitful years. Every day spent unjustifiably behind bars is a wasted day to many. But if quantifying the impact of such an insult on one victim is difficult, multiplying that scenario thousands of times will reveal the enormous damage produced on a society. Only a monster like Stalin could have made the convenient statement that "a single death is a tragedy," while "a million deaths is a statistic."

The paucity of printed material in English depicting the abuse that occurred within the walls of Eastern Europe's Communist prisons, which claimed—by most accounts—millions of lives, came as quite a surprise to me. Upon reflection, however, it made perfect sense. American society is made up primarily of descendants from Northwestern Europe, so it is only natural for general reader interest to be focused on topics pertaining to those countries of origin; Eastern European issues inevitably end up on the back burner. In the entire Western world, there continues to be—with notable exceptions—a predictable reaction of indifference and ignorance toward the Red Holocaust, and an international tribunal for those responsible is still lacking. Moreover, among former Communists, any personal acknowledgment of fault or gesture of reconciliation with the victims is absent. The implication is that survivors can condemn what they have experienced or witnessed but cannot expect justice.

In Romania, a major reason behind this lack of guilty verdicts or vindication was the persistence of disguised Communist elements in powerful positions well after the fall of Communism in 1989. Their efforts at keeping details of the past from public consciousness were unconcealed, exemplified in statements such as "anti-Communism is obsolete." The passing of several decades after the 1950s purge was not conducive to an efficient hunting of criminals—similar to that undertaken after World War II—either.

It is the responsibility of the person who has witnessed a truth to ensure its unearthing. "The destruction of the past" said French philosopher Simone Weil, "is the greatest of all crimes." There is indeed no single more precious and urgent duty than to establish historical accuracy. Because an undocumented event is one that did not occur—according to certain elements of Romanian society who have an interest in contesting the existence of the Communist genocide—this book will add to the body of evidence. It will challenge the denial and amnesia.

Jewish-Italian writer Primo Levi once remarked that learning about one personal tragedy often elicits more pain than absorbing a multitude of dreadful events. In addition, if we had to endure the suffering of every victim, we would not survive. Written in the form of a memoir, this book is by definition a subjective reflection of an individual experience, a narrative account according to the author's particular angle of view. Nevertheless, with its age-old theme of arbitrary detention, the story has a universal resonance, and the misfortune of "having been there" confers the writer credibility and authority on the subject.

My grandfather was just *one* of the innumerable victims of the Communist terror. Some were more, while others were far less fortunate than he was. Not all of the thousands of individuals unjustly imprisoned during those years survived the ordeal. Only a few had the courage, strength, and ability to report their suffering, and even fewer managed to publish their stories for the world to read. If one takes into account the survivors' advancing ages and dwindling numbers—in 1990, there were 98,700 registered members of the Association of Former Political Detainees, compared to 45,000 in 2005—the information gap is unlikely to ever be filled. That is why this chronicle, created out of respect for the truth, serves as a voice for the entire "Stalinist" generation. It is a documentary written in memory of all of the forgotten victims of Romania's Communist prisons—the nameless, faceless, and voiceless—who never had the chance to tell their stories. It is published for those who *do not know* what happened and are genuinely interested in finding out, and is particularly aimed at those who *do not want to know* but are pressed by reality to reconsider.

To forgive and to forget are entirely different concepts; one does not consequentially imply the other. A crime can be forgiven, but if it is forgotten, the victim's punishment becomes continual. The survivors must not forget, while those who have been spared must not ignore. Without subscribing to the notions of "competitive martyrdom" or "monopoly of suffering," the Communist repression has to at least be put in its proper perspective. And although I am equally appalled by other atrocities committed throughout the world—particularly at the time of this publication—I believe that the Stalinist crimes of the past century should occupy a well-documented and deservedly infamous place in the historical literature. Their significance has not faded over the last fifty years, and they represent a history lesson that ought to be told, so that the world learns from it and avoids a repetition of a terrible past. Ignorance is at the root of all evil—according to an old maxim; a clear understanding of how Communism was possible is crucial for our own self-preservation.

Prior to the manuscript going to press, I returned to Romania on a week-long prison tour looking for closure. I felt that the time was right to draw a line and put the story behind me. By publishing it, my grandfather was going to be redeemed; his suffering would finally have a meaning. What I found upon my homecoming, however, was a different country; not "my Romania," the Romania I grew up in, but a society on an irreversible march toward democracy, led by a younger generation disconnected from and unconcerned with the reality of the recent past. The fact that high school textbooks contained very little information about the Communist period was disturbing, and explained the high degree of unawareness I witnessed. In the greater scheme of things—the young generation claimed—Communism had been a mere blip on time's radar screen; years from now, it will barely be mentioned in history books. "We simply want to forget" was the lamentation of the elderly. Yet—I had to remind both groups—forty-five years of Communism destroyed millions of lives. While relatively short-lived, it was a monstrosity leading to some of the most atrocious crimes in history.

Is it wise to unearth a troubled past and analyze it, even if that implies facing an unflattering truth?—the reader is justified to inquire. Or is it better to keep it buried, adopt a tolerable version of it and focus on the future? To paraphrase American philosopher George Santayana, "those who cannot remember the past are condemned to repeat it." That is the practical value attached to all historical ruminations. Political theorist Neal Wood concurred when he stated that "the enlightening experience of studying history changes us and our views, and consequently has a direct bearing upon the way we fashion the future."

One can argue that it takes a multitude of socioeconomic and political elements, favorable internal circumstances, and a permissive or powerless international community for a radical government to emerge. Unfortunately, auspicious conditions develop frequently, and the results are painfully similar. This personal saga is an eye-opener regarding events with a true potential for recurrence if collective political vigilance fails. One glimpse at the current international situation is sufficient to reveal the present-day relevance of this memoir.

Anyone who has survived a totalitarian system, in which a small group of people imposes its extreme doctrine on the majority, will become tolerant and liberal by default. In tyranny, a person turns into an educated consumer of government-censored media, with an enhanced ability to read between the lines, to discern the truth—if there is one—from the myriad of lies. This individual develops an invisible "antenna," highly sensitive to rumors and speculations, serving the purpose of replacing the empty, newsless media. That skill, however, is often lost inside the comfort zones of free society and political pluralism. Within a democratic social order, people need to challenge anyone interested in restricting individual liberties to experience *one* day in an aberrant, dictatorial regime, which does not allow dissent and punishes all opposing views. If only feasible, such an experience would be the most efficient deterrent against deviations from democratic principles and practices.

Democracy may not be a flawless system, but one has to consider the grim alternatives offered by the twentieth century. Communism is one of them. Most human beings will reject all arguments in favor of that type of autocracy.

My grandfather first recounted the prison tales that constitute this memoir at my coming of age, after I turned 14, when he judged that I was mature enough to understand and sufficiently wise to keep them in secrecy. His stories may not have a special literary merit; after all, they were written for the eyes of his family, with no declared desire for publicity or intention for publication. Nonetheless, they are of sentimental value besides standing as documentation of what happened. These memories taught me that individual character matters and that a clear conscience is essential because without the two, man loses his soul. They also made me understand that liberty is indispensable because it gives us hope; and without it, we are in danger of losing our ability to survive. I decided to share the five fully written and well-guarded scrapbooks with the rest of the interested world as soon as I became an adult and had them securely in my possession.

Eighteen years had to elapse before I was able to follow through with my promise. As this effort proves, however, I have not ignored my Romanian roots and have healthy anchors in the past. I did not forget my grandfather's experience, and it was one of the many reasons I chose to leave my native country in 1990, three years after he passed away and within a year of the anti-Communist revolution. Mine was a decision he surely would have questioned—as any proud Romanian would—but without doubt would have understood and accepted because, above everything else, *Tatamare* was the greatest grandfather of all!

The notion that America is, for those who ventured into the unknown, a chance to escape oppression and injustice is not novel. My grandfather's legacy has helped me appreciate this new, adoptive land, where personal freedom is treasured and protected above anything else. And *that* is something—I am certain—he would be pleased to know.

Despite all that was unjustly taken from him, my grandfather preserved a good-hearted personality and a seemingly always serene look on his warm face and in his deep green eyes. He walked tall and confident, happy and grateful to be blessed with another day of life, and that is how he will be cherished in our memory. He forgave without malice and left this world reconciled with the past, proud of the younger generations and ready to be reunited with his lost wife, whom he missed so dearly.

Writing about the goodness of Stanciu Stroia has been effortless, since that is all I have known in him. As my family commemorates one hundred years from his birthday, it is my sincere hope that his memories will open the hearts and broaden the horizons of all those who read them.

That is why I entrust them to the printer.

Dan L. Duşleag
Bloomington, Indiana, March 2005

CHAPTER I—FAMILY

The Little Bag

Cred în Destin și în puterea cerească pe care o numesc Dumnezeu.
 I believe in destiny and in the heavenly power called God. That is the reason why I will fill this notebook with the moments of my life that cost me many years of freedom.

As they resurface in my memory, important events will be enumerated in imperfect chronology, and they are to be read only after I die. Until then, the manuscript will be placed in *săcușorul de cânepă*, the small bag made of hemp in which I saved my prison clothes, some of which I wore without interruption for almost seven years.

Today, that little bag can be found in Cacova, inside the large wooden chest, which is placed under the window looking out to the front street. At one end of the bag's lace is the needle that a fellow convict made from a booklet staple he found in the prison yard. This needle could be spotted only with a greater skillfulness than that of the prison guards who never found it, despite the countless searches they performed on me.

With the help of that needle, I sewed thousands of meters of thread taken from the seam of the mattresses, after I had used all of the thread from three pairs of socks. That particular needle and the sewing—I always had some *petece* (patches) that I took from wherever I could—saved me from an irremediable mental depression. When I was alone in my cell, in total isolation, and did not know what to do with my time, I sewed. The guards knew it because they could see me through the small cell door window, and they would shout at me, nodding their heads, sometimes in a lenient manner:

Iară coși, doctore? "You're sewing again, Doc?"

My family mailed me this little hempen bag in the spring of 1952, and it remained the only package—without a letter—I was permitted to receive during seven years of imprisonment.

There were so many political prisoners at that time—over three thousand in the Aiud Penitentiary alone—that it resulted in a serious shortage of undergarments. This left the prison officials with no choice but to order us to write to our families and request some. The dictated note that I scribbled on a small postcard was the only correspondence I was allowed to have with my family during all those years. It was saved by my wife—see the postal date on it—and it was kept in a leather bag that I inherited from my uncle, Ioan Lalu from Sibiel, who was married to my mother's sister, my good aunt Mina.

{The little bag joined my grandfather in his grave on August 1, 1987. I placed it on top of his coffin, tied with a Romanian flag ribbon, as he had requested.}

My Father

In that bag, along with my personal archive, I have safeguarded the last two letters my mother, my brother, and I received from my father, Dumitru Stroia. He wrote on February 8, 1906, that he was tired of living abroad and that he intended to sell his flock of sheep. He yearned to come back home, this time for good, after nearly ten years of hard work near the town of Rostov, on the Don River, in Southeast Russia.

{Sheep herding was a common trade for the people living in the mountainous regions of Transylvania. Practiced on a large scale, with shepherds owning thousands of animals, it was labor intensive but profitable. When the local pastures were inadequate or not easily accessible, the shepherds rented land in the Southern plains of neighboring Russia. Forming groups headed by a "staroste"—the brightest and most educated among them—they started the process of "transhumance" or seasonal moving of livestock from one region to another. Dumitru Stroia was the staroste of Cacova's shepherds.}

I was one and a half years old when he was murdered, on May 13, 1906. Street bandits had followed him, believing he was carrying a lot of cash. He was strangled and thrown in a barrel he was carrying in his wagon as he was on his way back from the Rostov post office, having just mailed a large sum of money home. The horses returned with the carriage and his lifeless body to his farm, twenty-five kilometers outside of town. From that money, the Sedria orphanage of Sibiu allowed me to withdraw a certain amount every autumn, at the beginning of the school year.

In April 1928, following the successful completion of my graduation thesis, I had to request the University of Medicine in Cluj to exempt me from paying taxes for my medical diploma. That was the last occasion during which I felt the pain and humiliation of not having a father.

The fact that I grew up fatherless as well as my mother's strict upbringing strengthened my faith during my seven-year detention. I could not have been a coward, an unworthy man, and leave my wife and children alone to face the hardships of life. It was difficult enough to helplessly watch my mother's struggle as a widow with two small children, when she was barely 26 years of age.

My Mother

My mother, Iosefina Stroia, was the daughter of the village priest and a young widow of modest fortunes. She never remarried, and I woke up every day listening to her cry. I must have been about three years old when I left our yard and wandered on the street to ask the first passerby to enter our house and stop my mother from weeping.

I was a rather busy, active child, and submitting to my mother's rules and restrictions was not an easy task. If she locked the small door to our yard in order to keep me from getting lost in the village streets, I opened the big gates and ran out. Or I escaped to my grandmother's house if I felt I was in danger of being disciplined.

When I was only five years old, I crossed the valley that divided the community and spent the day with a sister of my mother's until my mother came to fetch me back home. My aunt's husband, Uncle Nicolae, was very fond of me, and he used to send me to the general store to buy him tobacco, never forgetting to generously reward me with candy afterward. To my mother's exasperation, my unscheduled visits there became increasingly frequent.

I recall one particular summer evening in 1909, shortly before my uncle died, when I was sitting by a huge campfire with a group of carpenters, roasting potatoes. Uncle Nicolae had just arrived from nearby Ujbea Mountain, with a carriage headed by two strong oxen and fully loaded with giant wooden logs. That wood was used to build our barn, and despite my tender age, the entire event remained vividly registered in my memory.

When I was about 10, I developed the habit of returning home late in the evening, particularly on Sundays, after running around the village roads and hills with my friends. My mother would greet me with a wooden stick, not allowing me to provide an explanation for my whereabouts and prolonged absence. At 14, tired of the harsh treatment, I threatened her that I would quit school, run away from home, and get a job at the Rieger factory in Sibiu.

"So, how are you going to get along with your brother?" she would challenge me. "He will have all this schooling and you, nothing!"

Her crying tamed me quickly and made me forget about the perceived unfair treatment. But my rowdiness continued.

Fă bine, iartă-mă! "Do some good deeds and spare me of all this excitement!" my mother would implore me.

N-am vreme! "I have no time for that!" was my usual reply.

She was always terribly concerned that I would end up hurting myself in a serious manner, especially when I climbed all the way up the tall nut trees lining our street. Having to worry constantly, she never learned to trust my independent personality. Her parenting style was authoritarian, often critical of my high-risk behavior, and she would rarely offer a compliment or a caress. *Dragă* (dear) was a word she seldom used. Her deep faith, however, was unshakable; it was that of a very ambitious and energetic woman who eventually succeeded in sending both of her boys to school. That was a feat she managed to accomplish under enormously difficult financial circumstances, which she overcame through a lot of common sense and good judgment. Throughout her life, my mother maintained that perfect mental equilibrium.

I started elementary school at five, having my father's stepbrother as my first teacher, and then transferred to the larger school of Săliște in third grade, where every age-based classroom had an assigned teacher. Despite not knowing one single word of Attila's language, the following year I was obligated to attend the Hungarian middle school. This was my first encounter with a Magyar institution, the official purpose of which was to "Hungarize" the Romanian pupils. Three other children from my village were enrolled there as well, but I was not allowed to meet them during lunch break, so we could not converse in Romanian. That interdiction infuriated me tremendously.

{Transylvania was under Hungarian rule at that time. Austria-Hungary, also called the Dual Monarchy, was born following the "Ausgleich" or compromise act of 1867, through which the Habsburg Empire restructured its government into two distinct areas, one ruled by the Austrians from Vienna and the other by the Hungarians from Budapest. That led to an intense campaign of ethnic assimilation of the subject population through linguistic and cultural domination. Nevertheless, the chauvinistic effort to "Magyarize" the Romanian majority in occupied Transylvania was met with strong resistance and failed miserably.}

The strict, military-style regimen at the Roman Catholic Terezianum Institute was not at all to my liking, so I made an attempt to escape the dorms one night by jumping the tall iron fence surrounding the courtyard. After he caught me in the act, the Hungarian principal summoned my mother the next day. "Nothing will turn out of this boy with the behavior of a hooligan," he tried to convince her.

To my delight, the immediate consequence of that incident was that I had to move in with my older brother, a senior at Sibiu high school at that time. Nevertheless, my continued defiant attitude and unwillingness to learn Hungarian did not alleviate my mother's fear that I would be expelled from school before Christmas. That, however, never happened. My luck's name was Herr Krebs, an open-minded German teacher who accepted me without reservations. That vote of confidence empowered me to earn high marks based on merits, particularly in geography and mathematics. I could draw a map in front of the class and solve most mathematical quizzes instantly.

As such, I passed the grades with relative ease and in the fall of 1914, at the onset of World War I earned the right to enroll in the Sibiu Hungarian high school. There was a lot to be desired regarding the Hungarian teacher's attitude toward us—*valahi puturoși* (lazy Romanians)—and plenty to be said about the daily discrimination and humiliation we had to endure. However, all the pain was washed away in April 1919 during my freshman year, when the victorious, liberating Romanian Army passed through the boulevards of Sibiu on the way to occupying the Hungarian capital of Budapest. Following those events, I obtained my baccalaureate or high school diploma in 1922, scoring at the top of my class.

Another fortunate event during that time was my introduction to and the strong friendship I developed with Miss Valeria Grama, a student at the girls' high school in Sibiu. I eventually married Valy after years of intense courtship and upon successful completion of medical school.

Destiny rewarded my mother with the joy of seeing both of her children *cu școală* (with schooling), as she liked to say. The first son became a judge, the second a doctor. She was fortunate to see her older son once again, after he returned from self-imposed exile in Tsarist Russia. My brother, Mitică Stroia, fearing persecution by the Hungarian authorities, moved across Romania's northern border in 1916 as a refugee. Together with other intellectuals, young and old, he passed the Carpathian Mountains by the Cindrel Peak. And my mother was also happy to see her youngest son alive when she believed that he had died in Aiud—a rumor that was indeed circulating, claiming that I had succumbed in prison while hospitalized with scurvy—and to see him freed on Saint Nicholas's Day, December 6, 1957. On a postcard, which I saved in my archives, she ended a letter to her daughter-in-law with the following words: *Fie iertat Stanciu,* "God forgive Stanciu…."

A devout Christian, my mother never failed to follow the Orthodox fasting rituals. Out of 366 days in a calendar year, 192 were days of fasting, and only 174 were times when pork grease or animal proteins were allowed in the diet. The Easter Fast (seven weeks), the Christmas Fast (six weeks), Saint Mary Fast (two weeks) and Saints Peter and Paul Fast (about three weeks) were never missed, and every single Wednesday and Friday were also included in this regimen, which enabled my mother to live many years without symptoms of atherosclerosis.

Iosefina Stroia lived to be 82 years of age and passed away on March 23, 1958, three months after I was released from prison. By then, she had developed cardio-circulatory insufficiency, suffering from a dilated, hypertrophied left ventricle, which was surely a result of the many efforts and insults sustained throughout her life. During her last three days, her condition deteriorated into generalized edema and a massive cerebral congestion.

My wife and I agreed to have our tombs near that of my mother and close to the graves of my worthy ancestors, my grandfather and my great-grandfather, named Stanciu Stroia as well. In memory of my father, we added a plaque on the cross bearing the following inscription: "Stroia Dumitru, assassinated in Russia on May 13, 1906, at the age of 39."

My Great-Grandfather

I was told that my great-grandfather, Stanciu Stroia Sr., had served several mandates as the mayor of Cacova, a village small in size but large in traditions, numbering a thousand souls at that time. The people re-elected him both because of his business savvy and his good character. They referred to him lovingly as "Stanciu from Zăvoi," as his farm was located on the highest hill in town, the starting point to many of the paths leading to the mountains. A large field, where all the village horses fed freely, surrounded his well-groomed propriety.

Stanciu sent Ștefan Stroia, one of his younger sons, to college in Sibiu, where he eventually relocated and started a remarkable professional journey, all the way up to becoming the head notary of the entire county. The eldest of his eight children embraced a military career and following his bravery, was promoted in 1939 to general in the Romanian Army. That success came despite his lack of fortune in the First World War of 1916–1918, in which he had lost his left hand.

After my mother passed away, a senior lady from the village and a patient of mine, Ana Hanzu, told me a story about my witty great-grandfather at the conclusion of one of her medical visits. She was the sister of the famous General Alexandru Hanzu, former professor at the Military Academy in Vienna, Austria, and commander of the Romanian mountain troops during the First World War. He had been decorated for bravely leading his soldiers during the successful 1919 campaign of Tisa and Budapest.

"You know, Doctor," Ana said in a sad voice, "I lost a very good friend when your mother died…"

After praising her as a descendant of a worthy family and the proud daughter of Father Ioan Hanzu Sr., she continued:

"Both your parents were people with bright minds; but *cel mai deștept*, the smartest one in the entire family was surely your great-grandfather. Whenever there was an argument to be settled between villagers, his opinion was the first one sought," she recalled fondly.

Then she concluded with one of the famous episodes from the man's life, one I never got tired of hearing: It was on Easter Sunday, around 1880, and my great-grandfather was summoned by the inspecting Hungarian official to come to the City Hall for questioning. It was around ten o'clock in the morning following the Easter Mass, and according to the Orthodox tradition, family and friends had gathered for celebrations. That large Romanian crowd made the Hungarian authority very anxious.

After politely refusing the invitation, the mayor, in good spirits, told the foreign messenger:

Voi veni la primărie când vor fi Paștile Joia!…"Let the prefect come to *my* house instead, since I am already entertaining guests. As far as me showing up at the City Hall, tell him that'll happen only when Easter Sunday falls on a Thursday!"

Ce ținută demnă și corectă! What a stance! After hearing that story, I kept reminding myself of my great-grandfather's dignity and unwillingness to accept humiliation. And I embraced him as a model of behavior toward repressive authorities.

Once the older woman left my house, I recalled a conversation I had with her brother, General Hanzu, during my last year of medical school in Cluj. We met on a train in 1928, while we were both traveling in the same wagon from Sibiu to Cacova, and we walked side by side all the way from the station to the village. I asked him why he was not commuting by a chauffeured car; after all, he was "The General!" He replied that this trip reminded him of his youth, that he liked to be able to recognize the stones lining up the road, and that he simply enjoyed visiting with his sister Ana like in the good old days. If he would arrive by automobile, his driver would jump out of the car to open the door for "Mister General," which would leave a long-lasting impression on Ana. And that was exactly the kind of impression he was trying to avoid. He did not want to address his sister from the height of his military rank.

With honesty I can affirm that I have always strived to be correct and courteous in my relationships as well, and the common sense that guided me throughout my life offered much protection against unpleasant surprises. Modesty was the weapon I chose to employ against other people's vanity, and I believed that humility should remain a virtue even in successful individuals.

In life, one should not try to humiliate another. And that applies especially to youngsters, who have a fragile self-esteem but a clearly emerging personality. One's respect cannot be demanded or imposed, but rather earned and accepted naturally. Aside from the professional skills acquired by each according to his interest, drive, and abilities, there is something else separating individuals, even those with equal access to education and of the same culture: It is called the individual character!

That is why I think of my great-grandfather—a smart and courageous man—with such great veneration!

According to the inscription on his gravestone, he passed away in 1883.

CHAPTER II—ARREST

First Interrogation–Făgăraş, October 1950

It will soon be thirty years since that fateful day. It was on a Sunday evening, the first day of Easter, on April 30, 1951. I had just returned home to Făgăraş from Cacova, where I had visited my mother. It was a quiet and relaxing family night as I was telling my wife and children about the holiday I had spent in my mother's company. Even though it was getting rather late, none of us was interested in going to bed.

Around midnight, a persistent knocking on the dining room window disturbed the peaceful atmosphere. As I cautiously looked outside, I recognized the local Securitate chief officer standing in front of my window, surrounded by several militiamen who were quick to greet me. I also noticed two armed individuals in uniform right behind the chief and another man, an older officer, dressed in civilian clothes patiently waiting at the gate. He appeared to be carrying a gun as well and was not making any efforts to conceal it.

Without much introduction, the captain entered my office with one of the men and proceeded to perform a thorough search. He focused on the area around my working desk and spent quite some time in the library, reluctantly giving up his search after it proved fruitless. Disappointed by his failure to uncover compromising evidence, he ordered me to follow him to the Securitate headquarters "right now!"

Since the end of October 1950, when I had my first encounter with the secret police, I had been waiting every day for someone to return for my arrest, living with that unpleasant sensation of the inevitable. After six months of observation and analysis of my political situation had gone by, I sensed that I would be "picked up." I had been offered missions as an informer in the interim, but following my stubborn refusal to cooperate, I feared that the police had not given up on me. I could not have imagined, however, that I was not going to return home that night.

The local Securitate chief officer, Captain Teodosiu, had summoned me with a direct telephone call on a late afternoon that previous October to visit his office. I felt quite at home in the police building, where I had been invited to examine and treat a couple of detainees just a few days before. Confidence in the safety of my situation was aided by the detail that I was Captain Teodosiu's family physician, which included taking care of the medical needs of his two small children.

Proceeding straight to business, the chief started the interview by asking me if I had a large practice and was curious to find out what kind of people I preferred to see.

"I enjoy working with the peasants from the mountain villages, because I think they are more honest," I replied spontaneously, unsure where the conversation was heading.

"So, did you plan to become well known among these people?" the colonel sitting next to the chief, who had been quiet until then, suddenly intervened in the most improper Romanian, with a noticeable foreign accent.

Without waiting for my reply or taking his eyes off me, Captain Teodosiu explained: "He wanted to make sure that his children have a future."

The colonel went on: *Va să zică, ai tratat pe cei de pe munte?* "Does it mean that you have treated men from the mountains?"

I answered that I was not interested in the places my patients came from and that I approached everybody equally, serving anyone who needed my medical expertise.

However, as soon as that specific question about mountain people was asked, I understood the Securitate's true intentions and the ultimate purpose of my invitation there.

{Shortly after the Communists seized power in March 1945 with the backing of the Soviet Union, an armed anti-Communist resistance consisting of numerous groups of partisans took shape. Those detachments, neither large nor unified, oper-

ated with small arms hidden since World War II, under the cover of the night and the protection of the mountains and its inhabitants. The resistance emerged as a spontaneous movement with the common aim of opposing the Communist takeover of Romania. The partisans' continuous harassment of the Securitate troops sent to subdue them and their stubborn survival was an embarrassment to the new regime and seriously undermined its efforts to achieve total control of the country. In addition, this symbolic anti-Communist resistance had the real potential of becoming contagious. That must have surely been the hope and goal of those insurgents, who planned to overthrow the Soviet-installed power when international circumstances were deemed appropriate and when Western—mainly U.S.—help was on its way. Made up of former Romanian Army officers, farmers, students, doctors, lawyers, and members of the dissolved democratic parties, the rebels were tenaciously hunted down and executed, along with all who helped them. They managed to remain operational until 1962, when the last known active partisan was killed in the Banat Mountains. However, according to recent memoirs, a few individuals survived the hunt, were pardoned after the 1964 amnesty, and were still alive at the fall of Communism in 1989. The best-known example is former partisan and author Ion Gavrilă-Ogoranu.}

In that uneven contest, as I was well aware of recent stories of abuse toward arrested individuals, I had to protect myself from the cowardly acts the Securitate was capable of. Concerned foremost with my family's safety, I also feared serious consequences for my physical integrity and, especially, mental health if I did not cooperate. I eventually agreed to sign a short statement through which I accused myself of nonexistent crimes.

That first and last interrogatory at the Făgăraș Securitate office lasted about sixty minutes and ended the way the captain had planned it all along, with my name under a self-incriminating note. I obstinately refused to sign the first two dictations, but I felt I was not given much of a choice when it came to the third one, even though I realized I was signing my own sentence to prison. On that last document, I scribbled in a barely legible, nervous handwriting and under significant psychological pressure, as I could not fail to notice the big revolver strategically placed on a wooden table close to where I was sitting. *Securiștii*, the Securitate people, used to carry such guns, and I recalled the two officers who once lived in the upstairs bedrooms of my house who had one each. A thin door with window panels was all that separated our room from theirs, and I remember hearing the van stopping at our gate to pick the militiamen up, while they loaded their automatic guns and laughed on the way out the door....

Seeing that I was cornered, I tried in one instance—without asking for permission—to grab the telephone, wanting to inform my family about my whereabouts and reassure them that I was all right. I dared doing so because I thought I knew the Securitate chief well enough. But my hand froze on the receiver when the chief raised his voice:

Ce faci tovarășe? "What do you think you are doing, comrade?"

The moment I had to give him an explanation was the first time I started to wonder if I was still Doctor Stroia. Not only was my request to contact my home promptly denied, but I was also forced to sign another statement through which I engaged myself "not to say a word about what happened here, not even to my family." Otherwise, the note read bluntly, "I would be shot and my family would be punished." The entire situation appeared suddenly quite critical.

I have not spoken to anyone, not even to my loved ones, about what occurred that October afternoon within the walls of the Făgăraș Securitate office. This is the first time that I have written about it. And I would be extremely interested to find out if those statements surfaced *la dosar*, in my mysterious personal file, and what other accusations or derogatory information had been collected against me. Of crucial importance would be the declaration of Socol, the young partisan who was the first one to be captured, interrogated, and killed in obscure circumstances....

Three Young Men—Mogoș, Mazilu, and Socol

In order to save my family from an unpredictable future, I stated in writing that I had helped *fugari legionari*, "fascist fugitives" of my own volition and completely aware of whom I was dealing with. In fact, I never met any such men and had no true concept of what the Securitate was referring to.

The extent of my knowledge about the partisans' activity was similar to that of the average Făgăraș citizen—meaning very limited. The only suspicious individuals I had recently encountered were three of my son's former high school colleagues, Ioan Mogoș, Nicolaie Mazilu, and Silviu Socol, to whom I had offered insignificant help. I did not have any direct knowledge of their connections with the anti-Communist movement.

The three young men, whom I had never personally met before, showed up at our door on October 10, 1950, at around seven o'clock in the evening. Arriving home after my hospital rounds, I found them patiently waiting on the first level of our home, where I was running a private practice. They had introduced themselves to my wife as patients, and she signed them in despite the late hour. My daughter was home as well, whereas my son was not, having recently moved to the capital, where he was studying at the Bucharest Polytechnic Institute.

After a formal introduction, I quickly recalled that two years earlier on the morning of their high school graduation exam, they had been arrested by the Securitate. They were preparing an essay with my son, under the supervision of their Romanian language teacher. Zeno was not among the apprehended, and I never knew the nature of his friends' charge. I was also aware that prior to that incident, he had invited them to our house for *șezători literare* (book readings), and for a few birthday parties. That summed up the extent of the information I possessed about the three youngsters.

Socol was suffering from persistent strabismus in one eye, and I was quite certain that he was the son of father Socol from Berivoi, a nearby village. All Mazilu said to me was that he needed money in order to pay for a train ticket to return to his family in Timișoara, while Mogoș remained silent. We did not engage in any other conversations, but when I saw the students so poorly dressed and because it was very cold outside, I gave them a couple of shirts and pants, two of my old coats, a few aspirin and sulfonamide tablets, and some pocket money (about eight thousand lei, not a substantial amount during that period of inflation). Standing at the gate watching them leave our property, I advised them:

Nu vă încredeți în nimeni, și vedeți-vă de treabă!

"Do not trust anyone and mind your own business!"

Months later during my trial, I was repeatedly questioned about those words, and the court insisted that I explain exactly what I meant by them.

The young men returned ten days later, and I agreed to help them once more, this time with a handmade wool sweater, some medication, three thousand lei, and twenty blank pieces of writing paper they specifically requested. Once they had left, I suggested to our family members to be cautious in the future and not to welcome them into our house if they were to come back.

After a few days, I discovered that the alleged reason for their arrest in the past had been a vague accusation of "subversive political activity" and membership in the clandestine youth organization *Frăţia de Cruce*, "The Sworn Brotherhood." For that offense, they all had already served one year of prison time. When I provided the help, I was not aware of those particular details.

As more information about the young men surfaced during my imprisonment, I had a change of heart, wishing I had done more to help their cause. Three years into my detention at the Aiud Penitentiary, other inmates from Făgăraş informed me that Socol had died (nobody knew where, why, and how), and that the other two boys had been fatally shot through a pub window at night, right before they attempted to escape the country by swimming across the Danube to Yugoslavia.

During that first interrogation at the end of October 1950, the colonel threatened me with a face-to-face encounter with Socol. That confrontation never took place, largely because I insisted it should. Being naïve and having good faith as well as lacking diplomacy and political sense, I made the deadly mistake of appearing happy to come up against the alleged partisan who was imprisoned—the chief claimed—in the basement of the building. I pictured myself free of trouble and with a rapidly clarifying situation, as I was confident that Socol would confess the truth. Maybe at that time, he was already dead, but in any event, a statement made by him in front of the investigators could have only been favorable to me. Because no subversive exchange of words took place, I felt safe in my innocence. My interaction with the men had been simply an act of unconditional help offered to people in need.

{According to archived Securitate documents published in 2004 by Ion Gavrilă-Ogoranu, Silviu Socol was arrested in Toderița, Făgăraș County, on November 14, 1950, and Nicolaie Mazilu and Ioan Mogoș were shot to death during a fight with Securitate forces in Pădureni, Timișoara County, on December 16, 1950. All three were free when Dr. Stanciu Stroia was first interrogated, but already dead at the time of his arrest.}

These were the circumstances leading to my investigation, arrest, and subsequent sentence. Only now, decades later, do I realize that it took some courage and inner strength to navigate through that volatile period. In the difficult and anxious days following the interrogation, I continued to practice as an internist in Făgăraș as if nothing had happened. But I made the dangerous decision to carry with me at all times, carefully hidden in the left lower corner of my suit's lining, 10 grams of heroin, in the event I was detained and tortured. It would have been sufficient to intoxicate up to one hundred people....

No one in my family or any other person for that matter knew, until now, that I possessed such a large dose of the drug. Until the Făgăraș hospital pharmacy service was founded in 1947, I kept all of the controlled substances under my lock and surveillance and upon my subsequent election to hospital director, I remained in charge of the clinic medication safe.

Nevertheless, I flushed the heroin down the toilet a few days prior to my arrest.

My Arrest—Făgăraș, April 1951

The night of my arrest, on April 30, 1951, I was escorted in a civilized manner to the Făgăraș Securitate headquarters, located only a few blocks from our home. I did not object, argue, or even ask what was going to happen to me. Otherwise, I surely would have been handcuffed; the tall, intimidating officer waiting at the gate seemed ready to tackle me if ordered.

After a brisk walk in the cool night, I was delivered to the militiaman on duty, a middle-aged individual who had been my patient the other day. Lieutenant Tache and his subordinates strip-searched me thoroughly and took everything I had on me, including my pocket watch with its golden chain and my wedding ring. The latter must have been stolen, since it never followed me with the rest of my items to the Aiud prison. The watch, which I insisted be listed on the inventory of my personal belongings, was returned to me years later and is still in my possession today.

{The elegant Swiss-made Tissot pocket watch, more than half a century old, was offered to me on my coming of age and survived the transatlantic move. It is displayed with other family relics in my "Romanian room."}

After all of those formalities, I was shoved down the dirty basement of the building, with cement floors covered in urine and fecal excrements. The guard placed me in a small cell and locked the door; it was my first time in isolation.

After two hours of restlessly waiting in that cellar with countless thoughts spinning through my head, two Securitate officers arrived and blindfolded me. Without providing explanations, they guided me upstairs and pushed me into a police van, along with other detainees who had been arrested from their homes that night. Listening to their voices, I noticed that there were quite a few young people among them. They were obviously able to look around and recognize me; I heard them whisper softly:

Uite mă, doctorul Stroia! "Look, it's Doctor Stroia!"

Sitting on the back seat of the van, I was sandwiched and effectively immobilized between two Securitate officers, who ordered me *Să nu scoți o vorbă!*, not to make a sound. Any time I attempted to move, something iron-cold was pressed against my temple. The gun was evidently used to intimidate me and, probably more so, to frighten the prisoners with uncovered eyes.

Given the type of road the car was on, it was difficult to sense the direction we were heading to, maybe toward Brașov or Sibiu. At dawn, we arrived at Sibiu, a town I immediately recognized from the sounds of the streetcars' horns. Despite my efforts, I was unable to guess the location where we finally stopped.

Initial Detention—Sibiu

Eyes still covered, I was moved out of the van, walked a few steps outside, and entered a room where I was placed facing the wall.

"*Mă fascistule, legionarule!*" barked the guards, as they started their tirade, ensuring that I did not forget the gravity of the crimes I was accused of. Vulgar words, cursing, name-calling, and generally rude manners continued until they ended with blows on my back and boots hitting me on the bottom. *De!* Oh well!

Thanks to the epithets I was called by, especially that of *legionar* (Iron Guard member), I understood why I was so carefully watched and isolated from the others. Everything that happened during my incarceration time, and even long after my name was cleared by the courts nine years after I was released, was a consequence of those labels.

{The "Iron Guard" was a Romanian fascist movement, a political cult established in 1927 as the "Legion of the Archangel Michael." Organized into paramilitary units, its members committed acts of violence, vandalism, and political assassinations, including that of the illustrious historian Professor Nicolae Iorga. Promoting nationalistic and Eastern Orthodox values, it enlisted the support of the clergy and became a mass movement. The parliamentary elections of 1937 saw the Iron Guard evolve into the third-largest Romanian political party, with a leader, Corneliu Zelea Codreanu, who captured the masses through his mystical devotion to Christianity and his commitment to anti-Semitism and anti-Communism. In 1941, the Romanian Army, under the command of Marshall Ion Antonescu, suppressed a military rebellion organized by the Legion, and the organization's demise followed quickly thereafter.}

A few hours later, still blindfolded, I was dragged toward a basement, as I counted ten steps down. At the last one, I was told to keep my head up so that I would hit the stone ceiling, after which I was pushed and locked in the first cell on the left of the stairwell. There, one guard uncovered my eyes, which adjusted easily to the very poorly lit surroundings. The room was located in the basement of the Sibiu Securitate headquarters and was called *talpa iadului* (bottom of hell), a term I found out about later from fellow Sibiu Penitentiary inmates. It was a very small space with no windows to the outside world, filthy, with mud on the floor, putrid walls, and water dripping from the ceiling. The intermittent flushing noise emanating from above meant that the toilets were placed right above it.

Apart from this cell where I spent half a day, the Securitate basement had another larger room, divided into ten improvised spaces, five on each side of a small, narrow middle hallway. The jailors had baptized these ten cells *cele zece porunci* (the Ten Commandments).

Later that night, eyes covered again, I was moved to a so-called *celulă mormânt* (grave cell). There were three such rooms at the bottom of the basement, roughly fifteen meters away from the stairs and to the left of the hallway, in a cave that had been dug in the ground. These makeshift spaces were supported by wooden boards and had no light. The third cell was divided into another three rooms, each about one meter by a half-meter in size. I was ordered to head toward the last one, which resembled a tomb-like structure. Once the guard locked the door behind him, I was forced to sit on a board a half-meter in size (which I measured with the palm of my hand), supported by a wooden post. One could only enter this cell when the sitting board was raised at the guard's orders.

There was mud and dirt on the floor, and the brick walls were unfinished, without paint or plaster covering, so rough that you could not lean against them. And then there were the rats swarming at my feet, quite a few and very lively. All this for the purpose of intimidating me, of course!

I was not allowed to talk to the neighboring prisoner even in the softest tone of voice, because there was constant surveillance by the jailors working in short shifts. You could hear them only when they would sneak in, slowly and carefully opening the hallway door, guided by a flashlight, an essential tool in that completely unlit environment. These cells were built with the evident intention of breaking down the psychological resistance of the prisoners, in anticipation of further questioning.

When my neighbor called me in a whispering voice, "Stanciu," believing I was one of his colleagues from Olteț, who happened to have the same first name, I had to reassure myself it was a human being speaking to me and not a ghost. Unfortunately, the prison guard heard him before I could answer, so the poor man was ferociously beaten and repeatedly hit against the hard stonewalls.

I spent three full days isolated in that area, from Monday morning until Thursday morning. Only God and my interrogators witnessed the extent of my physical transformation during those seventy-two hours of no eating and no bathroom privileges. I refused to eat the small daily pieces of bread thrown at me, and when I grew tired of sitting, I placed them as pillows under my head. They ended up eaten by the rats, the biggest specimens I have seen in my entire life. Only at the Sibiu and Aiud prisons have I encountered rats thirty to forty centimeters in length, not to mention the other forty to fifty centimeters of their tails!

The quality two-layer raglan coat that I had bought in Brașov in 1936 and was still wearing at that point kept me from freezing. Years later, from what was left of it I made a small vest, which I still wear today, during the summer, in Cacova.

On the fourth day, a Securitate man opened the cell door and addressed me, while talking in total darkness:

Na mă, întinde palma! "Hey you, stretch your palm out."

Responding to the first human interaction in days, I took the slice of bread handed to me and gulped it down with an extraordinary appetite and speed. I felt as if I had just returned from the dead, as if I was brought back to life. Eating the 50 grams of bread, I instantly regretted the slices I had wasted on the rats. From that moment on, bread became and has remained until this day the most delicious nourishment in my diet.

Second Interrogation—Sibiu

Around eight o'clock that morning, a guard handed me a pair of black eyeglasses and roughly hustled me upstairs, pale and exhausted, as I must have looked. He held me by my arm as he guided me through the hallway and the stairways, reminding me to raise my head just in time to hit every stone sticking out of the ceiling. It was time for my next interrogation.

The chief investigator in charge of my case was Securitate agent Gheorghe Mezei. His assistant, a senior lieutenant, motioned me inside but never introduced himself, so I do not know his name. Interestingly and undoubtedly prearranged, another lieutenant from the Făgăraş office whom I knew very well attended my interrogatory as well. He was sitting comfortably on a chair in the back, and I recognized him the moment I entered the interrogation chamber. Alexandrescu had lived in our house in recent months, in one of the upstairs bedrooms with his wife, who used our downstairs kitchen. A native of Roşiorii de Vede, he moved in upon his arrival to Făgăraş, before he could find a suitable flat. At the time of my arrest, the local authorities had ordered me to house as many as three Securitate officers on the second floor.

The familiar presence initially gave me courage and a sense of relief. I was neither afraid nor in low spirits that morning, but my face was probably disfigured from the three days spent in total darkness. To my bewilderment, Senior Lieutenant Alexandrescu, dressed in civilian clothing, appeared to be pleased to see me looking so deplorable. He moved to the same table with me, to my right, only a meter away, with an arrogant grin on his face. At that hour, I must have been the stellar captive of the Făgăraş Securitate! I do not recall ever having to interact with a more ill-intended individual.

As soon as I sat down, I asked Alexandrescu for a cigarette—we had smoked together many times before—but he rudely refused. (My eternal naiveté!)

Hoping to get the entire ordeal over with quickly, I agreed to write on a blank sheet of paper a statement dictated by the investigator. But when Mezei got to the description of my "bourgeois" house, my private property that I had built between 1936 and 1938 from scratch and after many years of hard labor, I refused to continue. It was then that Lieutenant Alexandrescu interrupted the dictation to inform the investigator that he was very familiar with the topography of my house and the three different entrances it had. He ordered me to write that I had sought the help of anti-Communist partisans to capture and execute the Securitate officers who lived upstairs.

Outraged, I tore apart my two and a half pages of self-incriminating declaration and to everybody's dismay made an attempt to get up from the chair. Captain Mezei quickly summoned me to sit down and dictated another one. The exact words I put on that piece of paper I cannot recall, since my exhaustion at that time had reached a critical point. I signed that statement in the end—what else was I supposed to do?—while pointing out my indignation and disbelief to Lieutenant Alexandrescu. I stated that I did not admit to what I was forced to write, and that he would be tormented all his life by the fabricated accusations he brought against me. Predictably, my interjection had no effect, and I did not even have the strength to read what I had just written. Apart from his search for the proper accusatory words to be included in the dictation, Captain Mezei paced around the room without asking me anything. Somehow, I escaped that session without being beaten.

Four hours later, I returned to the grave cell, glasses still on, but this time I was told to look out for the steps and the ceiling so that I would not hurt myself. As I was being taken back to the basement, I noticed a desk with a telephone in the middle of the hallway, surrounded by several prison guards. I heard the phone ring, saw an officer nodding his head: *Da, da!* "Yes, yes!" and all of a sudden the jailors were less brutal with me.

I smelled food, a sign that they were serving lunch at noon, and I sat down on the bench of the grave cell with the door left partially open. A few seconds later, another guard came along with a bowl full of thick sour soup and a piece of bread weighing about 250 grams. The cup was excessively full, with the content spilling over, and the potatoes and pieces of cartilage the soup contained gave it an added consistency.

Before I had a chance to eat, the guard removed my glasses and led me—carefully carrying my bowl in his hands—toward the door of the hallway. I was pleasantly surprised by his almost humane behavior. I did not know what was going to happen next, but when I saw the blue sky through the door of the first room on the right, at the entrance of the basement, and the daylight coming from the stairway, I was almost certain I would be freed.

A Frightening Encounter

My happiness was short-lived, however. The guard pushed me into the next cell, and when the door to the basement suddenly closed behind me, I found myself in the most frightening situation of my entire period of detention. The first thing I noticed as I entered that room was a tiny window with iron bars and about twenty empty and ravaged black metal beds, some on top of each other. It was pitch black, the air was thick and foul-smelling. For a moment, I thought I was going to be murdered: A bulky young fellow sitting on a bench in the corner of the cell near the door, about 24 years old and over two meters tall, charged me like a madman. Through a miraculous balancing act, I managed to save my bowl of soup from spilling and my piece of bread from falling to the ground.

The man, unshaven and looking at me with big, bulging eyes, had a frightful appearance and wore the lost expression of a crazy person. I was convinced he was a Securitate hit man, sent to exterminate me. He grabbed my left arm violently and started to groan, his breath wretched. I pleaded with him to let go of me, but he kept moaning and mumbling nonsensically, unable to utter a clear word. He appeared to have had a shock when he saw me and was speechless as a result. My immediate thought was to hit him hard in the groin or testicles, and then attempt to make my way to the small cell window looking out onto the yard, with the intention of shouting or crying for help in case I was badly hurt.

After a few agonizing moments of wrestling, the man, who appeared to have calmed down, realized that I failed to recognize him and started to talk to me, looking me straight in the eyes while shaking me by the shoulders:

"*Doctore, doctore!*"

Still very suspicious, I firmly replied: *Lasă-mă în pace! Nu te cunosc!* "Leave me alone. I don't know you!"

But he insisted: "Of course you do. It's me, Lae Greavu! I'm married to Melita Balthes, the butcher's daughter from Făgăraș!"

I recollected instantly that she was one of my patients, and I knew that her husband was the only individual in Făgăraș with that unusual name. Lae Greavu was a theology student and a native of Olteț village, where several farmers and students had recently been arrested. He told me he had been isolated in this cell for several days and felt as if he were losing his mind. The room we were in was a horrible mess, with the twenty iron bunk beds in total disarray. Depressed and exasperated at his lengthy isolation, Lae had tried to hang himself, but he could not manage to get his sizeable head through the loops of the bed frame.... My fear, at least, had vanished.

Years later I returned to Făgăraș to discover that Lae's wife Melita, a German girl, had divorced him—as many wives were coerced into doing by the Securitate—despite raising his child....

After a couple of days, another dozen prisoners were brought into our cell, mostly very young men. One of them was Ion Roșca from Râușor, the birth village of my wife, a detail that made the entire situation harder to tolerate. Officers stopped by frequently to inspect our room, always making a point of asking the younger detainees in an ironic and tendentious manner about the plans they discussed with *șefu'*, "the chief from Făgăraș."

{*A distant relative of Dr. Stanciu Stroia and a classmate of his daughter, Ion Roșca was arrested while a senior in high school. "As we awaited our interrogation in that crowded environment"—Roșca recalls—"we abstained from talking. The detainees did not trust each other since the distinction between a true prisoner and an informer was impossible to make. I first recognized Dr. Stanciu Stroia's voice as he wrangled with a guard about the rough treatment. The two of us decided to discuss only medical issues." Accused of "conspiracy to destroy the popular regime in*

Romania," Ion Roşca spent twelve years between Sibiu, Jilava, Gherla, and Aiud prisons; a stone quarry at the Danube-Black Sea Canal; and forced labor camps in Periprava and Grind. Released in 1963, he returned to high school and obtained his baccalaureate diploma. As of January 2005, he was alive and well at the age of 73.}

Around the same time, another native of my city was being held in the first room near the entrance to the basement, on the right side of the hallway. Curious about the activity on the corridor, he dragged a long bench to the door and looked through the cracks in the upper wooden boards. That is when he heard the phone ring in the guards' room and tried to listen to the instructions the men were getting from their superiors. We met later in a different cell, and he recounted how he had witnessed when I was led to the interrogation chamber and had watched the hallway until I was brought back four hours later, looking terribly exhausted. I was wearing my own street clothes then, including the beige raglan coat, by which I was recognized in the entire city of Făgăraş. He also recalled that as soon as I was brought back to the grave cell, the phone rang again and the sergeant on duty took a standing position while replying to his orders:

Da, să trăiţi, am înţeles! "Yes, sir. I understand, sir!"

The guards appeared relaxed and were talkative as if they had just accomplished a successful mission.

Friends and Foes

The food we were given while I was jailed in Sibiu had few calories and included no fresh vegetables or fruits whatsoever, but it was—as I was going to find out—of slightly better quality than that at Aiud. Our daily meals consisted of a mold-free piece of corn mush and over 200 grams of wheat bread. We ate the porridge in the morning with a great appetite, but the most filling meal was the evening piece of bread.

On a few occasions, fresh food came through the cell window: peppers, onions, or fruits from the pantry, thrown by the youngest son of the prison director, an eight-year-old playful and seemingly always happy boy. He sympathized with us, maybe because he saw a few young students among the inmates in our group. Our cell's windows were located right across from the kitchen and the adjacent director's house; they had narrow iron bars at the time, without the wooden shutters added later. The boss's wife, a clerk of the court, was gone most of the day, so nobody supervised the boy.

As we were taking the infrequent, brisk walk through the prison yard, the child threw any food he could find in the pantry at us, watching our procession pass by his window. The younger inmates quickly and discretely collected the leftovers, and upon returning to our cell, we all shared and consumed them with great pleasure.

Other times, the boy climbed up on the prison wall, near the sentry boxes; from there he threw half-smoked cigarette butts discarded by the officers. Throughout all this, the guards on the prison wall looked the other way, pretending not to notice what the director's child was up to. However, there were other individuals responsible for supervising the jailors themselves. These counter informers, who watched from hidden locations throughout the compound, reported directly to the chief.

Eventually, the all-powerful director, who went to great lengths to avoid any contact with the prisoners, was informed by the cleaning woman, a young Saxon girl, of his son's activities. The father saw fit to solve the problem by physically punishing him, which outraged the inmates but eventually proved to be effective.

In an attempt to get even, the boy sang to the housekeeper: *Ecaterino, vedea-te-aș moartă, cu dric la poartă și cai mascați!* "Ecaterina, I wish you were dead, with a black hearse and masked horses at your door!"

When he got beat again the next evening, we voiced our disagreement by shouting through the windows of our cell. We carried on for many minutes. Sadly, after a while, the child stopped showing up in the yard or at the window....

As I was trying to occupy my time standing near the basement window of the Sibiu prison, I could hear and count the steps of the guards patrolling the prison court. Invariably, accompanying their steps were those of a dog, a German shepherd named Loprich who belonged to Captain Mezei, my former interrogator. This dog was famous at the Sibiu Securitate headquarters. If prompted by the commands *burghez* or *chiabur* (bourgeois or rich), it would rush upon that person. The story goes that this accidentally happened to the captain himself during a training exercise, when the animal tore apart his coat.

Another torment at Sibiu was the shaving we were given by a regular convict who mistrusted and disliked us, the "politicals." His favorite activity appeared to be shaving our group every ten to fourteen days, which he accomplished with laundry—rather than shaving—soap and without any foam. Under the watchful eye of a prison guard, he first got our faces barely wet, and then finished the job hastily with a sharp razor. Some of the depressed inmates would have cut their own throats if they had ever managed to get their hands on that razor!

As I continued living in this challenging environment, I was moved at one point into another cell, crammed with at least forty other prisoners. Some of them were sleeping on a platform above the bunk beds. That is how I met the notary from Săcel, a village near mine, who was sentenced to four years in prison because the county tax collector denounced him as having *un defect de comportament față de autorități*, "a behavioral defect toward the authorities." The same individual accused him, among other things, of having hidden in his garden guns seized after the German retreat, none of which were found by the Securitate men during their search.

Throughout the days that followed, more and more prisoners were crammed into our cell, most of them from Făgăraș. A local "gangster" was among them. He was a repeat offender convicted of various petty crimes, busy telling stories about his adventures to the youngsters in the cell who were eager to listen and learn. He claimed to have been caught stealing a bag full of important documents from a German businessperson as the man was boarding a plane. What a good education one can receive while wasting time in prison, I thought.

I could hardly stand the atmosphere of that basement room, which had a little vault in the middle of the ceiling. This was arguably because I was only at the beginning of my years behind bars; the grueling period was yet to come, after my trial and conviction.

When you are incarcerated, the most difficult thing to endure is not the lack of physical liberty per se, as one might think; rather, it's all of the other continuous restrictions imposed on your daily life. The regimen was unbearable for political prisoners in particular. The norm was to isolate them and to force them into hard labor to the point of exhaustion. In addition, various prisons had different rules and regulations one had to obey and comply with, which made any attempt to adapt unlikely to succeed.

CHAPTER III—TRIAL

Sibiu Penitentiary—May 1951

One day in May 1951, a few weeks after my arrest, we were all transferred from the Securitate jail via police vans to a new location for our trials. During our leaving of the compound, I discovered that the basement in which we had been detained, located adjacent to the Sibiu Courthouse and Military Tribunal, was a part of the headquarters of the 7th Army Corps.

Throughout this transportation, my eyes were not covered, so I thoroughly enjoyed the clear daylight and took plenty of deep breaths of the fresh morning air. As I passed through the prison yard, I felt almost free and very upbeat, despite the watchful presence of Securitate officers all around me. I could not see how and why I would be sentenced to long years of imprisonment. This was a reflection of my good faith and political naiveté, which I suffered from my entire life. I imagined that I would receive some type of punishment, but I was also confident of a suspension of that sentence, given the frivolity of the charges brought against me.

Looking back, I realize how unprepared I was, from a physical standpoint and even more from a mental one, to face what was to come. I had never spoken with ex-political prisoners, and I was not aware of the severity of the regimen imposed in Communist jails.

Once we entered the Sibiu Penitentiary, the prisoners who were allowed to light cigarettes were advised to finish smoking. A few of us were introduced in one of the rooms on the first floor, where I found four other men still dressed in their civilian clothes. I made the assumption that they had not been sentenced yet. One of them was Cornel Balaj, a recently married young man of 24 years of age from Ilia, Hunedoara County. I ended up working with him at the Ilia polyclinic years later, upon my release, and we managed to avoid disclosing that we knew each other from before.

{Cornel Balaj was accused of "conspiracy against the social order." "At one point"—Balaj recalls—"Dr. Stroia and I shared adjacent cells, so we climbed up on our beds at night in order to talk through the iron bars by the ceiling. We also indulged in quick conversations during the yard walk. When I informed Dr. Stroia of my four-year sentence, he reassured me with a sigh of relief: 'It will be a piece of cake! Four years will pass before you know it!'" Cornel Balaj spent his entire sentence at the Danube-Black Sea Canal, between 1951 and 1955. Despite the official interdiction and potential repercussions, the two enjoyed a long-lasting friendship well beyond the prison years and kept a regular correspondence on family and medical matters. Suffering from a chronic muscle disease, Balaj became Dr. Stroia's patient in Ilia in 1958. He was still in good health in January 2005, at the age of 82.}

All of the inmates in that cell appeared depressed and subdued after weeks of imprisonment and uncertainty about their immediate future. I tried to be a bit cheerful and managed to raise their spirits with the bread and ten cigarettes I had just received from Mr. Balaj. Moreover, as I noticed some straw mattresses worn to shreds in one of the corners of the room, I asked nonchalantly:

Unde-i dormitorul meu? "Where's my bedroom?"

They all burst into laughter.

The Germans

One of my new cellmates was a tall and robust man, around 36 years of age. He claimed to have been a wartime employee of the German ambassador to Romania, Manfred von Killinger, at his former residence by Lake Snagov, near Bucharest. He recalled how his former boss committed suicide in 1944, to avoid capture by the Soviet troops storming his embassy. A gendarme sergeant in the German official's guard, my roommate had been arrested once before; the first detention took place in 1947, when he was apprehended while attempting to flee across the border into Yugoslavia, carrying his gun and all of his military equipment. The second time, he was taken into custody for saying *un banc*, a rather innocent political joke!

Many individuals were jailed in those days for ridiculing Communist officials in sarcastic stories, quickly spread from person to person, with some people arrested at their places of employment after being denounced by colleagues. In 1948, this man was sent to join a battalion of former gendarmes, camped at Orăștie, in order to be "re-educated" and retrained. As soon as he arrived at the site, he met some old friends, and when asked to tell what news he had, he replied with the comic story about "RPR." One of his friends did not fail to report him, so he was re-arrested and transferred to Sibiu, where he was serving a sentence of one and a half years.

{This is a play on words: RPR or "Rau, Petre, Rau" is translated as "Bad, Peter, Bad" but could also mean Popular Republic of Romania. This was a subtle hint at the hardships experienced by Romanians during those years.}

The sole advantage of being constantly moved between different cells was the chance to interact with interesting people. Former active military men were among those jailed at the Sibiu Penitentiary, awaiting their trial by the military court. In July 1951, a rumor was circulating that three recently arrested generals would join our group. A German non-commissioned officer was brought instead. It was easy to recognize the man's background because of the way he greeted us, with a typical German salute, and by his peaked military cap. We received him with hospitality, and I offered him a cigarette from the seemingly endless pack carefully hidden in the cell's chimney. I thought the young man would enjoy it, as I knew that transported detainees were not permitted to smoke. Besides, nobody was allowed to bring cigarettes into the cells.

The German had been arrested when he attempted to flee the country and return to West Germany, like his other compatriot. He had been a Nazi pilot engaged on the Russian front, but when his air force regiment was defeated in 1943, he began flying supply planes from Sevastopol, in Southeast Russia to Constanța, on the Romanian Black Sea coast. With the German Army retreating and the Soviet Army reclaiming previously lost territories, he had to change his route to Constanța—Budapest, Hungary. On his sixteenth flight, above Agnita, near Mediaș, his plane ran out of fuel, and he was forced to land on a farm field. Of the four-member flight crew, one died during the emergency landing and the other two were shot by pursuing Romanian gendarmes. He was the fortunate one who managed to escape with the help of the local Transylvanian Saxons. Under their protection, he survived by hiding in the tall cornfields until the fall. At harvest time, when the crops were collected and the hiding place vanished, he was left with the sole and bleak choice of surrendering to the Romanian authorities. He endured forced labor as a sweeper in the city of Sighișoara and later, because he was a mechanic by training, he was transferred to a factory near Caracal. After five years, he escaped the camp but was eventually caught at the border.

He was a high school graduate, so we found some topics of mutual interest, in particular chemistry subjects, our conversations being aided by the presence of a chemistry student in the cell. The German was very intrigued by our general knowledge and culture, because he thought that all Romanians were backward and uncivilized. What surprised me even more and made me recall this encounter was his lack of accurate information regarding the history of the Romanian people and their existence in Transylvania. He was convinced—because it was what he had always been taught—that all of the cultured inhabitants of Transylvania were Germans, dispersed over one hundred square kilometers to the right and to the left of the road connecting Arad, Oradea, and Brașov. Consequently, the German soldiers came to Transylvania to defend their own people!

A thorough education and good geography lesson courtesy of the Third Reich!

{An explanatory note about the German migration to Romania: Transylvania or Ardeal is the northwestern region of the country, a fertile, picturesque, and wooded plateau surrounded by the Carpathian Mountains, also called the Transylvanian Alps. In the twelfth century, it was part of the Magyar Kingdom, which persuaded German colonists by means of free land and tax incentives to settle in strategic areas, in order to defend the crown's southeastern frontiers against the Turkish Empire.

Saxons arrived in southern Transylvania from Flanders and the Lower Rhine, and a number of predominantly German cities emerged in a region inhabited by a Romanian majority. They included Sibiu (Hermannstadt), Cluj (Klausenburg), Brașov (Kronstadt), and Sighișoara (Schäßburg). Fortified towns and churches (Kirchenburgen) were built to guard the mountain passes, and the Transylvanian Saxons (Siebenbürger Sachsen) grew prosperous by dominating the trade routes to Asia. A second migration occurred centuries later, between 1712 and 1815, when the Habsburg Empire settled farmers from Swabia in the western part of Transylvania, in cities such as Timișoara (Temeswar) and Satu Mare (Sathmar). They were to repopulate territories devastated by wars and epidemics and cultivate land regained from the withdrawing Ottoman Turks. These settlers were known as the Danube or Banat Swabians (Donauschwaben or Banater Schwaben). Some Germans intermarried and assimilated over the years; others became fierce nationalists and were the ancestors of the Germans accused of pro-Hitler sympathies. While the German population in Transylvania reached a peak of 745,000 in the 1930s, the post-World War II enslavement of thousands in forced labor in the Soviet Union, followed by the repatriation of many to West Germany, led to dwindling numbers of less then 20,000—by the most pessimistic accounts—and ensured the virtual extinction of a culture.}

Three Romanian Generals

After three weeks spent within the walls of the same cell, the German was removed from our group. From the standpoint of the prison establishment, friendship-building was undesirable because it could lead to solidarity and unrest. A division general—as anticipated—was introduced in his place in June 1951. He was an older man of medium height and light build with a gentle face. He introduced himself as General Radu Băldescu, former commander of the 18th Infantry Division of the Romanian Army. He had fought at Sevastopol and was decorated with the Michael the Brave Order and the Iron Cross. I was told that the maneuvers this general orchestrated on the battlefield were filmed and shown in all movie theatres in Berlin as a model of modern and efficient warfare tactics.

He was a quiet, dignified, and reserved man, who appeared to be in great emotional suffering. He kept looking through the window the whole time—there were no wooden boards to cover our outside view then—trying to get a glance at the little granddaughter of his that he used to walk to school until only a few days before. The separation from his family was an overwhelming torment.

Days later, he suffered a small stroke, resulting in right-sided hemi-paresis and significant speech difficulty. We notified the prison physician, and he agreed to send anticoagulant medication over, albeit with some delay. Beyond that measure, he showed total disregard for the case and made no attempt to hospitalize the general in the infirmary, designated for critical situations such as this.

A change of his fortune occurred when a major from the M.A.I., the almighty Ministry of Internal Affairs, inspected the facility and ordered the jail administrator to arrange for beds in our cell. The condition of the general improved visibly after a few days of adequate rest.

{General Radu Băldescu was born in 1888 and was the son of an Orthodox priest. An Officers' School graduate, he took part in several World War I campaigns and by 1941 was promoted to the rank of general in the Romanian Army. Assigned the 18th Infantry Division, he guided it to great military success during the siege of Sevastopol in June-July 1942, fighting alongside German armies. His units broke the Soviet lines, seized their objectives, and repulsed all enemy counterattacks. For his skills and bravery, he was awarded multiple medals and orders. However, because of his refusal to execute defecting Romanian soldiers, his hostility toward politicizing the army, and especially his open criticism of Communism, he was compelled to resign, lost his rank, and was arrested by the Securitate in June 1951. He died in Jilava prison in December 1953.}

After separation from General Băldescu, I was surprised and delighted to meet General Calețeanu, whom I had worked with at the Military Instruction Center in Făgăraș. I had been briefly dispatched there during World War II while he was still a colonel. We had kept in touch for a while, and he stated that a few days prior to his arrest and upon his transfer to Sibiu he had sent me an Easter card.

"Now I know why you didn't reply to my note," he said in a forgiving voice.

I had already been imprisoned when he wrote the card. Caleţeanu claimed that he was the 104th high-ranking military official discharged and detained by the Communists since the end of the war.

Another few weeks passed, and in July 1951, I landed in a different cell, where I met General Gheorghe Marinescu from Sibiu. In comparison to the previous military men I had come across, he appeared depressed, demoralized, and lacked self-respect. He would bow several times and lie on his belly in front of the guards, even after the prison director finished his routine morning inspection. All inmates were forced to get down to the floor during the cell chief's report to the guards, but that was the extent of it.

Moreover, the general was very disappointed by his arrest, since he had published an ode dedicated to Stalin in a local Sibiu newspaper. But he had forgotten that he pushed the limits of acceptable wartime behavior in order to get decorated and advanced in rank. He failed to remember that in the letters and photos sent to his wife, he bragged about the capture and gruesome execution of the leader of the Ukrainian partisans he had been ordered to apprehend. Upon returning home, he chose to divorce his wife. She denounced him in return, right around the time when reports of his division's misconduct were surfacing in the army headquarters.

All kinds of characters, with various backgrounds and behaviors were imprisoned during those days, and the lack of liberty brought out either the best or the worst in them....

A Man "Known to the People"

My arrest and imprisonment took place in total secrecy, and that is how I was held captive all those years. I was not allowed to speak to my family at any point in time or to receive direct news from home. No packages were sent to me (with one notable exception), even though other political prisoners were entitled to receive such mailings. They kept transferring me from one cell to another on an ongoing basis, to prevent me from befriending other prisoners who had not been sentenced yet and advising them about the trials. I was always watched very strictly, and I was kept in isolation on numerous occasions, mostly all alone in an empty cold cell. During my 1956 trips to the Sibiu Courthouse for the revision of my trial, solitary confinement was the norm whenever I was taken out of and brought back to the Aiud prison.

My overall physical state deteriorated gradually over the first months in captivity, and my fatigue was debilitating. This asthenia never ceased to progress, and I started to suffer from stubborn headaches associated with dizziness. Aware of possible complications of my condition, I requested to be seen and examined by a doctor. I was informed that the Sibiu prison physician was someone by the name of Dr. Grigorescu, but that he refused to give me any attention. Where were his medical ethics and his conscience? I wondered. He denied me the benefits of medical help during the months spent in Sibiu, even though I was in great need of a tonic and especially of multivitamins. Furthermore, I noticed that he was consistently giving me the cold shoulder and even reprimanded me that, as a physician, I was not familiar with the common, expected symptoms developing in inmates as a consequence of prolonged imprisonment. That line—a recurrent theme—represented the only therapeutic plan ever instituted by the Communist prison doctors on my behalf.

By staging my arrest, the Făgăraș Securitate was seeking praise and recognition from the Bucharest headquarters and was trying to maintain its prestige, as well as attempting to intimidate the inhabitants of the city of Făgăraș and the surrounding county. Sending a high profile intellectual to prison, one "known to the people" or *cu priză la popor* ("admired by the locals"—an expression repeatedly used by my interrogators), was going to accomplish the task.

In October 1950, during our first encounter, the Făgăraș Securitate chief had inquired if my goal was to build a successful practice and if I wanted to be praised by the county inhabitants. My honest reply was—as one would expect—affirmative and was presumably music to my captors' ears.

My Career

The people of Făgăraș are not reactionary, but traditionalist, hard-working Romanians, with a strong sense of freedom stemming from the knowledge that they are the masters of their land. They are an ancient people and a part of the larger *Țara Făgărașului* (Făgăraș County), which has been under Romanian rule since the fourteenth century, from the time of Mircea the Old, who reigned between 1386 and 1418.

As a Romanian from *Ardeal* (Transylvania), I had only one motto in my life: to be an honest man who does his duty in a position that society sees fit; the suitable man in the suitable place.

Even though I grew up fatherless, my tenacious mother made sure I received a proper education. After graduating from medical school, I became well known in the city of Făgăraș, as well as in the entire county. I earned my popularity and excellent reputation after intense medical activity over a span of twenty years and because I was the first practicing internist in Făgăraș when I arrived there in 1931. The respected Romanian Professor Dr. Iuliu Hațieganu from the University of Medicine in Cluj, under whose guidance I had trained, had chosen me to be *deschizător de drum* (a pioneer), to organize the new department of internal medicine at the Făgăraș Regional Hospital. Prior to leaving his clinic and transferring to my wife's home city, he taught me the right work ethic and how to become a good, compassionate doctor.

{Dr. Iuliu Hațieganu (1885–1959) was the most prestigious Romanian internist of the interwar period, author of numerous textbooks and original articles. He was elected dean of the University of Medicine in Cluj, Transylvania, in 1919 and subsequently became the first acting professor of internal medicine at the same facility. He started giving lectures in the Romanian language, thus founding the higher Romanian medical education system. The professor is said to have replied to a Făgăraș patient visiting his Cluj clinic in 1935: "Why are you coming to me, when you have Dr. Stanciu Stroia practicing in your town?"}

Without displaying a lack of modesty, I concluded that the sort of person I became as a result of my upbringing in Cacova and the prestige that I had acquired throughout Făgăraș County contributed to my harsh sentence. It was not by accident that my activities received great recognition; I practiced medicine with the scrupulousness I had assimilated during my years at the university, where I had been a lecturer and later an assistant professor. My success was due to both my medical knowledge and my candid desire to help those who were ill and who came to me with trust, in spite of my young age.

Military Experience

My medical career took unexpected and interesting turns in August 1940, when for the second time within a year, I was called up to join the Army Reserves for a period of two months. The goal was to familiarize civilian doctors with the military regimen, as the country was preparing for its inevitable entry into World War II.

I was assigned to the 16th Mounted Division in Bucharest, which was part of the royal squadron of cavalry. Soon, I was transferred to Bolintinul din Vale, only to return to the capital on September 6, escorting the victim of a near-drowning, a soldier whose horse collapsed while he was crossing the Argeș River. After transferring the patient to the Central Military Hospital, I was ordered to return to the royal riding hall.

Once there, I was puzzled to see the commander of the royal brigades, Lieutenant Colonel Sturza, standing in front of the entire unit, pale and visibly moved. As soon as I joined the ranks, he started taking the loyalty oath to the newly installed king of Romania, Michael. I learned that Carol II, his father, had just been deposed and had left the country by train that morning. As I was leaving the riding hall, his portraits were being removed from the walls.

{In 1866, amid evidence of the autocratic reign, corruption, and incompetence of their elected leader Alexandru Ioan Cuza, Romanian politicians called in a Prussian to be their ruler, Carol I (Karl I) of Hohenzollern-Sigmaringen. Practical

politics led to the decision to bring a prestigious prince from a reigning European house, in order to amplify Romanian's voice at the European meeting table. This was done in line with the country's quest for independence from Turkey, which was eventually achieved twelve years later. It also represented the beginning of a constitutional monarchy that included several successors: Ferdinand, Carol II, and Michael. The political reputation of Carol II did not survive his attempt at forming a royal dictatorship and Romania's territorial losses of 1940, which occurred under his watch. He was toppled and fled the palace in September 1940, with a priceless collection of art stacked in his train, leaving his teenage son Michael in charge of the Romanian crown. The monarchy was dismantled in 1947 with King Michael's forced abdication under Communist pressure.}

Back in Bolintinul din Vale the next morning, I saluted my unit commander with an enthusiastic: *Trăiască Vodă Mihai!* "Long Live King Michael!"

Clearly surprised and concerned at the same time, the commander pulled me to the side to reprimand me:

Ce-ai pățit Doctore, să nu te audă cineva! "What went into you, Doc'? God forbid somebody heard you!"

Apparently, I was the first to bring the news of the political change into my regiment, which was sworn in later that day. Despite being only one of two officers not of royal descent, thus lacking the "blue blood," I noticed that I was shown increased respect after that incident. The plain epaulets on my shoulders remained the same, but my status had changed.

A week later, during dinner with the other fifteen officers, I observed that the lower ranking ones were squeezed at the corners of the tables and served significantly smaller and inferior quality meals. Displeased, I requested a "normal" portion. The commander, a colonel with a delicate personality and considerate conduct, requested my presence after dinner for explanations. Speaking from a physician's perspective and without the timidity expected in a young officer, I stated my dissatisfaction with the unfair treatment. After listening carefully, the colonel ordered:

"From this moment on, you'll be in charge of the officer's diet! Dismissed!"

Unfortunately, I discovered that the sergeant cooking in the officers' kitchen used half the number of ducks he claimed on the dietary sheet and charged the unit ten times the customary price (a detail I remember thirty-nine years later!). Given the circumstances, the commander put me in charge of the feeding regimen of the entire unit, not merely the ill or hospitalized soldiers. And on my discharge papers, he scribbled an addendum that read: "Deserves to be advanced in rank, for his display of personality and courage." Regrettably, it proved insufficient in conferring me immunity from subsequent political troubles.

My short and circumstantial military exposure ended in 1943, after I served six months as a promoted captain and infectious disease control commander of the same unit, stationed behind the front, in Transnistria.

{Transnistria is a strip of territory in the Republic of Moldova, located east or "across" the Nistru (Dniestr), between the river and the Ukrainian border. This region, with its capital at Tiraspol, is inhabited by a Slavic majority and Romanian minority and was briefly (1941–1944) under Romanian and German control during World War II. It became a breakaway region in 1991, after Pro-Russian separatists declared independence from Moldova.}

During those months I befriended Dr. Vasile Mârza, a former assistant to renowned Professor Constantin I. Parhon from the Iași Medical School. The captain served under my command together with eighteen other soldiers, despite being a few years my senior and having had a lengthier military service. A Communist acting in illegality, he managed to arrange his transfer out of the country and to Transnistria in 1942, in order to avoid legal trouble. Informed by my superiors that I was directly responsible for his deeds, I decided to protect the man and took him under my wing. He was a trained histologist and pathologist, so I granted his request to be stationed at the local military hospital, supervising our cases of typhus exanthematicus, (a bacterial, louse-born disease prevalent in times of war and famine), rather than joining me on my long rounds at the regional clinics dispersed throughout Oceacov District. We developed a courteous relationship based on mutual respect, and in August 1943, I made the effort to deliver a heavy package to his family in Iași, during my short, five-day leave for home.

Captain Mârza's fortunes changed substantially after the Communist takeover of Romania in 1945. Then, by 1948, as the newly installed health minister, he refused to grant me an appointment. I did not plan to ask him for any favors. My genuine intention had been to congratulate him on his success. To this date, Mârza's gesture continues to bewilder me....

After the months spent in Transnistria, my career experienced a rapid downfall.

Patriotism and Persecution

Within five years of serving the inhabitants of Făgăraș County, and after having had the opportunity to treat thousands of patients, I started to sense an emerging professional envy among some of my colleagues:

"Invidia medicorum pessima." *{Latin maxim: "A doctor's envy is the worst kind."}*

I was never a chauvinist, and I was well received by citizens of other nationalities, whom I treated with all due attention and respect. But the good reputation came at a hefty price and brought a lot of hatred from my foreign peers, who ceased to see me with good eyes. I was eventually "combed out" of medical leadership positions. The reasons invoked were that I was pro-German, anti-Soviet, and an Iron Guard member. Those were accusations without merit destined to fail when faced with reality. But who was going to listen to my defense?

The Saxons from Făgăraș would remind you of the protest they staged against me in 1936 through their association because I chose to purchase an old German house against their wishes. And can you really imagine any Romanian in those days, especially one from Transylvania, daring to be a German sympathizer after the Vienna Dictate?

There goes my German affiliation!

{The infamous Vienna Dictate or Second Vienna Award refers to the annexation of Northern Transylvania to Hungary in 1940, decided during a meeting in the Austrian capital between representatives of fascist Germany and Italy. It was Hitler's effort at settling the dispute between the two countries, the help of which he had enlisted for his future military ambitions in the Balkans. This temporary settlement was reversed after the Romanians turned their arms against the Nazis and was rectified through the Peace Treaty of Paris in 1947. Romania's post-World War II borders with Hungary remained identical with those set out in 1920.}

My medical activity in service of the Russian population of Transnistria, where I was stationed for six months in 1943, speaks for itself against any perceived anti-Soviet attitude. The people of the Oceacov District, whose medical well-being I was responsible for, regarded me as a wizard after I correctly diagnosed a liver cancer patient and predicted his demise two weeks later. That accuracy impressed them so much that they offered me a lot of credit and had the highest regard for my work.

The machinations of the Iron Guard were far from my interest, and anyone who knew me at all was acutely aware of my aversion and general distrust toward politics, in which I saw only dishonest affairs, corruption, and demagogy. I chose never to become a member of a political organization because I despised their false rhetoric and found the fighting between the parties disturbing. Political activity was never on my agenda, and I was reluctant to be engaged in any polemics. My only field of interest and activity remained the medical one, so I must have been involved in the "politics" of being a physician! *{Even Dr. Stroia's inmate file at Aiud—dated May 31, 1955, and obtained courtesy of historian Ioan Ciupea—referrs to him as being "apolitic."}*

Between 1926 and 1927, while studying medicine at the University of Cluj, I became the president-elect of the *Societatea Studenților în Medicină* (Cluj Medical Students' Society). In that capacity, I was interested in the social issues and professional problems the student body dealt with. That position compelled me to closely monitor the evolution of the student movements and their 1920s strikes. Those efforts were in favor of increasing government spending and assistance for Romanian college students enrolled after World War I. In Bucharest, for instance, no dormitories were available, and scholarships were few and infrequently awarded on merit. Foreigners appeared to be privileged, many enrolling with fraudulent baccalaureate diplomas. Once the student movement degenerated into a political struggle, however, I distanced myself from the organization. Despite being their leader, I refused to take part in the demonstrations staged at the Oradea Congress in 1927, which turned into hooliganism, because I was hostile to the students' desire to join right-wing movements. Preparing for my future, I cared primarily about the quality of my training as an internist at the university clinic.

Overall, the days spent as a young Romanian in Cluj had a determining influence on my evolution into a fierce protector of the essence of the Romanian spirit. Listening to great Romanian artists and orators such as Octavian Goga at the National Theatre was an electrifying experience. *Mustul care fierbe* (the boiling wine) is how the students referred to his passionate yet tactful speeches. The entire generation of the 1920s grew up under the influence of that clean patriotism.

The Romanian people were the owners of the proud claim that they had never staged an aggression outside of their borders, which in turn they always had to defend. We knew that *Țările Române* (the Romanian Counties) avoided dissolution as a political unit despite four hundred years of Ottoman Turkish invasions. And we were also aware—even under Austro-Hungarian occupation—of the tumultuous history the Romanians endured with an untainted conscience, resisting the countless assaults from East and West, because they were blessed with worthy and courageous leaders.

We had been a free and independent nation merely for the past century, since the 1877–1878 Independence War against Turkey. And our unity was completed only at the time of Transylvania's unification with Romania in 1918, through the Great Romanian Assembly of Alba Iulia and after the World War I victory over the Germans. The return of Transylvania to Greater Romania resulted from the defeat and eventual collapse and fragmentation of the Austrian-Hungarian Empire.

I recall these historical facts now because I am trying to convey the grandiose feelings I was overwhelmed with as an adolescent and youth living in Cluj. It is because of those patriotic sentiments that I was persecuted after World War II.

Quoting from Octavian Goga, a native of Rășinari by Sibiu and *poetul pătimirii noastre* (the poet of our sufferings) seems appropriate in the context:

Dar de ne-am prăpădi cu toții, Tu, Oltule, să ne răzbuni!
"And if we all shall perish, You, Olt Rriver, should avenge us!"

{Octavian Goga (1881–1938), "The Bard from Rășinari," was a militant Romanian poet. "Oltul" is a patriotic poem abundant in metaphoric language, about a personified Olt River who witnesses Transylvania's foreign oppresssion and struggle for independence.}

"Lacking High Political Level"

My dismissal in 1945 from the presidency of *Casa Cercuală*, the Făgăraș Social Services, hardly disturbed me; quite the contrary, it gave me the opportunity to concentrate on my clinical duties and my forty-bed hospital with its busy tuberculosis section. Following an inspection organized by the Ministry of Health as a result of my reports, that floor had been opened for admissions in 1936. Transferring the tuberculosis patients out of the general infectious disease area turned out to be to everyone's health benefit.

Prior to my social services discharge, I had not been spared from controversy either. In 1942, after I had treated several cases of severe toxic exposure, I made a request to the director of the local ammunition factory to allow workers in the triton section to rotate every three months. Rather than following my medical advice, he accused me of "production sabotage" and forbade me to set foot in the building, most notably during an inspection by the Ministry of Labor. Later, the factory administration threatened to sue me when an intoxicated worker with pulmonary congestion succumbed from the abscess he developed as a complication while under my care. They claimed that he acquired tuberculosis while he was an inpatient on my ward. The patient died following three years of suffering and despite intensive care, since at that time antibiotics were not readily available. His wife and two children were compensated adequately, but I refused to give in to the political pressure. Years later, I paid a heavy cost for my oppositional but principle-based attitude.

Then, during 1945, a lengthy legal process initiated by the Ministry of Health led to accusations of financial wrongdoing by the previous hospital leadership. Medical supplies had been unaccounted for during a thorough inventory. The facility eventually was nationalized. Its administrator, Gheorghe Bârsan, had to resign, and the director, chief surgeon Dr. Gheorghe Cornea, was forced into retirement. Fortunately, the penalties imposed were relatively easy to pay given the rampant inflation at that time. There was no evidence of wrongdoing against me, so I was left to reorganize the inefficient and anarchic facility. I became the fourth elected director since its opening days in 1904.

The scrutiny intensified during a late evening in May 1949, when an extraordinary ad hoc hospital union meeting was called by a few of my colleagues to discuss my position in the organization, whose former president I had been in 1947. Everything came as a big surprise; it was shocking but by no means demoralizing, though it never crossed my mind that I would be forced to leave the hospital prior to retirement.

The chief of staff in charge of all of Făgăraș County, recently installed in that position through a Ministry of Health directive, presided at the meeting. Up to that moment, I had been the house doctor of his own father, who suffered from diabetic complications. The other fellow who spoke against me was a younger physician, whom I protected against a lawsuit after he performed a paravenous injection on a hospitalized patient, leading to an extensive necrosis of the man's right elbow. He was the same individual whose stay in our institution I had facilitated when a wartime transfer to Basarabia became imminent.

The ingratitude of both peers was bitter, and so was my recompense. After I was characterized as a "bad man," the accusation brought against me and the ensuing discussion reached a few conclusions: I was "not attentive to the hospital personnel's needs" and "gave them poor evaluations;" I was "lacking a true democratic spirit" and I was "too authoritarian, like a dictator."

How could I have been the "arrogant director" when I was the only doctor in town without a motorized vehicle? The one-horsepower carriage was my only means of transportation. And my family members were always so humble in attitude and attire; my children's ability to survive the hardships encountered during my absence is further proof of that fact.

And since when did professionalism become undesirable? Yes, compared to my predecessor, I showed little tolerance for negligence on the job, incorrectness, lies, or treachery and rejected the emergence of "cliques." And I tried to lead by example, never missing work even when I endured a debilitating lumbago and decided to pass on a paid vacation to Techirghiol Resort. But those were all insignificant details, when the meeting concluded with the additional charge that I was "lacking a high political level!"

Lipsit de un nivel politic ridicat.... Now, what could I have said in my defense in response to that outrageous claim? That the only line I was taught during political science class in high school was that Marx wrote a treatise called *The Capital* and contributed to *The Communist Manifesto?* Or that there was no political teaching in medical school and my subscriptions included solely the *Presse Medicale, Clujul Medical*, and other professional journals?

Years ago, a friend asked me if I wished I were young again. *Da! Sub 24 de ani!* "Yes, under 24 years!" was my instant reply. My youthful idealism during my college years enforced the conviction that hard work would lead to success regardless of the opposing milieu. What a deception that belief turned out to be! In real life, one has to adapt to the social environment because as soon as one rejects it, he is sacrificed. Superiority in any domain will not be forgiven by enemies, and mistakes will be dearly avenged.

Yes, I had been politically ignorant, and under those circumstances I was relieved of my duties as director of the Făgăraș Regional Hospital. Revoking my privileges as an attending physician in the internal medicine department was an unproblematic step further. Left unable to find employment in any state-owned facility, I accepted a position as a consulting internist in a—still functioning then—private clinic, where I worked with all my skill and conscientiousness until the day of my arrest.

Prior to 1949 and the many changes in my life, I used to meet with a few men of my age and social background at "Casina Romana," a local tavern, for a couple of hours on Friday evening, when everybody's job obligations ceased. It was a fascinating mosaic of individuals; some were busy professionals, others were retired, a few were in between jobs, but all enjoyed *un pahar de vorbă* (a glass of conversation) in a quiet, secluded room. Rarely, when one of us was in a particularly good mood and willing to treat everyone at the round table with beer or wine, did the gathering last beyond nine o'clock.

I avoided going to those reunions after I was dismissed from the hospital. That proved to be my bad luck, because I arrived home on a Friday, in October 1950, a little earlier then usual to find three young men waiting in my living room....

And that is how I became an example of our emerging history. As Gheorghe Bica, a witty peasant from Cincul Mare once put it:

Fraților, am luptat să dărâmăm o dictatură regală, dar am dat de una și mai a dracului.... "Brothers, we fought to demolish a royal dictatorship, but I fancy we have stumbled over a worse one...."

Character and Conscience

I cannot continue without mentioning an old friend of mine, Aurel Moga, son of the Veștem notary, whom I first met in the fall of 1918 on the benches of the Gheorghe Lazăr High School in Sibiu.

"De mortuis nil nisi bonum!" *{Latin maxim: Let nothing but good be said of the dead}*, our ancestors, the Romans used to say.

My friend died in 1977 of myocardial infarction, while still functioning as president of the Romanian Medical Academy. He was erudite, a great scholar, an expert in internal medicine, who dedicated his life to the intense and thorough accumulation of medical knowledge. A treatise in six volumes regarding the diagnosis and treatment of hypertension is the most valuable work he left behind. He studied with me under Professor Hațieganu, but failed to find interest in the students' struggles.

Sadly, my schoolmate proved that he lacked both courage and character when he read—in a 1947 university union meeting—a statement of defamation against our great professor and founder of our medical school. That led to Dr. Hațieganu's dismissal from the clinic he had headed with such dignity and skill since 1919. It took several years and the intervention of Soviet scientists familiar with the professor's works and publications for Dr. Hațieganu to be politically rehabilitated and reinstalled in his deserved tenure position.

When I saw Dr. Hațieganu again in March 1951 shortly before my arrest, the master did not criticize his apprentice; he simply asked me with disbelief in his voice:

Vezi ce a făcut nenorocitul de Moga? "Did you see what poor Moga did?"

Everybody who knew them both from the old days was stunned by Moga's attitude. Yes, he made it to the top of the medical academy eventually, but he did so through the back door. *Pentru un ciolan, și-a vândut conștiința!* For a nice berth, the man sold his conscience!

Because he had been my childhood friend, I took his side every time he was criticized by his peers or by his own students. As if he needed my defense. His behavior toward my family did not prove more humane, either. My old friend—dean of the Cluj medical school at the time—denied my daughter, who aced her medical school entry exam, an admission spot. While I was attending "my second university," my political situation had earned her an "unacceptably low social grade." Only after the telegraphic petition of Nicolae Popescu-Doreanu, the minister of education himself, who considered that an applicant with a perfect score deserved unconditional acceptance, was my daughter given justice. She finished medical training at the top of her class, the same way she started.

When I returned to life seven years later, I found Mr. Moga very diplomatic, with a note of farce in his gestures and compassion for my unfortunate fate. He lamented about the difficulties he encountered when he allowed my daughter to start medical school. But his assistants, who knew and trusted me, told me a different story; if it had been so hard for him to enroll her, it was apparently easier to eliminate her from a postgraduate position in a Cluj clinic, when she passed the exam but the job was given to somebody else.

At the opposite pole, I will place the venerable Professor Emil Țeposu, a great urologist and distant relative of mine, who chose to commit suicide rather than cooperate with the Securitate in bringing down his teacher, Professor Alexandru Pop....

People and people, with or without character, with or without conscience, with or without the courage to fight injustice....

"Fear protects life!" says a popular aphorism.

"Sic transit Gloria mundi!" *{Latin maxim: Thus passes the glory of the world.}*

Where is parody writer Ion Luca Caragiale or Grigore Alexandrescu with his witty fables? One is certain to find an applicable example:

"The large dog bites the small one,
But it sometimes happens that
The small one bites back...."

My File

The mode in which I was convicted was without witnesses and solely based on the "suspicion" that I had engaged in "subversive activities" against the security of the Romanian state.

I do not know the content of my political file. I have never read one single page of it, but I am certain that the statements collected and notes inserted by the Securitate and other elements foreign to the Romanian people were false and malicious. The "proofs" used to make up my file were invented and accused me of deeds I had never dreamed of doing. Since I was a representative of the intellectual elite, the intention was to compromise and sentence me in the most severe manner, as one would do with a traitor of the working class. I was a humble physician from Făgăraș transformed into great bourgeois exploiter overnight, turned into an example of Communist might and justice. I became an "enemy of the people."

Nor was my court-appointed attorney allowed to look over my file, which was the newly introduced procedure, the Communist "fashion." With the exception of its creators, nobody was familiar with its pages, unless the panel of judges had access to them.

A lot of scattered information that had been used against me surfaced within four years of my conviction, introduced by new prisoners from Făgăraș arriving at the Aiud Penitentiary. Newsworthy data was spread from man to man through the use of the Morse alphabet. It was the only communication method suitable in the austerity of our jail environment. And I was probably the only prisoner—despite being one of the oldest—who did not learn how to decipher coded information, which was transmitted through short and long knocks on the heating pipes and the cell walls. Each letter was assigned a special code, and skilled prisoners were able to interpret up to fifty words per minute. But fellow inmates made a steady effort to keep me updated. That is how I found out that the Ministry of Internal Affairs had released the initial warrant for my capture on March 15, 1951, but the actual arrest had been postponed until April 30 for "tactical reasons." In addition, when Făgăraș natives made the rounds with the bucket or the water barrel, they kicked my metal cell door courageously (despite the interdicition) and shouted my name, in order to greet me. Then, when my turn came around, I would reciprocate the salutation.

Upon release from prison, I further discovered that a particular page in my file contained misinformation of enormous proportions. The Făgăraș Securitate fabricated a note in which it was stated that I had left my medical practice in town in order to move to the mountains and fight alongside the partisans during each of my temporary absences. A baseless accusation documented as if it were an undisputable truth!

And there was another piece of information that always eluded me: the indication on my file denoting me as a dangerous, dark element. I base this assumption on the experiences I endured during imprisonment on every occasion somebody glanced at it.

"Abortion of Făgăraș Society"

My trial was scheduled for January 8, 1952, the days prior to which I spent in total isolation.

The main reason for a weak presence in court and my decision to portray myself as an unintelligent person was concern for my family's safety. I had not seen my wife and college-bound children in months and was desperate to find out how they were holding up. Thoughts of severe repercussions against them triggered by my protestation were constantly spinning through my head. I had to remind myself of the statement I had signed, promising I would not say a word about what went on during my visits at the Făgăraș Securitate headquarters.

After reading the beginning of the accusation, the military prosecutor pointed to me and declared to the audience in a belligerent voice:

Priviți această lepădătură a societății din Făgăraș....

"Look at this abortion of the Făgăraș society...."

From the moment I heard that statement, I suffered a mental block and was unable to utter a word in my defense. I kept silent and replied only to the questions posed by the president of the panel of judges. I admitted to all of the crimes I was accused of. Given the way my investigation had gone so far, I realized that any vociferous attempt to defend myself would be futile. I understood the potential of creating a worse situation for my family, and I resigned myself to my fate.

Physically, I felt frail, but I managed not to be intimidated or frightened. After the prosecutor labeled me a villain, I sensed a sudden strengthening of my morale, which has helped me throughout my entire detention.

The authorities in Bucharest had already decided the outcome of my trial and the duration of my sentence. Only after arrival at the Aiud prison did I discover that important detail, well known to all the seasoned detainees. Before any political trial took place, the prison director was summoned to the Ministry of Internal Affairs in Bucharest, to be briefed about the cases scheduled to be sentenced the following week. On the day before my trial, I was brought to face the director himself in his office, and he assured me that if I admitted my guilt, my sentence would be more lenient. He instructed me to confess to any and all accusations brought against me and to abstain from any protest; otherwise I would jeopardize my situation even further. Lacking the required legal knowledge and having good faith, I believed what I was told.

The night before the trial, when I was being taken back to my cell, in the prison hallway I came across a senior lieutenant, a very tall and thin man, asthenic in appearance, with an angry look and a mean expression on his face. I imagined that he was an officer on trial by the military court. And I recall telling my cellmates that I was afraid he would not survive in prison for more than three months if he were convicted, because he appeared weak and the perfect candidate for catching tuberculosis. I felt sorry for the man, as I was making this naïve observation based on my medical experience.

To my astonishment, I recognized the same individual the next morning in court, occupying the seat reserved for the prosecutor! Before I actually saw him there and stared at his face while he was spitting his venomous accusations, I had believed in a softer punishment.

Furthermore, the defense attorney appointed by the court was *un caraghioslîc* (a ridiculous character). None of the prisoners were permitted to contact their personal lawyers or to discuss their case with the appointed one. The detainees were kept in a defendant's box, about four by five meters square, and were brought to the court in groups of four to six people. I was escorted in with five peasants from Făgăraș County I had never met before who also were accused of providing aid to the partisans. The lawyers were seated across the room, in the opposite direction from their clients, in a box of a similar size, and three guards were lined up between the two areas. A narrow hallway roughly one meter in width separated the prisoners' boxes from the rest of the room and was surrounded by barbed wire extending up to the ceiling. When the attorney asked the defendant a question, the guards interrupted the prisoner if he attempted to answer, so that nothing made any sense at all. *Stranie farsă!* It was a strange farce indeed!

My "lawyer" was a former high school colleague who was a freshman when I was in my senior year. He accused me more than he defended me in his short plea. He stated that he remembered me as an eminent pupil, that

I had been the president of the Cluj Medical Students' Society and a successful internist and respected assistant professor at the university.

Despite all of the above, he proclaimed in a grave voice, *A făcut greșeala de a ajuta fugarii* "He made the mistake of helping the partisans."

Then he concluded that a man of my stature should not be allowed to make errors in life, particularly of a political nature.

"Favoring the Crime of Plotting against the Romanian State"

My trial was a grotesque show orchestrated from the top, with serious accusations invented to impress the jury. It was a setup, a scheme, and a flight of the imagination with the clear intention of crucifying me and ruining my life and the life of my family. I was accused of "hostile intentions toward the working class."

The quickly reached sentence, number 12, from January 8, 1952, had the following headline:

Favorizare la crimă de uneltire împotriva statului Român.

"Favoring the crime of plotting against the Romanian State."

That statement was followed by other attacks and invectives, as the prosecutor continued with his tirade:

Dacă nu era el și alții ca el.... "If it wasn't for him and others like him, paratroopers would not have had to land on the Negoiu Mountain to fight those partisans. They would have never existed in the first place, hidden in the mountains!"

And further: *Banii ce i-a dat fugarilor....* "The money he gave to the rebels was not his own, but money received from the reactionary government in Paris." *Altă enormitate!* (What nonsense!)

Those are the words by which the Sibiu Military Tribunal prosecutors accused me. After a well-planned frame-up by the Făgăraș Securitate, I was sentenced to seven years of "correctional imprisonment," without witnesses or a pertinent defense.

With great clarity, I sensed the tremendous determination of elements foreign to the Romanian people to exclude me from society. These same individuals had maltreated, tortured, and killed other innocent people and good patriots. Now they were targeting a large group of intellectuals, of which I was a part, who disagreed with the events that took place in Romania in those days.

Despite being deceived on many occasions, I have tried to aid the unfortunate and oppressed throughout my entire existence. Using my conscience as the sole guide proved to be a misstep in judgment, because my considerate behavior betrayed me. *Mă credeam Om între oameni, Om de omenie.* Prior to my arrest, I thought of myself as a worthy man. Given my civil and responsible attitude toward society and toward my fellow human beings, I had never imagined being in the situation of facing trial in a court of law or needing a lawyer to defend me in a civil, criminal, or political case.

I had always strived to help the needy and the poor, but certainly not those who were "against the security of the Romanian state." I had tried to help people at odds with their fate, not at odds with the law. Based on their appearance, I had suspected that the three youngsters were in trouble with the new political regime, and I thought of them as adventurers, but I was not aware of the extent of their involvement with the anti-Communist movement. Frankly, I still regret that I did not offer more support to their cause.

Despite all that had been declared at my trial, I was certain that having just been accused of aiding the insurgents, I was going to receive a lighter sentence, of maybe one or one and a half years of detention. And I was fairly confident that I would eventually receive a suspension....

Instead, I spent many years at the Aiud Penitentiary, a special facility operated by the Ministry of Internal Affairs and reserved for members of the Iron Guard—two thousand of them—and for dignitaries and ex-ministers. The Iron Guard leaders were puzzled to see me among them and distrusted me because I was an unknown entity among the intellectuals who were members of their organization.

Somehow, I managed to survive, especially from a mental point of view, carrying out my entire sentence not in a corrective jail—as decided at my trial—but in a dreadful prison set up for political detainees. Most important, however, I overcame the name by which the prosecutor addressed me during the trial: "an abortion of society...."

"Suspect without Vices"

Not even today do the honest people of Făgăraș understand why I was arrested, let alone why my sentence was so harsh and, above all, why I was treated as if I were a common criminal. The Securitate henchmen appeared confused in their effort to categorize me, so I became—by accident—part of a group of peasants from Făgăraș County accused of hiding and supporting Negoiu Mountain rebels. I was made *șef de lot*, the leader of this "abortive group," as the Aiud authorities labeled us. Seven farmers constituted it, and I was appointed chief of the bunch. The peasants all lived in villages scattered around the base of the mountains, in small localities such as Ohaba, Ileni and Netotu. A few were well-trained former army soldiers; others owned guns, which were seized during searches performed on their properties, while some had direct contacts with the partisans.

Yet none of them was deprived of more than five years of liberty and some of only two. I, on the other hand, was sentenced to six years of imprisonment, and eventually to seven, for the help that I had offered to those fugitives, for not denouncing them to the authorities, and for failing to report facts that I did not know. In other words, I was accused of "scheming against the Communist regime."

I might have been purposely confused—a fact never admitted by my prosecutors!—with another, younger physician from Făgăraș, who—as it surfaced later at Aiud—was apparently one of the sought-after leaders. That individual was caught in 1953 and sentenced to twenty-five years. If that was the case, and if everything was an honest blunder, why was it not admitted to? Why did I remain locked up until 1957?

Other doctors had been arrested as well under similar charges: Dr. Lucian Stanciu of Viștea de Jos and Dr. Vasile Munteanu of Lisa, among many others. The latter had been accused of treating a wounded partisan and was sentenced to fifteen years. He ended up on probation and forced labor on state farms rather than in isolation, as had frequently been my case.

Throughout my incarceration and for many years after my release, I was suspected of continuing operations as the shadow leader of the Negoiu Mountain partisans. At least that was the chosen pretext used for my uninterrupted monitoring and harassment. Five years into my freedom, a secret police officer dressed in civilian clothes invited me politely to follow him to the Ilia Securitate headquarters. I was working at the local clinic at the time, enjoying a quiet and secluded life, socially isolated from the inhabitants of the city and surrounding villages. At his office, the officer inquired about a malpractice case, asking some completely irrelevant questions. Then he acknowledged that he was aware of my innocence and that he knew that I had nothing to do with the partisans. Despite all that, as if to deny what he had just said, he wanted to know if I had found out anything at all about their leader! That person, of course, I had never met.

Why the Făgăraș Securitate demonized me, declaring that I was a hidden boss, an enigmatic chief of the regime's enemies, why I remained an eternal suspect will remain beyond my comprehension. The truth of the matter is that I have never met or seen any of the partisans I was supposedly coordinating. My file contains just the title of *suspect în observație* (suspect under surveillance). The only guilt that I could possibly have had was that of not betraying my people or my conscience.

In my short autobiography requested by the Ministry of Internal Affairs in 1948, the party official wrote an addendum which he shared with me prior to sealing the envelope and which read: *fără vicii* (without vices). From the conversations I had with other intellectuals imprisoned at Aiud, I understood that this lack-of-vices label worsened my prognosis. A clique from Făgăraș wanted to find the appropriate moment to dispose of Doctor Stroia and his family and that time had just arrived. The Făgăraș Securitate had reasons to be jubilant at the announcement of my lengthy sentence, used as a *sperietoare* (a scarecrow) to further subdue the population of my town.

{*My grandfather was tenaciously watched during the years after he was released from prison. Various individuals performed this surveillance, by constantly showing up and searching for information from the superintendent of the building he lived in, from his neighbors and acquaintances. Every one of his moves was spied on in order to prevent "anything he might do." In 2002, our family finally gained brief access to his previously classified file, which contained detailed documentation of his monitoring well into his retirement and as late as 1980. My grandfather was referred to as "the objective" and fictive or unidentifiable names of informers were repeatedly mentioned: agents Ștefănescu, Niculescu and Georgescu, next to those of cooperating physicians Drs. Petre Ambrus and Ion Bordeianu. The identity of the "abortive group" my grandfather was purportedly a part of was also revealed: Ion Dobrin, Ștefan Idomir, Matei Iaru, Vichente Norel, Tănase Crețu, Ionel and Toma Barbu, together with that of the elusive partisan leader Ion Gavrilă-Ogoranu. The alleged harmful note on the cover of his folder was never found.*}

The Betrayal

Să nu-ți bagi în cojoc păduchii altuia!

"Do not transfer somebody else's lice to your own coat," says a popular aphorism. Unfortunately, that is exactly what happened to our family with Maria Pascal.

At the end of April 1944, after its success in the Ukraine, the Soviet Army's offensive against the retreating German forces reached Basarabia and Moldova. As the front was approaching the city of Orhei, the local Romanian population, which included many students, was ordered to evacuate south, to Făgăraș. That same night, the bridge over the Prut River was heavily bombed by the advancing Soviet troops, turning the evacuation process into complete chaos.

That is how Maria Pascal, a sixth grader at the Orhei School, ended up being a student at the Făgăraș School for girls. My daughter, then a fifth grader, suggested that we should invite "the refugee girl from Basarabia" over for Sunday dinner. Naturally, we agreed, especially since we used to house other unfortunate children in the past. For a full two years, from

1936 to 1938, we took care of a 12-year-old boy and a 10-year-old girl, both of whom had become orphans as a result of heavy flooding in Cahul, a county in Southern Basarabia.

In our attempt to ease Maria's loneliness and feelings of abandonment brought on by her refugee experience and the lack of contact with her family, she was welcomed as our Sunday guest for several weekends in a row. Maria's mother had died two years earlier, and her father was fighting on the Eastern front. Two of her younger brothers remained in the care of her aging grandfather in a village near Orhei.

Maria was a good student and adjusted well to our family life, slowly becoming almost like our third child. Because our daughter and a son were so close to her age, the high school director asked us to allow her to live in our house. She happily moved in and took summer classes to recover school time lost during the war. She passed her high school diploma with ease, and I took the initiative to write to the dean of the University of Cluj, requesting him to facilitate her college enrollment. In 1949, Maria was admitted to study philology on a full scholarship, which included meals and housing in the dorms.

The last time I saw her was in March 1951. Anticipating a possible arrest by the Securitate, I paid her a visit on a hasty trip to Cluj. I bought her a few items, including clothing, and advised her to keep up the serious studying.

That same year, it was my daughter Tita's turn to start college while my son Zeno, who was four years her senior, had just finished the Bucharest Polytechnic Institute. Following my arrest, he was not permitted to sit for his graduation or certification exam, and this restriction continued for three years after my release from prison.

{Dr. Stela Stroia, Zeno Stroia's wife, recalled in 2004: "Despite graduating first in his class, Zeno was expelled from college after his father's arrest. Unable to find employment, he accepted an engineering position at a factory in Băița, which exported uranium to the Soviet Union. Because he refused to become a member of the Communist Party and was forbidden to take his certification exam, his salary was low compared to his qualifications and volume of work. In 1986, as part of

Dictator Nicolae Ceaușescu's 'resettlement program', his private property was demolished, and we were forced to move to a state-owned apartment. A generous and faithful man, Zeno died in 1995 of spleen cancer, primarily as a result of his uranium exposure in the 1950s."}

When I was being investigated, several false and tendentious claims were made to the Securitate by an individual close to our family. Maria Pascal, now on the path of becoming a professor, appeared to have quickly forgotten where she had spent the previous eight years. On top of that, she was supposed to be the only defense witness at my trial, but failed to show up....

Upon my return from prison, I sent the remainder of her belongings, carefully wrapped and safeguarded by my family in a wooden container, to Turda, where she was a professor of philology. She replied late, stating just the following: "I received the package, which brought back many memories."

By pure chance, Tita, a physician employed in Turda as well, came briefly across her in the hallways of the local clinic. Maria gazed the other way. Perhaps her guilty conscience stopped her from looking my daughter in the eyes. Wouldn't it have been good for her to have a close friend who cared for her, after losing her entire family?

This deception was not my first one, but surely the most painful I have suffered in my entire life. Growing up without a father, I managed to become a successful individual after years of hard work and then tried my best to help the less fortunate.

The result: a clear conscience, but also painful betrayals.

The first handwritten page of Dr. Stanciu Stroia's memoir, dated January 24, 1979.

View of the village of Cacova, nestled in a valley in the heart of Transylvania. With one main, horseshoe shaped road, the settlement was first mentioned in 1366.

Continuing a centuries old tradition, a Cacova shepherd leads his sheep to greener pastures, in this November 1995 photograph.

Built on Church Street in 1906, Dr. Stanciu Stroia's childhood house in Cacova became his grandchildren's vacation paradise.

The Transylvanian style interior suffered little change over the past century.

Last letter from Russia sent by Dumitru Stroia, before he was murdered by street robbers at the age of 39. Dated "1906 February in 8 days" it was addressed to: "Wished for wife and little children…" Stanciu Stroia was less than two years old at the time of his father's death.

Stanciu Stroia's parents, Dumitru and Iosefina Stroia, with their first born son Mitica, in 1902. Four years later, the family became fatherless.

Iosefina Stroia remained a widow for fifty-two years.

Stanciu Stroia, nine years old, Cacova, April 1914.

Father Ioan Hanzu Jr., Stanciu Stroia's maternal uncle and mentor.

Maternal grandparents
Marina and Father Ioan
Hanzu Sr., in 1902.

Stanciu Stroia
at 18 years of age,
in 1922.

Stanciu Stroia as a fourth year
medical student, in 1926.

Judge Dumitru (Mitica)
Stroia, Stanciu Stroia's
brother, in 1920.

Postcard from Mitica Stroia to
"Mr. Stanciu Stroia, 2nd year medical student, Cluj"
dated February 22, 1924:
"Dear little brother,
It's been so long since you gave me a sign of life.
I'm trying to wake you up from your stupor. Write me,
how have you been? How's your second college year?
You've enrolled, right? Has the students' struggle
calmed down, or is it boiling again? From home,
I don't have any news. I am good and healthy.
Embracing you with love, Mitica."

Dr. Stanciu Stroia (center of second row, seventh from the right) in 1928, heading the Cluj Medical Students' Society. Professor Dr. Iuliu Hatieganu is in the first row, sixth from the right.

Dr. Stanciu Stroia, in the center of student leadership.
University of Cluj, 1928.

Clujul Medical, a specialty journal from 1928 addressed to Dr. Stanciu Stroia, clinical instructor, and *The Statute of the Cluj Medical Students' Society* signed by the president in 1927. Both are examples of the "subversive material" he enjoyed reading.

Letitia and Clemente Grama, Valeria Grama's parents, in 1899.

Father Vincentiu Popa Grama (1852-1920), Valeria Grama's grandfather and decorated hero in the 1877-1878 War of Inderpendence against Turkey.

Valeria Grama and Stanciu Stroia on their engagement day, April 17, 1928.

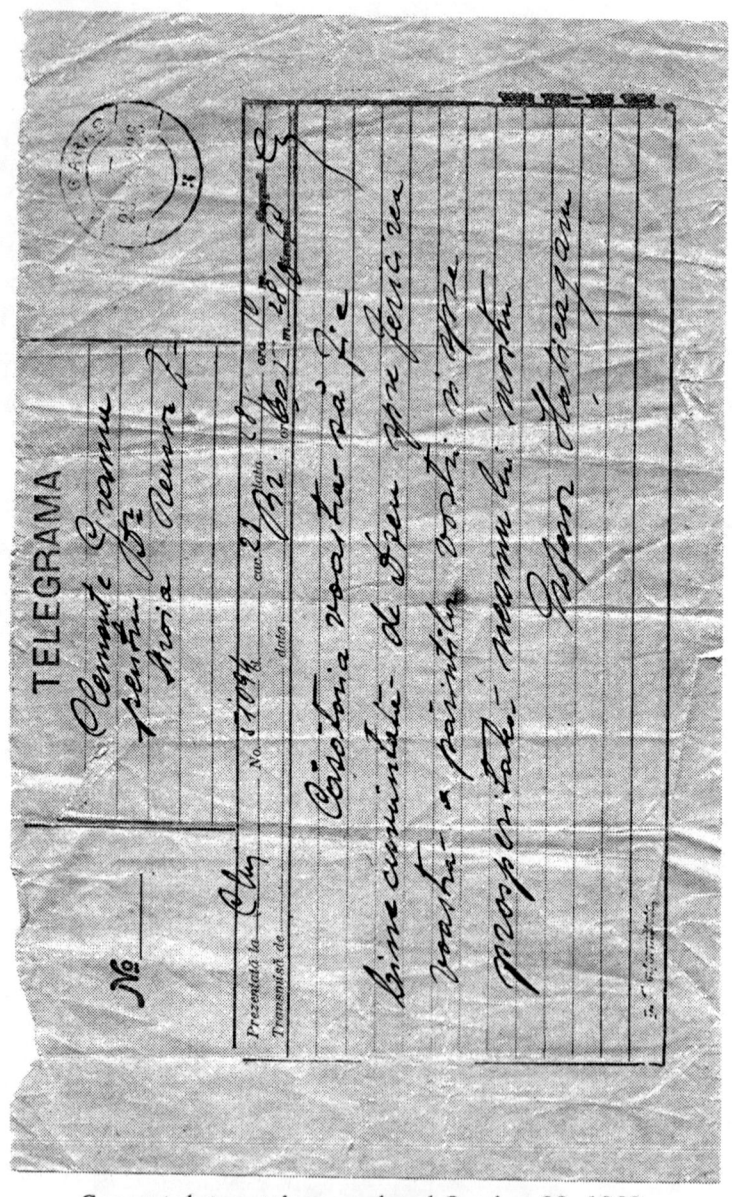

Congratulatory telegram dated October 28, 1928,
sent by Professor Dr. Iuliu Hatieganu to Dr. Stanciu Stroia
on his wedding day:
"May your union be blessed by God, for your happiness, that
of your parents and for the prosperity of our people."

Valeria Grama and Stanciu Stroia on their wedding day: October 28, 1928.

Lucia and Zeno Stroia, in Romanian National Costumes, 1939.

A happy family in 1935: Valeria, Zeno, Lucia and Stanciu Stroia.

Dr. Stanciu Stroia and son Zeno, surrounded by workers at the construction site of his two-story house and clinic, in 1938.

Dr. Stanciu Stroia in 1932, at the start of his medical career in Fagaras.

At work in his office in Fagaras, in 1938. The art above the bookcase depicts a doctor's struggle to save a patient from death's grip.

In 1943, during World War II, as Infectious Disease Control Captain in the Romanian Army.

Postcard written in Romanian, sent by Polish Captain
Dr. Antoni Firlej on March 14, 1940 from Split, Yugoslavia
(Croatia). It is addressed to Dr. Stanciu Stroia, who
facilitated his release from the Fagaras refugee camp:
"Dear colleague, for your good heart, many thanks! I am in
Split now, where the weather is beautiful. Greetings to you
and your entire family."

When Dr. Stanciu Stroia was elected director of the Fagaras Regional Hospital in 1945, the facility had forty beds, employed one hundred people, and served a population of 100,000.
(Photograph courtesy of Dan Dragolea and Mircea Ivanoiu)

Dr. Stanciu Stroia (center), among the patients and staff of the tuberculosis section, which opened under his initiative and guidance in 1936.

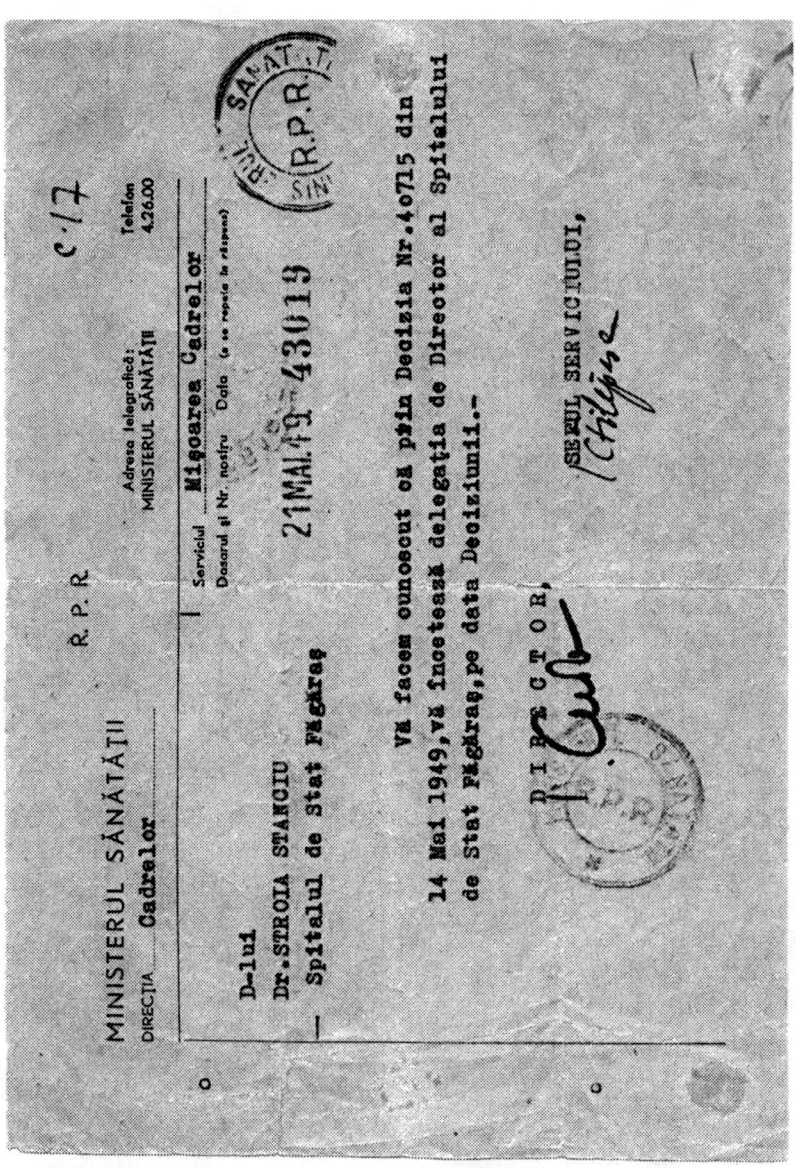

Official termination letter from the Department of Personnel Placement, Ministry of Health, Romanian Popular Republic, recorded on May 21, 1949: "To Dr. Stanciu Stroia, You are herby informed that pursuant to the decision number 40715 dated May 14, 1949, your mandate as Director of Fagaras State Hospital ceases immediately."

CHAPTER IV—IMPRISONMENT

Jilava Transit—December 1952

Eighteen months into my sentence, I was still being held at the Sibiu Penitentiary. Then, toward the end of December 1952, I was selected in a large group of prisoners to be transported to the Jilava Penitentiary. The purpose of that trip by special train was to sort the inmates into categories and then ship them to various jails throughout the country, according to predetermined criteria and irrespective of the nature of their sentences. The triage of prisoners was simple. It was of little importance if the verdict read "corrective imprisonment" or "hard labor." What mattered was the note on the personal file issued by the Ministry of Internal Affairs, which sealed the individual's fate.

The harshest prisons were at Aiud and Gherla—the rumor went—with Galați and Sighetul Marmației worth an infamous mention as well. Iron Guard members, former magistrates, and "reactionary" elements resisting all attempts at "re-education" were concentrated and safeguarded at Aiud. It was a remarkable collection of the regime's most feared political opponents.

When our train arrived in Bucharest, the intimidating shouting of the transport guards frightened the prisoners the most. As for me, I was terrified when our van came to a halt, and I read the name on the gate to the new prison: "Jilava."

This place, part of a former defensive fort built on the outskirts of the capital by King Carol I, was dug in the ground and consisted of large hallways and spacious cells, some built to hold up to one hundred-fifty detainees. I was placed in one of those crowded rooms, with water dripping from the concrete ceiling on ice-cold, cement floors. It was similar to the notorious Gherla prison, which made me recall the threat mothers used to frighten (as a last resort, of course!) their misbehaving children with:

"Be good, or I'll send you to Gherla!"

Every cell had a barrel of drinking water and a bucket used for urination and defecation, which was emptied and washed once a day in the morning, rarely twice. When full by the end of the day, such a bucket would weigh up to 200 kilograms. Four athletic individuals were hardly able to carry it into the yard, to be emptied in a designated area.

Some convicts spent many months in those basements; our group stayed there only a few days, prior to redistribution to other jails, each prisoner according to his file.

On Christmas Day 1952, about a hundred of us were herded to the railway station once again, to begin our new journey. We did not know where we were heading, and most of us were separated from our former groups, so we did not know each other. We were confined to one train wagon for three days, travelling with very few stops, and we found out that we could each survive on 500 grams of bread and 200 grams of jelly. Then, by the third day, as we got closer to Aiud, and with our guard—a first sergeant—certainly aware of that, we did not receive our daily ration. The protests of a few who were familiar with the formal rights of transported convicts were in vain.

Despite forgiving him, I sometimes wish I could recall the name of the individual who took possession of one hundred food portions, so his eternal sleep would be disturbed. Because it is difficult for me to forget the date of December 25, 1952, the day I almost starved to death....

Aiud Penitentiary

The entrance to the Aiud prison had three large gates made of solid cast iron. The first faced the street, the second allowed access to the administrative offices, and the third was the actual prison door leading to the compound itself. When I arrived from Jilava in the middle of the night, with my fellow one hundred inmates dragging their feet, the guard prompted us to look closely at the entrance and pointed out:

Uitați-vă bine, că de aici nu mai ieșiți toți câți ați intrat!
"Most of you will not walk out through these gates alive!"
What an encouraging welcome!

Passing through the main, older section of the prison, I noticed that it was built on three levels and—as I soon found out—consisted of over three hundred cells, all small in size, each roughly four and a half meters long and two and a quarter meters wide. The cells had rotten wooden floors and a central heating system that functioned—apart from when it was defective—only twice a day, one hour in the morning and one in the evening.

Next to the main facility stood two one-level structures of similar size, unwholesome and unsanitary, with bare dirt floors, forming the so-called "Zarca" compound or older wing erected in 1770, during the reign of Maria Theresa. Zarca was the Hungarian word for prison, adopted by the Romanian authorities.

{Maria Theresa, 1717–1780, was the Archduchess of Austria, Queen of Bohemia and Hungary, and Empress of the Holy Roman Empire. She reigned over Romanian Transylvania during the Austrian-Hungarian occupation. According to the gate guards at Aiud, as of September 2004 Zarca was still in use, housing common criminals.}

Those buildings housed primarily members of the Iron Guard and ex-ministers, together with a few inmates relocated from the main cell section as a punishment.

As soon as we arrived, we were escorted to two cells in the basement of the old prison building. We slept on straw mattresses and almost on top of each other, unable to find a comfortable position, as over forty of us were crammed in spaces of five-by-six meters square. That night I understood for the first time what life in prison truly meant. As we were trying to rest, ten of us were moved to a different location, a cold cell submerged in total darkness. It was so chilly, we started searching for anything we could cover our freezing bodies with, and in order to keep us warm, we positioned ourselves in small groups, sitting next to each other. I discovered an item that felt like a blanket and had a strong starch odor. When I woke up the next morning, I noticed many other such pieces of cloth lying around on the floor. I recognized the *basoldine* (dowdies), rags used to wash the stairs and the hallways of the penitentiary!

Trying to prepare for what was to come, I said to myself: *Ține-te bine Stanciule!* "Hang on tight, Stanciu! You'll have to endure many other things, and you'll have to overcome them all!"

I recalled the days when I was the Făgăraș prison physician in charge of the inmates' personal health and hygiene, and how different my experience of treating people sentenced according to the penal law had been. I was now the one behind bars, and that was a fact still difficult to come to terms with.

{Located in the center of a small town in Alba County, Transylvania, some 187 miles northwest of Bucharest, the infamous Aiud was one of Romania's harshest penitentiaries and theater of brutal incarcerations and Communist atrocities. The elite of the anti-Communist resistance, thousands of intellectuals, peasants, students, and elements of the pre-Communist government are believed to have perished in this place. Former Iron Guard members were also concentrated there. Hunger, cold, and terror reigned. The detainees were denied medical attention, endured bitter winters, sleeping often without cover, and ate spoiled, infested food. Cells were secretly monitored, and the inmates were encouraged to inform on one another. The individuals refusing to recant their anti-Communist beliefs were placed in solitary confinement and beaten. Their families were harassed, and their wives persuaded to divorce them. In 1992, under the sponsorship of the Association of Former Political Detainees, the city of Aiud erected a monument titled "The Ordeal," made up of multiple crosses, to watch over the peaceful rest of unidentified martyrs buried in the local cemetery.}

Hungarians and the Iron Guard

In my first days at Aiud, I shared a cell with a group of people who knew each other well from years spent together. All were quite old and carried on their conversations only in Hungarian. Former municipal authorities from Cluj, the Transylvanian capital, they used to be in charge of the city during the Vienna Dictate. The prefect, the president of the appeals court, the police chief, and other members of the city council had been returned to Romania by the new Hungarian government in Budapest, to be tried and sentenced for crimes they had committed against the Romanian population while they governed in Cluj.

The prefect was Count Bethlen, brother of the former Hungarian prime minister bearing the same last name (Istvan Bethlen), who headed the government prior to 1940. He appeared to enjoy talking to me because I could speak broken Hungarian, the little I still remembered from high school. The count was granted the unusual privilege of spending hours outside of the cell, so he swept the prison yard every day along with other fortunate people, such as Nichifor Crainic, the Romanian ex-minister from 1939. We watched those lucky inmates when we were escorted to the yard for our daily ten- to fifteen-minute walk. They had fresh air in abundance and ate leftovers from the nearby kitchen.

{Nichifor Crainic (1889–1972) was a writer, philosopher, professor at the universities of Bucharest and Chișinău, director of the cultural journal "The Thinking" and a member of the Romanian Academy. His imprisonment was a result of his political activity during the interwar period.}

Count Bethlen and I met again in 1960 on a side street in Cluj. We recognized each other and talked a little bit, out of courtesy. He seemed well, appeared healthier than me, and maintained his proud stance.

I also recall that crowded room because of the strong garlic odor that suddenly filled the space one day, a smell I could not stand before my imprisonment. A convict recently transferred from the forced labor camps of the Danube-Black Sea Canal, managed to conceal a piece of garlic, and he generously offered me half of one of its roots. I ate it over a few days with a tremendous appetite, because my nutrition was completely void of fresh vegetables or fruits. From that time on, my taste for the root changed forever and *usturoi* (garlic) became one of my favorite dietary herbs.

About ten days into my time at Aiud, once the head guard had finished studying everybody's file, the newly arrived prisoners were redistributed. I was the only one transferred to the large prison section, in a secluded area where I did not know a soul. I shared my space with Iron Guard members, who were surprised to see me among them and thus grew suspicious, avoiding my presence when I first arrived. My file must have indicated that I was more dangerous than the typical member openly enlisted in the organization!

Finally, I was stripped of my old, worn-out suit, which was taken to the storage room, and I was handed a new inmate uniform, striped clothing in the so-called "Franko style."

My misery at Aiud was about to start.

The Factory

Once detainees set foot in Aiud, those capable of physical labor were sent directly to the prison factory. I was among them. We operated in three shifts, seven to eight hours long, each shift consisting of up to eight hundred workers. Most of us were involved in unskilled labor, building wooden ammunition containers—eight hundred boxes a day—headed for Communist North Korea, in the middle of a fierce war at the time. I vividly remember how I had to hit twelve hundred nails in those boxes over eight hours! Every time I failed to pay close attention to the task at hand because my mind was on my family, I hit my left index finger, which was always black and blue from the ensuing bruises.

The work quota was enormous and kept getting bigger. There were serious consequences in case it was not met. At the first offense, the daily ration of bread was cut in half. Other means of punishment were solitary confinement, imprisonment in the basement, and, ultimately, chaining in a group of thirty to forty people forced to stand up in a narrow cell for three to four days in a row. On top of that were the unfavorable notes added to the personal files, with "lack of re-education" signifying more penalties.

During November 1953, the prisoners were ordered to work in two shifts of twelve hours each. The jail officials argued that this measure would increase production, but, in fact, it was applied in order to exhaust and exterminate the weaker individuals. Some inmates staged a protest, particularly a couple of engineers and a professor, but it was to no avail, and they ended up spending the next three weeks in chains.

Once in a while, as I entered the factory during the winter months, I noticed up to fifteen piles of clothing belonging to working inmates from the previous shift. The wrongdoers were being disciplined. They were locked undressed in the basement, for an entire night, so they had to stick to one another and move as one, in order to warm up and survive the freezing temperatures.

I also recall the trembling I suffered every morning as I entered the factory because of the terrible cold that winter. Around the same time, I developed troublesome symptoms for which I could not find an easy interpretation. I consulted a few medical colleagues regarding the tension and anxiety I felt and about my not being able to stand still. I constantly had to move around in response to this unexplained hyperactive state.

Then there was the blonde senior lieutenant who stood at the entrance to the factory and who hit every single one of us in the buttocks with his boot. This was his way of counting us, like sheep in a sheepfold. He was careful not to miss any one of the eight hundred people who entered the building in one shift. I almost felt sorry for the man; I thought that after a while, given the repetitive motion that activity employed, he must surely have had serious muscle cramps in his right leg!

When we left the factory, the jailors counted us once again, this time with the so-called *"ia pe cinci"* (five at a time) system, supposed to minimize mistakes. If the number resulting from the exit count was not the same as the one listed in the prison files, the process was repeated twice or even three times.

On our return to the cells, we were forced to run toward the main prison gate, so that we would not have the chance to see each other for too long, to share words, ideas, or news. I was the last one to arrive more often than not; my exhaustion made hurrying impossible. So I always entered the gate cautiously, out of fear I would be hit again. Raising my hands up and mumbling a lamentation proved usually effective in avoiding the beating.

Even back then, most of us were aware of the existence of the Prisoners' Act, still in force today, which was written in such a manner as to encourage the inmates to work. According to that piece of legislation, a day of labor in captivity was equal to a day and a half deducted from the sentence.

That law, however, never applied in my case.

Butcher and Executioner

While in the factory, I worked alongside a convict employed as a mechanic, with whom I shared the same cell. I was horrified when I accidentally glanced at his casebook once. A very short, bulky man, less than 160 centimeters tall, with accentuated facial features and aquiline nose, my roommate had been sentenced in 1945 to seventeen years behind bars for murder. To say that he had been a dangerous element of society would not be an overstatement. If he found me asleep upon his return from his late factory shift, he would drag me out of bed, mattress included!

I asked him on one occasion about his past, and he eagerly told me all about it. He fondly referred to himself as a "surgeon" or a "butcher" in the *Sumanele Negre* (Black Shirts) battalion led by a lawyer named Olteanu from Brașov. A paramilitary group with a strong nationalistic and anti-Communist agenda, the Black Shirts advanced behind the Transylvanian frontline in 1940. After liberating villages where Romanians had been massacred, they captured the Hungarian soldiers who had participated in the killings. Following a verdict given by the battalion court, they executed them on the spot. In one village, they were given orders to put sixteen Hungarians to death by beheading them. The butcher, whose real name was Traian but whom I called *cel groaznic* (the gruesome), chopped off the head of the first condemned man with an axe, but fainted before getting to the second.

He reminisced a lot about the comfortable prison life he enjoyed during the monarchy, prior to 1948, after which harsh restrictions were imposed.

With great disappointment, he recalled the introduction of *vigilența* (the vigilance). He claimed that during the war, Communists and Iron Guard members, both representing extremist organizations acting illegally, fraternized in jail. They were entitled to sell half the goods they produced in the prison factory on the outside market and retain the proceeds. They communicated with their families through letters, and—if there was an urgent need—they received packages. The Communists were also granted access to the "red help," a miniature prison library with censored books, and they were kept informed through newspapers.

The most repulsive individual I ever met in prison, despicable in every aspect, including his hideous face, however, was Lax, a former executioner at Auschwitz. He had been a prisoner in the concentration camp but accepted to perform the job of hanging his fellow inmates. He put the noose around their necks or took the chair from under their feet. No hint of remorse was present in his voice when he recounted his deeds. Lax was sentenced to twenty-five years of imprisonment but was free to walk in the penitentiary yard. He was such a sadist that he would throw oil on rats he caught and set them on fire for the sheer pleasure of watching the spectacle. We were all on the edge for the three nights he slept in our room, sent by the prison authorities as *turnător* (an informer), reporting on our conversations.

I met him again in Ilia in 1965, when he showed up at my clinic's door asking for an appointment. He was employed in construction at the time, paving the road from Ilia to Arad. I was terrified to see him even if he looked pale and weak, but he fortunately failed to recognize me in the white lab coat. He was in the company of a middle-aged woman claiming to be his wife, who was ill as well and introduced herself as Mrs. Dumitrașcu. Without losing my composure, I asked him for his last name but he replied evasively that he was "not married to the lady yet."

A couple of weeks later, Mr. Lax came back for a follow-up visit, bringing along another sick coworker. I had advised the clinic clerks to receive him well, without mentioning his past activities. He claimed to have been promoted chief of the workers' group and to be their medical orderly.

To my great relief, that encounter turned out to be our last.

Air Force Men

I was soon moved again to a cell with four iron beds, this time with mattresses *and* blankets. There, I found myself in the company of a peasant, a gendarme sergeant, and a Romanian Air Force colonel. The latter, Boldur Voinescu, was a robust young man with a friendly, engaging personality and, like any pilot, very courageous.

We never met after our liberation, but I heard that he managed to open a tinker's shop on the periphery of Bucharest. In spite of the obstacles prison graduates faced in starting a business, the news came as no surprise to me, knowing that Boldur was such a skillful and versatile character. He consistently finished his quota on time and even brought me a piece of cheese or an extra slice of bread he obtained somehow, inviting me to eat with him by saying:

Mâncă doctore, că altcum te cureți! "Eat, Doc, 'cause otherwise you'll perish."

Boldur Voinescu's father had been the chief prosecutor for the Supreme Court. He challenged Ion Brătianu in a duel and had to resign from office as a result.

{Ion I. C. Brătianu had been the leader of the National Liberal Party in the interwar period and ruled Romania as a premier between 1909 and 1927—with interruptions—in a dictatorial style.}

"See, Doc, what fate can bring in an instant to a man and his children?" he used to lament, reminiscing about his family's history.

"Had my father not left the magistrate, he would have been a governor in 1927, and all this would not have happened."

Despite the situation we were in, he was always in a good mood, and I liked him for his high spirits and honesty. Unfortunately, we never shared the same team, as he was a mechanic and I a mere unskilled laborer.

Many other air force pilots were housed at Aiud, and I had the chance to meet a few at the start of my shift while briefly waiting in the factory courtyard. They were all young, cheerful, and witty. I remember one captain who always asked me why I was losing weight and growing tired, encouraging me to stay healthy. He joked a lot, and the last image I have of him is his smile, with a wink, as he confessed to us once:

"I *finally* got a piece of a sow's pussy in my sour soup today!"

Unfortunately, that man died of tuberculosis just prior to his scheduled release.

I also recall a pilot in isolation, whom I saw for a split second when the guard opened his door to clear the room. His cell was covered in countless drawings of planes, smeared on the walls with dark coal. This must have happened during the nights when he endured severe migraines. I could hear him shout out the window in the direction of the railway station located within 200 meters of the prison compound:

Mă mecanicule, mă doare tare capu', nu mai fluiera! "Hey, you, the train mechanic, stop that whistling; it gives me a terrible headache!"

In line with prison policy, the doctor refused to provide the man with painkillers. His yelling awakened me, but besides providing encouragement, I could do nothing to ease his suffering....

Escape and Protest

The next cell I was transferred to was located close, less then four meters away from the outside street, adjacent to the six-meter high wall surrounding the prison compound. Armed guards positioned at every fifty meters were on duty along that fortification, and there were four sentry boxes on top of the wall, one in each corner.

One night, I woke up from a deep sleep with painful palpitations, shortness of breath and bradycardia, an abnormally slow heart rate. In addition to being tormented by a chronic enterocolitis with abdominal cramps and bloody diarrhea, I was also hypertensive, which I was not fully aware of back then.

We were ordered to sleep with the lights on at night, so that the guards could observe our every move through the small, cell door window. This procedure had been introduced the year before, after a few convicts managed to escape from Galați Penitentiary under the cover of night by cutting the window bars with a makeshift hacksaw and sliding along the gutter.

Seconds after I got up that night, in total darkness and in discomfort, heart pounding in my chest, I heard several gunshots coming from right outside my cell. An odd case of telepathy, I thought. Concerned, I knocked on the door, asking the guard what had happened.

Au tras de pe zid securiștii de pază. "The guards on the wall fired some shots," he replied nonchalantly.

The next morning, I uncovered the chain of events: At midnight, three imprisoned captains escaped from the jail. Despite acting quickly, the men were noticed by the electrician doing his nighttime inspection as they were leaning over the generator with an iron bar, prepared to tear it down. The inspector was an ex-commander who had just finished five years of imprisonment and was a couple of months away from being released. They hit him on the head and killed him instantly, along with another prisoner, a worker from Basarabia who was part of the electrical team as well and happened that moment to walk down the hallway.

Overwhelmed by panic and making poor choices, the three men removed only the fuse of the generator, hoping to leave the prison in darkness. They made it to the prison wall, and two of them were successful in escaping by climbing a ladder they had positioned there during the day. The third captain was shot, non-fatally, while crossing the fence, once the fuse was replaced and the light was switched back on. Most inmates were dumbfounded and sad when they heard what the three escapees had accomplished: They had killed a fellow prisoner and an innocent bystander.

Naturally, the authorities intensified all security measures the next day. We were subjected to a regime of terror for the next six months, after which a military prosecutor, newly arrived at Aiud and speaking in broken Romanian, made an official announcement. He gathered all the prisoners in the yard and read them the accusation act by which the three escapees were sentenced to death. Then he informed everybody of the two fleeing captains' fate: They had been chased and apprehended in Bucharest, one of them while he was trying to contact his estranged wife, who had divorced him and had married a Securitate colonel.

My cellmates at the time were all Transylvanian peasants and former members of the Iron Guard. After the escape incident, they were prevented from leaving the cell for factory work, and the guards nailed wooden boards on our windows. With the outside view entirely blocked, the room became pitch black, and the ventilation was inadequate for maintaining a breathable atmosphere. I quickly discovered that man has the organism of a superior animal and adapts to the harshest conditions.

Nervous tension was visibly on the rise. When it was announced through the Morse code that one of the fellows next door had been taken out of his cell, and no one knew the reason, a signal was given for everybody to hit the iron doors and yell. All prisoners started to scream in unison from the top of their lungs, but one could not understand a word they were saying. Only Richard Wagner could have imitated the incredible noise created! Overcome by the charged atmosphere, I moved my bunk bed, climbed on it and started to fiercely hit the cell door with both fists.

The commotion lasted a quarter of an hour and must have been heard throughout the city of Aiud, certainly at the local train station. It took me a number of minutes to calm down. Once the last inmate became exhausted from the shouting and kicking, the jailors opened the small feeding doors and glanced at us with the caution you would approach a wild beast. They demanded to know who the instigators were. They saw I was older and some knew I was a doctor, so they asked me first:

Tu n-ai bătut, așa-i? "You didn't kick the door, right?"

A short pause followed.

Bine ai făcut! "Well done!" one of the guards complimented me, after I instinctively shook my head and mumbled *Nu!* "No!"

Fortunately, given the extent of everybody's involvement, no one could be singled out for punishment that day.

Mental Health and Body Searches

After furious prisoners succeeded once in throwing a guard over the railing, iron gates with wire nets were introduced between the hallways separating the second and third floor. The instances when inmates were rude, cursing at the jailors, or agitated and violent were not infrequent. Some detainees became depressed and refused to eat; others were paranoid and delusional. The outcome of their misbehavior was not always easy to guess.

At times, when I chose to be silent for several hours, my worried cellmates would ask me:

Unde ai plecat doctore, cu ursu'? "Where have you gone, Doc? Are you walking with the bear?" or similar statements like that, implying that I have lost my mind.

Somebody who has never been imprisoned believes—as I did before my sad and undeserved sentence—that a convict is left alone, isolated in a cell. He is given food as if he were an animal, albeit the food is of inadequate quality and insufficient amount for a normal human being. As for the rest of the time, he is sitting quietly, ignored and forgotten, left in peace. But, in fact, a prisoner experiences continuous uncertainty, total lack of control, as he is moved from one cell to another, unable to make friends and unsure of what to expect next. To survive, he must be *numai ochi și urechi* (all eyes and ears).

During my incarceration, we were routinely harassed and removed from cells for interrogations. We were asked to report on conversations with other inmates. In the process, many prisoners were coerced into becoming informers for the authorities.

In order to demoralize them, the prisoners were promptly told bad family news. The worst case I recall was that of a young fellow who was informed that his wife had left and divorced him the day the event occurred. The man, a native of Râușor, whom I knew from before and whose family was well respected in town, cried and lamented for days in a cell located a floor below mine. I encouraged him as we communicated through the separating wall. Years later I saw him again on the streets of Făgăraș. Despite that devastating experience, he claimed to have recovered his personal life. Another great example of human resilience.

Then we had to endure unwarranted body searches indiscriminately performed on us as frequently as the prison administration saw fit. Despite the draconian security measures employed, the officers' biggest fear continued to be that we would be able to get possession of items from the outside world. Consequently, after we were stripped naked, the search was so thorough and humiliating that it included an inspection of the anus!

When my hat was taken off my head once, exposing my short hair, and I was asked, *Ce ai acolo?* "What's under there?" I replied, *Mintea ce mi-a mai rămas!* "The mind that I have left!"

The fellow next to me gave a more intelligent answer to the same question: *Un tun!* "A cannon!"

Any items that you did not conceal were confiscated, as was anything labeled prohibited. I remember the imprisoned colonel returning from forced labor at the Danube-Black Sea Canal who hid some antibiotics that would have saved his life. He was standing next to me when his medications were taken away. Ironically, he developed a pulmonary infection shortly thereafter and succumbed after a few days of inadequate infirmary care. I learned about his fate from inmates who worked late at night in the prison yard, inspecting the wagon carrying corpses to the cemetery.

In the middle of one night, several jailors stormed into my cell, pulled me out, and brutally pushed me toward the guards' room because I was suspected of having hidden something in the collar of my shirt. In fact, I had just sewn a new patch to it and was trying to make it fit by stretching it. One guard had seen me through the small window, and he promptly informed the officer on duty, convinced he had discovered something extraordinary. As soon as the door was locked, five individuals rushed at me, stripped me naked, and frantically searched through my items. The officer cut the collar of my shirt zestfully only to be very disappointed. I was then returned to my cell with a boot kick.

The whole scene was witnessed by a convict who was in solitary confinement at the end of the hallway. We called that the bottom of the T, which was the shape of the prison facility. He told me cheerfully during next day's yard walk that the failed outcome of the search made his day.

In the course of another search performed on me, the guards found a half-dozen tiny pieces of broken glass in the pocket of my jacket. When I was asked why I kept them, I responded that I used them to rub and shorten my fingernails. As he confiscated my inoffensive but useful tools, one of the jailors demonstrated how I should cut my fingernails with my teeth! Only when you are imprisoned do you realize how precious an object can be, no matter how small, if it has proved its usefulness.

Well, I guess Lenin was the one who advised his friends not to fall prey to small and unimportant things in life!

Doctors and Informers

The solitary confinement chamber was a cell roughly two meters long and half a meter wide. It was build of wooden boards and placed at the very end of each basement hallway. These desolated cells functioned continuously, occupied by punished inmates under a regimen of isolation and starvation. Sips of stale water and 150 grams of bread were all the nourishment an inmate could expect per day.

The grounds for confinement were often trivial. In June 1955, I had broken the row during a yard walk in order to straighten a wild rose that had been beaten by the rain and had fallen to the ground. Three hours was the amount of time I was forced to spend in such a cell as a result.

{My grandfather had a true passion for gardening, and the endless variety of beautiful flowers he planted and nurtured during his retirement years in Cacova were a proof of his love.}

Fortunately for me and my family—to whom I eventually returned alive—destiny protected me from being put in chains, as happened to many political prisoners. Even though I generally avoid contact with former inmates, I enjoy talking on the phone to one of them, a retired physician as well. I am very fond of Dr. Remus Doctor—who, obviously, has the most appropriate last name!—and prize his great sense of humor and perfectly lucid mind at the age of 88. We converse once a year but have no intentions of meeting in person, since we are aware of the Securitate's distrust of us, two old, harmless, genuine patriots. The exchange of ideas with this distinguished colleague is short and intense, but it never fails to bring a smile on my face.

Dr. Remus Doctor was an assistant professor of internal medicine at the University of Cluj in 1924, when I was in my second year of medical school. His wrists and ankles were chained for days during December 1954 after he was denounced by one of his fellow physicians for offering macaroni and cheese—out of his own ration—to a seriously debilitated prisoner under his care. The informer was one of six doctors selected to serve with Dr. Remus Doctor in the improvised, rundown, and under-equipped prison infirmary.

Dr. Ghiță Iriminoiu, a former colleague of mine from Cluj, was apparently the culprit. I previously had been granted permission to see him as a patient, on a late evening after my factory shift. He was serving fifteen years for having hidden a Romanian Army defector in the basement of his house. He seemed unpleasantly surprised when I greeted him by his first name, "Ghiță," as I was glad to see a past collaborator in that environment and did not consider that way of addressing improper. He stated that although he was not a trained internist, he attempted to perform the work expected of one. Aware of my professional credentials and the infirmary's need of a specialist, he promised reluctantly to ask the administration to add me to the staff. This was a tremendous favor, because the selected doctors enjoyed a tolerable diet and were granted fresh air during unescorted walks in the courtyard. My ailing health was in need of that milieu. Given that the official (outside) physician responsible for the facility was hardly ever there, I could at least have alleviated my fellow inmates' medical problems.

On my second visit, however, Dr. Iriminoiu appeared more reserved, so our encounter was limited to discussing my deteriorating health and the lack of treatment options. During the third appointment, a month later, he informed me that my request to join the medical staff had been rejected because I was "a dangerous, suspect character." He paused briefly after that statement and waited inquisitively for my reply. Aware of the rumors circulating about him being an informer on matters such as attitude and behavior of patients and fellow doctors, I abstained from any comments.

I also knew that watching *his* every move was the counter observer—the dentist of the compound. That is how my colleague Ghiță Iriminoiu, nicknamed *Criminoiu* (the criminal), fell into disgrace one day and was subsequently removed from the physician group and transferred back to the cells. There, everybody despised him, and the poor man died a few months later, from a rapidly progressing cancer of unclear etiology.

At about the same time, a radiologist and former assistant professor at the University of Bucharest was released from the medical staff as well and put in chains when his attempt to mail a letter to his family was uncovered by the dentist. The radiologist was four months away from being set free! A prison sergeant was supposed to be the letter carrier, as he was responsible for delivering the mail from the penitentiary to the Ministry of Internal Affairs. He was followed by the Securitate, who had been tipped off by the dentist, and was arrested as he tried to enter the radiologist's house.

Given the new circumstances, the prison director, knowing about my internal medicine and radiology training, appeared interested in appointing me in that capacity. He asked me if I knew what the radiologist had done and what my obligations were. When I cautiously replied that I did not know either, he dismissed me without explanation. Seriously ill with scurvy and hypertension, I continued to suffer without help.

Such was the extent of informer infiltrations in our ranks that incidents like the following were not uncommon:

Să iasă din rînd turnătorii! "All foundry workers step forward!" a guard ordered the lined-up prisoners one morning. *{In Romanian, the words "informant" and "foundry" are pronounced identically.}*

There was a lot of mumbling and commotion, but no one dared to move. Then silence reigned for a few seconds.

"Hey, I was not referring to who you think I was referring to!" the bemused guard continued, sensing the confusion.

"I am talking about those of you who work in the foundry. I have to give you some soap."

The many informers planted by the Securitate in virtually every larger cell spied on anything and everything, paying particular attention to what was discussed. The ultimate goal was to discover our sources of news and information, the faintest connection to the world. The authorities were also interested in prisoners' personal conduct, to conclude if they were being "re-educated" or were in need of further correction. The presence of those informers created the most unpleasant atmosphere, difficult for the rest of us to endure.

I spotted one such individual in my cell once, after he tried unsuccessfully to stir my roommates into starting a riot during dinnertime. We were six people in a room at that time, and three of us were doctors. After that incident, we decided to ignor "Mister Student," a native of my hometown of Făgăraș and a first-year University of Cluj student at the time of his arrest. His persistent arrogance toward a humble Macedonian blacksmith from Dobrogea, whom he harassed and insulted, made his situation worse. We wanted to protect the older man from the abuse, so none of us spoke to the youngster again.

That was easier said than done, because the student was sleeping to my right, his head at my feet. Trying to extract information out of me, he made several attempts to start a conversation, waiting for the right moment to look me straight in the eyes. To avoid showing my displeasure, I turned my head the other way each time that happened. Then I found myself whispering *Diavole!* "You little devil!"

Needless to say, the young man was not very successful, and luckily, six weeks later, following a redistribution of prisoners, we were separated. Despite the authorities' intention, there was no friendship disrupted on that occasion.

Smokers and Cold Temperatures

By 1953, every time the guards escorted me to the infirmary—and there was one on every floor, attempting to meet the needs of the countless ill inmates—I brought back into the cell anything one of the helpful doctors dared to give me: a cigarette, a slice of bread, some news. I volunteered for medically unnecessary injections as well, in order to make me walk with a believable limp, so that the guards would not notice the bread I had stuffed in my pockets. The cigarettes I hid in my drawers, which I was careful enough to tie well prior to leaving the sickroom.

Inside the cells, one could light a cigarette only with a spark obtained by rubbing two rocks against each other, then setting a small, well dried piece of cloth on fire. In the factory, the grinder was of real use. It was interesting to observe the truly pathological passion displayed by the heavy smokers. Some readily gave up their share of food for a couple of cigarettes. Others puffed from stubs discarded by the guards throughout the yard, which they could spot from a great distance, then collect discretely and conceal carefully. The smokers' addictive behavior was very apparent; some spent all day in search of the next nicotine dose.

On a rare occasion, someone—we never figured out who it was—threw an entire cigarette through the window. This rare treat we shared as a group, gently passing it from one to another while hiding in the most distant corner of the cell. One of us stood guard in front of the door window, blocking the jailor's view with the back of the head.

{My grandfather never picked up a true smoking habit, but I recall the joy he experienced every Christmas evening, sharply dressed with a red bowtie and telling a fascinating tale to a captive family audience, in the company of an imported Dutch cigar.}

Aside from moments when we sought our privacy, we were always curious to hear and see, if at all possible, any activity going on in the hallways. Temporarily removing the corks from the wooden boards nailed to our windows enabled us to briefly peek through the holes; that was usually the extent of our glance at the yard. Despite the risk of being seen by the guards, we also tried to pull the lock from the cell door window with the help of a threadlike piece of wire. Working hours at a time for about ten days, an older convict had the patience to bore a small hole through the metal door with a thin cable. As soon as he finished his labor-intensive work, the guard on duty caught him in the act as he was attempting to gaze through the tiny opening. The prisoner apologized for his deed and, surprisingly, was pardoned by the officer, who was terribly amused when he heard the prisoner bemoan:

Mă scuzați, dar n-am putut prinde "goanga" din vizetă!

"I am so sorry! I could not catch the 'bug' [the guard's eye] I saw through the hole!"

Throughout my time at Aiud, I was unlucky to be confined—always, it seemed—in the northern part of the main prison. We called it the "Alaska Wing." Regardless of the season, the sun failed to grace that northern wall with a warm ray. I must have spent a total of four years moving between cells in that area. There were times when the inmates from the southern section wore only their jackets in the middle of February, while we were shivering with cold, dressed in everything we could find, including the striped cloak without a lining.

One evening in the fall of 1953, eight of us were relocated from various cells into a larger room on the first level of the northern section. As the key turned in the door lock, making that sinister, screeching noise, we discovered that the room had been emptied of beds, had no light, and was extremely cold. We were not given winter clothing, so we started searching in the dark, hoping to unearth some blankets. Under the covered windows, we discovered what felt like rough pieces of cloth. We lay on the bare floor that night using our boots as pillows and covered each other with every item we found in that room. The next morning I woke up—once again—under a bunch of cleaning rags, used for washing the prison hallways before inspections. Fortunately, they appeared to have been rinsed after the job!

Then, for the duration of two months, in January and February 1954, the heating system froze and broke down. While the outside temperatures reached record low levels, no heat emanated from that malfunctioning device whatsoever. At one point, we measured on the inside of our windows ten centimeters of ice buildup, which melted only after mid-March. At least we were allowed to smash and break the dirty icicles. As if our endurance was not tested to the limits, the guards decided to confiscate our straw mattresses, so we were forced to sleep directly on the ice-cold iron beds, covered by flimsy blankets.

That entire winter I spent in the company of three Macedonian farmers from Dobrogea. One of them complained that his toes were frostbitten, but all I could do was reassure and encourage him. Following another terrible winter night, during which I was unable to stop the cold from piercing my insides, I woke up with frozen lower extremities and pain in my insteps. Looking at my feet, I noticed three red stripes, very sensitive to touch, that had appeared on my soles. My misery was completed by unbearable aches in both heels, which had coarse skin and marked prints, left by the wooden clogs I had to wear while working in the factory. My skin, which suffered third-degree frostbite, never completely recovered.

Because of the cold weather, the jailors' daily routines had to be gradually modified and then cancelled altogether. The officers stopped entering our cells every day as they used to so that they could check the window iron bars with wooden hammers, in order to detect a fresh cut from a makeshift saw. The lack of oxygen and the unbearable pestilential smell emanating from our room kept them away from the door in the morning, when they performed the prisoner count and listened to our report. The malodorous gases from the buckets that served as toilets and were emptied only twice a day worsened the atmosphere. We had no choice but to get used to that environment, but I wondered quite often how an organism could adapt to such conditions....

During those six months of severe imprisonment, from late September 1953 to mid-March 1954, we never left our cells and were deprived of *plimbare* (the outside walk). When circumstances obligated the officers to get closer to our door, they all lighted cigarettes and were busy smoking them. Except for the guard who took the bucket full of urine and fecal matter and handed us water in a barrel, the only person permitted to open the cell door was the officer on duty. Certain prisoners were appointed to hand him those buckets, and when I was assigned to that duty, I could observe how abnormal the prisoners' digestion was.

When we finally took a walk outside on the 15th of March, we found a mountain of snow standing in the middle of the yard as proof of the long and harsh winter. Shortly thereafter, the higher outdoor temperatures melted the ice on the ceiling of our room, making it fall to the ground in shattered spiky pieces. It was an interesting, noisy spectacle that lasted several days.

How we survived that merciless winter, God only knows!

Ocnele Mari Episode

During the spring of 1954, an unprecedented level of terror was directed against the political prisoners, especially those housed in the three hundred cells of the main section. None of us knew why the cruel regime was imposed at that particular time. We suspected an unusual political occurrence in the outside world, such as an assassination attempt against Ana Pauker or Vasile Luca, the infamous Communist leaders. We did not know back then that both had been dismissed from the party leadership in 1952. Another year passed before we managed to unveil the truth, with the arrival of a new batch of convicts at Aiud.

"Pătrășcanu's trial has taken place!" they whispered. "He has been sentenced to death and executed!"

Without further clarification, that was all that surfaced. Vague details were all I was able to muster, even years after my release. Another half-century will pass before the history books will undoubtedly describe, with accurate documentation, the precise circumstances leading to the sacrifice of Pătrășcanu. Until then, we are left with a street in Bucharest that still bears his name.

{What an accurate prediction! Lucrețiu Pătrășcanu was a genuine nationalist among Romanian Communists. A founding member of the party in 1921, he was an intellectual, which in itself made him a highly suspicious individual. Chants such as "Pătrășcanu to power" at the party's first public rallies in 1944 attested to his rising popularity, and he consolidated his position by declaring that he was "first a Romanian and only then a Communist." Being a patriot who placed his national identity over party loyalty, the serving minister of justice was labeled "anti-Soviet" and "under the influence of the bourgeoisie." A show trial was launched, identifying Pătrășcanu as a U.S. and British imperialist agent, with evidence made

up to confirm the accusations. The death sentence was a predetermined verdict, and Pătrășcanu was executed in April 1954 in his prison cell. Details of one of his acquaintance's persecution are found in Lena Constante's memoir The Silent Escape: Three Thousand Days in Romanian Prisons. *Both stories represent familiar scenarios in those unfortunate times.}*

At the end of 1953, there were only members of the Iron Guard in my section of the jail, after the authorities forbade them from working in the factory. The leaders of the group continued to distrust me, puzzled by my presence among them. This was a consequence of the fabrications by the Făgăraș Securitate regarding my affiliation with the organization.

A new prisoner triage took place during that winter, at the conclusion of which it was ordered that the elders and those incapable of physical labor be send to Ocnele Mari prison. In addition, fifteen hundred Iron Guard members in restricted confinement had to make room for working inmates who were going to replace them.

Most of the soon-to-be transferred prisoners were glad to leave Aiud. Based on the rumors that were circulating, they were at Ocnele Mari to receive parcels from home and communicate with their families through a glass door over the speakerphone. On the other hand, the place was motley and strange, with predominantly ill, older people, most of them incapacitated and depressed, and was infested with informers. I kept thinking how difficult it would be for my wife to come and visit or even to mail me a package, if that was indeed permitted. On the other hand, my failing health would have benefited tremendously from an extra couple of hundred calories per day. Yet again, imagining the misery my wife was going through, where was the additional food supposed to come from?

Lined up for inspection next to my roommates, I waited for the penitentiary director to arrive in front of me. Flipping through the pages of my file, he asked, without looking at me, why I had been sentenced.

Pentru ajutor și nedenunțare. "For helping and not denouncing," I answered.

Raising his head to bless me with a brief, disgusted glance, he ordered his adjutants, before he made his way to the next transfer candidate:

"He'll stay here! Move him to another cell!"

In retrospect, remaining in the same surroundings proved to be the healthier choice, given the tremendous problems my wife was facing, the full extent of which I was not aware of at that time. And I never regretted having to live behind bars with Iron Guard members, despite the extremely harsh conditions that almost killed me. At least I was in the middle of educated people I accepted and by whom I—eventually—felt understood and supported, even if I was not "one of them." The camaraderie that developed among us, the decency in everybody's behavior, the continuing exchange of opinions and knowledge, all meant the least upsetting environment possible. Making true friendships remained difficult, however, because every few months, we were separated and redistributed. And most of my cellmates were quite young, if one takes into account that I was over 50 at that time.

Prison Guards

Moved to yet another cell, I found myself in the most acceptable and respectable company. I could not have done a better job if I had been allowed to choose my own cellmates. This time I shared the space with three physicians and two professors, with whom I spent true quality time, pleasant and intellectually challenging. We talked a lot, each choosing a topic of general interest from his area of expertise, and then we quizzed each other, answering questions in a low tone of voice, while paying attention to the prison guards eavesdropping through the door.

One evening around eight o'clock, one of the doctors was having a longer than usual debate with one of the professors. The jailor, noticing the solemn manner in which the two men were speaking to each other, opened the door with a sudden swing and demanded to be briefed on the subject.

Despre ce vorbiți, mă? "Hey, what are you talking about?" he inquired, eager to report on the subversive discussion. The professor's angry answer took him by surprise and made him give up his monitoring for a while:

Despre capra cu trei iezi, Dumnezeii mătii! "About the fairy tale with the three goats, damn you!"

That is why the guards were formally forbidden to engage in talks with us, make comments, or reply to our protests or requests, even reasonable ones, the type one would make to a fellow human being. The regime they were working under was one of tension as well, in some respects almost as harsh as that imposed on us. I mention here body searches, performed on the guards themselves by their superiors, in order to eliminate any chance they might introduce items to prisoners they befriended.

Among the guards, there were a few kinder people, or at least that is how I saw things. One individual, who I believe took this position out of genuine curiosity, given that he acted interested in the conditions in which the detainees lived, spoke to us one morning in the friendliest voice and manner:

Poftiți, serviți apă, vă rog! "Help yourselves with some water, please."

The well-meaning guard was—as one would guess—an exception, confirming the rule of rudeness, which explains why he lasted only a few months on the job. His way of addressing the prisoners was unheard of among his colleagues.

Then there were the jailors at Zarca, the most unattractive area of the penitentiary, both in terms of its appearance and conditions. Back in 1953, the inmates who were unable or forbidden to work in the factory were restricted to that section. The Maier brothers were two notorious employees who continuously terrorized the prisoners there. They entered the cells in the middle of the night and at their own discretion, having no authorization to do so in the absence of the officer on duty, carrying big metal rods with which they hit the ground in a menacing way, barking at the half asleep, frightened detainees:

Suntem puși aici să vă distrugem! "We're here to destroy you, bastards! We represent the Republic! Who doesn't listen to us, doesn't respect the Republic!"

Surprisingly, they were fired and convicted of abuse of power.

Years later, as I was traveling by train from Cluj to Ilia, I met one particular guard from whom I had received slaps in the face. We recognized each other in an instant, but there was nothing to talk about. We both maintained an awkward silence, sharing seats in the same compartment. We could have had an argument, an angry exchange of words, but would that have mattered?

Chief and Thief

Șef de celulă (cell chief) was a position I involuntarily found myself in one too many times, and it brought me mainly problems. While in that capacity, I was put into solitary confinement because the guards were displeased with the quality of my cellmates' floor-cleaning. I lost count of the number of occasions I was ordered to scrub the hallways myself—especially if the guards knew I was a doctor—turning the stairs white with an old rag. The traffic on the prison stairs connecting three floors was heavy, and not one visible footstep was tolerated after the job was done.

Washing the toilets required extreme caution to avoid getting dirty and bringing the soiled clothing with the pungent smell into the cells. Because we were not allowed to use toilet paper, we had to wash ourselves with a small amount of water, according to the so-called "Turkish system." Our bodily hygiene was always inadequate, with a trip to the common showers allowed only once every two weeks, in groups of twenty prisoners. The time under the lukewarm water was so brief one could barely get the skin wet. All of this represented a challenging exam on cleanliness, which I passed with obvious difficulty, given my standards and expectations as a physician.

In the summer of 1953, after being released from my factory job because of illness, I was held in the old section of the penitentiary. I was the chief once again, still failing to comprehend why the prison guards seemed to always pick me for that role. Despite the misery I had to endure, my personal reward was the extra help I could offer fellow inmates, along with my medical advice.

We were fifty-six people in the room at that time, and I was the one responsible for counting the food portions received through the cell door window. Under the risk of being denounced, I faked mistakes in my counting, with the help of a couple of other prisoners, who came to the door with two bowls each. The sour soup was brought in a large pot and poured into bowls with a ladle, while the liquid was constantly stirred. When I got to number five, for example, which I had to say aloud, I dared to say "Five" for a second time while telling the prisoner *hai mai repede!* (hurry up!). Repeating the trick enabled us to obtain as many as four double helpings per meal, which we shared in an established order among all of us.

During my efforts to fairly distribute the food, problems emerged because of a mischievous man, a semi-educated individual whom we nicknamed "Mister Intellectual." When his turn came to fill the bowl, I witnessed him snatching with his finger a piece of gristle, maybe the only one in the entire pot. Revolted by his shamelessness, I raised my voice and reprimanded him in front of the whole group after the door had closed.

He was a tall man, about 55 years old, dark-haired, and with a rude look on his face, who slept up in the bunk beds. My open disapproval upset him. I had already admonished him once for stealing pieces of clothing soap, cigarettes, and even the bread some prisoners—*fomiștii* (the starvers)—chose not to eat entirely during one meal. These people would consume the food in small pieces, despite my advice that it was physiologically unhealthy to constantly stimulate the stomach, causing discomfort and leaving one always feeling hungry.

From a heated discussion that followed the stealing incidents, I found out that Mr. Intellectual had been a prosecutor in the city of Râmnicu-Vâlcea who was promoted judge at the Timișoara Court of Appeal in the 1940s. Even though I was experiencing difficulty in acquiring new information, and I had to write everything down in order to memorize it, I found it easy to remember his Latin-based name: Tarciniu.

After his neighbor caught him stealing again in the middle of the night, I was so outraged I made a request to the guards to move him out of our cell or replace me as chief. The added anger and protest of my cellmates led to his quick removal. But he kept on with his old habit and was caught in the act once more; this time, his new mates threw him out of his bunk bed. The leg fracture he sustained during that incident healed without surgical treatment but left him with a long-term defect: He limped and could walk only with crutches.

Whom did I meet again nine years later, in 1962 at the Băile Bazna Resort? Tarciniu, that devil! It ended up being an anxiety-provoking encounter. I had just arrived at the spa and was ready to check in. He was in the company of a young blonde, a Saxon woman who claimed to be his wife. We were in the same waiting room, and I avoided his sight, retreating into a corner where I stood patiently until the last tourist was taken care of.

With his arrogant demeanor and impertinent style, he demanded to be given a room on the ground floor, with two beds, even though his request was impossible to honor unless someone vacated such a room, the hotel clerk explained.

Cum, tovarășe? "What are you trying to say, comrade?" he yelled back at the clerk, an ex-county chief forced by illness into early retirement.

Pe mine nu mă serviți, care sunt invalid pentru Republică? "You're saying that you're refusing to serve me? Me, a disabled veteran who fought for the Republic?" he asked, continuing his tirade.

Fui! How about that! I thought. He of all people had the nerve to make such a claim!

As a result of his tantrum, he was checked into a single room on the ground floor, and his wife was temporarily offered another one. After he left, I discreetly asked the clerk the man's name, in order to confirm his identity.

For the entire week I spent there, I made a conscious effort to avoid him during mealtime, picking a table at the opposite end of the dining room, where I ate in the company of strangers. But eventually, it happened. He must have caught my eye one day, because as soon as I left the mud baths and sauna, he was waiting for me around the corner of the building!

Raising his walking stick in the air and waving it toward me, he shouted: *Tovarășe!* "Comrade!"

Taken by surprise, I had to stop. What was I supposed to do? Failing to walk toward him would have raised suspicions, so I did it, albeit with some hesitation.

To be recognized was not a choice either, if I were to maintain my tranquillity, because he was the type of person capable of harming me. All it would take was a denouncement to the Securitate for an invented reason. That possibility alone was a real threat.

Îmi păreți tare cunoscut! "You look so familiar," Tarciniu addressed me as he was getting closer.

Acting a bit confused, I replied politely that I had never seen him in my life.

"Where did you go to college?" he continued, staring at me.

"In Cluj," I answered calmly.

"Have you had any other schooling?" he asked with a wink. I pretended not to understand his question.

But he insisted: "What is your name?"

"Stanciu," I said.

Semănați mult cu Stroia. "You look a lot like Stroia, a man I used to know.... I am sorry. I have mistaken you for somebody else."

Only God saved me that day! Tarciniu continued to watch me as I was walking on the lone paved street in Băile Bazna. Fortunately, I managed to avoid him from that point on.

Such stressful moments were at the root of my hypertension. And despite my prudence and moderation in life, there have been a lot of them, too many....

Baia Sprie Episodes

I managed to escape from another memorable prison incident without being physically harmed. God rescued me many times, but on this occasion, he did it in a miraculous fashion.

The event took place in the autumn of 1953, as the Aiud prison administration was responding to an emergency order to ship sixty prisoners to forced labor in the Baia Sprie lead and copper mines, located in Maramureș County, Northern Romania. Given that all inmates in decent physical condition were employed in the factory, the officials had to select individuals from the group working in the kitchen and yard and around the horse stable. When the final count proved insufficient, a few ill prisoners had to be picked out, too. In conformity with established routines, the chosen ones—me included—were isolated for three days while each personal file was reviewed.

As I was suffering with scurvy, I was naturally concerned about the prospect of leaving for the mines. A former lawyer, who slept right next to me, noticed that I was not tolerating the corn porridge and played the Good Samaritan, exchanging it for his slice of wheat bread. I am still grateful for his kind gesture, which temporarily alleviated my discomfort. He had just arrived from the prison kitchen where he had held a job, and now was scheduled to leave for the mines in the morning.

The next day around noon, a Securitate lieutenant entered our cell with a list of names in his hands. He was a likable guy with a smile on his face. According to the rules, when one's name was called, the prisoner had to answer clearly and in a normal tone of voice: "Present."

Upon my turn, however, I yelled: *Acii*! "Right here!" badly mispronouncing the words at the same time.

Annoyed, the lieutenant raised his eyes from the paper, searching the room for the culprit.

Care ești ăla, mă țărane? "Which one is the peasant here?" he asked.

Io! "Me!" I screamed in the same manner.

I do not know what got into me, what I was thinking, or why I chose to be so obstinate. I am not quite as stubborn as my grandson Dan, but I think I was trying to act as a native of my village of Cacova would have in that circumstance.

The lawyer and everybody else around me started to laugh, knowing that I was an educated person.

"How many years have you been in prison?" the lieutenant continued, trying to make a point.

Trii! "Three," I said, like an illiterate.

"You could have learned three foreign languages by now, but instead, you don't even know how to correctly answer an appeal!"

There was cheerful laughter from all prisoners. Even the lieutenant appeared visibly pleased by the effect of his joke.

Looking back, I still wonder what my response would have been had the lieutenant made the decision to continue with his interrogatory. If he had asked me about my studies, could I have possibly answered, *Facultatea de Prostologie?* "The University of Stupidity?" Imagine the consequences....

Two hours later, the director of the penitentiary arrived with our files. When he looked over mine, he had a sudden change of mind, and I was removed from the departing group.

What can I add to that fortunate instance? Only that it was my destiny. I doubt that I would have survived the mines, especially the climbing involved, as I am certain that my heart would have failed in such conditions.

A few months later, while I was in isolation right across from the main entrance, I witnessed another dire prison scene related to Baia Sprie. It must have been around nine or ten at night, when somebody pulled the alarm and yelled an order directed to all of us:

Toată lumea culcată! Nu se uită nimeni pe geam! "All inmates lie on the floor! Nobody look out the window!"

The prisoners, alarmed and dismayed, grew more attentive to the activity outside their cells, rather than following the instructions. After a few minutes of calm, I recognized the indistinguishable noise produced by feet dragging metal chains, together with similar but lighter sounds. Trying to adjust my eyes to the dark, I peeked through the window and caught a glimpse of a long procession of newly arrived convicts. Aside from the chain noise, there was total silence: no sounds, no voices. The men appeared exhausted and subdued, unwilling or forbidden to say a word. All were promptly escorted to the highest floor of the compound.

Around six o'clock the next morning, I heard the upstairs guard reply to the kitchen person when asked about the number of pieces of bread he needed.

Optzeci! "Eighty!" he yelled.

I soon discovered that the chained prisoners had been transferred from the Baia Sprie mines, and that neither the chains nor the handcuffs were removed after the transport. The cruel treatment was a result of three convicts from the group escaping a night before and killing a Securitate officer in the process.

Given my isolation, I was unable to obtain more details about their fate.

Despair and Suicide

Several evenings later, I heard an unusual amount of noise coming from a cell adjacent to mine. Following a few minutes of attentive listening, ear glued to the wall, I realized that a new inmate had been brought into a previously empty isolation chamber. The poor man kept whining and crying without interruption for over an hour. Our rooms shared the same heating pipes, lined along the upper part of the wall, so the sounds were easily transmitted from one cell to the other. I reacted as any doctor would in that circumstance and demanded assistance, but the jailor showed no interest in my request or the fellow's plea.

After about three days, I got tired of hearing the cries, so I pushed the bed to the wall, got on top of it, and removed the pipe with little effort. Then I invited my neighbor to do the same; that way we were able to see each other. He was a short old man, dressed in a riding coat, with black, stripped pants, who appeared to be in significant emotional distress. He explained that he had been a minister in Iuliu Maniu's government in 1929 and was worried that his transfer out of Zarca and to this isolation cell was due to the authorities' intention to execute him. He appeared anxious and disoriented, as if he had lost his mental balance.

{Iuliu Maniu (1873–1953) was the leader of the National Peasant Party, the main political opposition group in the interwar period, representing the needs of the emerging middle class. He served as Romania's prime minister between 1928 and 1930. Maniu's party won the 1946 national elections, but the Communists falsified the results, dissolved the party, and arrested its leadership. Maniu died in

the high security Sighetul Marmației prison located within two miles of the Soviet border and reserved for the democratic political elite.}

By reassuring him that the individuals moved to this building were those likely to be freed soon, he calmed down. Our conversation ended at that point, and I never heard him cry again. A couple of days later, he was removed from the room next door, and I was transferred into another cell as well. We never met again, and I could only hope that my predictions were accurate.

Later that month, I glanced at a row of prisoners brought out into the courtyard for a walk, eyes looking to the ground. All of a sudden, gunshots that appeared to originate from one of the prison's corners disrupted the silence. Loud booing and shouting followed instantly, accompanied by mayhem in the cells. It was all directed at the commander of the penitentiary, Colonel Magistrate Kohler, who made his appearance in the yard. I heard people rushing to the windows of their cells and agitated guards running up and down the hallways. Caution aside, I lifted one bed on top of another and pushed both right under the window. With a decent view, I noticed a lot of armed guards running toward the cell section. Unable to figure out more, I speculated that the gunshot noise and the ensuing chaos must have been caused by a serious incident.

It took days for the news to reach me: A political detainee, a former worker from Teiuș who was serving a seventeen-year sentence had been shot to death. He could not tolerate the imprisonment anymore, so he had reported his desolation to the commander just a day before. He was directed to the prison physician, Captain Bogățean, who was indifferent to the man's anguish and advised him that instead of trying a futile treatment, he should throw himself into the barbed wire that surrounded the penitentiary!

A sand field four meters wide, always carefully levelled off so that the guards could identify the faintest footprints, encircled the prison building. A sharp barbed wire fence surrounded it, with metal boards hanging from place to place displaying the message: *Împușcare fără somație!* "Shooting without warning!" The actual six-meter high prison wall was built around the entire compound, with strategically placed guard observation posts in every corner. This particular inmate was so exhausted and so desperate that he took the first opportunity to throw himself into the barbed wire, where he was instantly shot by the guards on the wall.

A few weeks later, I was removed from isolation and placed together with three other inmates in the room previously occupied by the prisoner who had been shot. The cell had been empty, except for personal items wrapped in a blanket on the bed closest to the window. The guard instructed me not to open the package or remove any items, since it belonged to "the dead man" and had to be handed to the authorities. The "dead man" who had lost his life at his doctor's recommendation....

English Professors

At one point, two English professors were imprisoned in the northwestern part of the T-shaped prison. They were excellent conversationalists, endlessly arguing and loudly debating on various subjects. Confined in adjacent cells, they sat in opposite corners of their respective rooms. When the officer doing the rounds overheard the detainees lecturing each other on intellectual matters, he attempted to stop them:

Care vorbești acolo, mă? "Hey, who's the one doing the talking down there?" he barked his threatening question.

Visibly annoyed by the sudden interruption, the neighboring prisoners, all carefully listening to the entertaining chat, started to shout in chorus, creating a deafening clatter:

Huo, huo, huo! "Boo, boo, boo!"

The uproar continued for a while, to the exasperation of the guards.

Consequently, an interrogation of every inmate from that section was started on the spot, in order for the culprits to be identified. Through the Morse code, as if it was ordered, the entire prison population was informed about it within minutes. No one confessed to having started the clamor, and it was too difficult to look into thousands of files.

As a result, security measures were increased once again and so was the surveillance of the prisoners. Writing on the walls was prohibited, including scribbling with makeshift animal-bone pencils, which were confiscated when found. English words and mathematical calculations were especially forbidden, and no prisoner was allowed to have the tiniest piece of paper in his possession.

Because there were many highly educated individuals around, and the abundant time had to be killed somehow, we tried to teach the youngsters French or English, by writing words on the walls with pointy wooden sticks. This lasted until the authorities noticed our activity and covered the walls with paint one could not make a scratch on.

Proving our resilience, we turned to fragments of an English version of the Bible (Eremia and Ezekiel), miraculously introduced inside our cell by a gutsy new inmate and carefully hidden under the toilet bucket, nailed to some slats. That location was chosen because the guards avoided lifting the bucket upside down during searches, as they did with the water barrel. All the prisoners interested in English used those pages to learn the language.

Around the same time, I met the son-in-law of Mihail Sadoveanu *(celebrated Romanian historical novelist, 1880–1961)*, who was suffering from a compensated mitral valve insufficiency, and whom I managed to reassure and calm down. Medical advice and psychological support were the only tools I could use to alleviate a cellmate's suffering.

The Postcard

During seven years of detention I was never allowed to communicate with my family, and all I ever received was a small package containing undergarments and weighing less than two kilograms during the winter of 1952–1953. My wife mailed the hempen bag in response to the one postcard I was permitted to write on December 9, 1952, at the request of the prison officials. That correspondence only took place because the authorities were constrained by severe shortages of personal items, for the ever-growing number of political convicts overcrowding the prison.

I found the safeguarded note resting on the dining room table upon my return home on December 8, 1957. Scribbled with strong lead pencil marks by an unsteady hand, with slanted lines and letters increasingly reduced in size, it read as follows:

"Dear Valy,

I am healthy. Please send me the following items: one scarf, one pair of drawers, two pairs of wool socks, two pairs of cotton socks, two towels, one roll of wool thread, one thick needle, one pair of boots, shoe polish, a shoe brush, a rubber shoe lining, laundry soap, tooth paste and two hankies.

Kisses from Stanciu."

This was the only access to pencil and paper and the only words I wrote in all those years. Out of the parcel delivered to my jailors, only the undergarments ended up in my possession.

Priests and Bishops

In 1953, because of my deteriorating health, I was released from factory duties. Together with fifty-six other individuals, mostly elderly, I was transferred to a larger cell located at the end of the prison's oldest wing. We were all considered *elemente periculoase* (dangerous elements). There were two Orthodox priests among my new roommates. One of them was Father Zosim Oancea.

{Father Zosim Oancea was a remarkable personality of the Romanian Orthodox clergy. He was a graduate of the Bucharest Theological Institute, a professor of religion, and a priest at the Sibiu Orthodox Cathedral. A noble and generous soul, he provided financial support to impoverished families of political detainees. As a result, he spent fourteen years, from 1950 to 1964, within the walls of Sibiu and Aiud prisons and at the forced labor camp of Periprava. Upon his release, he preached in the village of Sibiel, near Cacova, and founded the local Museum of Stained-glass Icons, the most representative of its kind in the country. Father Oancea shared a lifelong friendship with Dr. Stanciu Stroia and paid him a final respect in 1987 by officiating at his funeral. He was still alive in 2004 at the age

of 93, having just published his memoir The Prisons of an Orthodox Priest. *Father Oancea reminisced fondly: "I remember Dr. Stanciu Stroia's efforts in helping other detainees with medical advice and his interventions on their behalf at the prison infirmary, requesting medications. His intelligence and medical knowledge, his commitment to people and his honesty and warmth in communicating with others impressed me the most. His sound judgment had its roots in the mountain people's wisdom, whereas his gentle soul and healthy humor provided moral support in many difficult, hard-to-imagine circumstances."}*

Every Sunday morning, the priests withdrew to a corner of the room, seeking privacy from the jailors' watchful eyes, trying to perform the Orthodox liturgy, entirely from memory. The service coincided with the sounds of the nearby church's bells, sounds that contributed enormously to our survival. Son of Iosefina, daughter of a priest, I was exposed to the Orthodox service at an early age and knew the religious ceremonies well by the time I was 14. I paid particular attention to the Sunday mass and the vespers and remembered what was read and sung during processions for the dead. Hence, it was no surprise when I quickly became the chorister in our improvised church, reciting wise words that had persisted in my memory:

Cu adevărat deșertăciune sunt toate..."Everything in life is futile, like the desert...where all of us are troubled.... When we finally hold the world in our hands, we pass into our graves...together, the rich and the poor." A statement reminiscent of the Communist ideology, from Christ's own times!

Learning a new prayer, on the other hand, proved to be a formidable task, given my troubled memorization process. Only after two weeks of efforts, by repeatedly listening to it and scratching it on the cell wall multiple times, was I able to remember the Saint Ephraim prayer:

Doamne și Stăpânul vieții mele...
God and Master of my life,
The Spirit of idleness, worries,
Self-love and empty words,
Do not bring upon me.

The Spirit of purity, humble thoughts,
Patience and love,
Do give Your servant.
Help me Lord acknowledge my sins
And forgive my brother,
Că bine ești cuvântat în vecii vecilor...
For You are blessed into eternity,
Amen.

In that larger room, the youngsters slept on worn-out mattresses in the upper bunk beds, while the old and the ill rested on the cots below. I occupied the space next to that of a former manager of the Astra Petroleum Society, who was serving a sentence of twenty-five years, as a result of an industrial sabotage indictment. There were five executives from major oil producing companies in that cell, all of whom were serving lengthy prison terms for similar, fabricated accusations. My other neighbor was a younger doctor, a poor fellow suffering from Potts disease, the humpback of which I had to help keep warm on several occasions. The man's condition was caused by a bone and joint infection, a complication of late tuberculosis leading to a debilitating spine deformity.

We also enjoyed the company of six Roman Catholic archpriests, all German-Saxons, one of whom was a former bishop from Timișoara. They had lost an enormous amount of weight, over 50 kilograms each, so that loose skin was hanging from their abdomens and thighs, as if they were wearing aprons. I had to sew their vests in order to make them tighter and warmer.

Two young Greek Catholic deacons completed the group. They held doctorate degrees in theology from Rome, but were jailed upon their return to Romania, after the content of their published religious dissertations was deemed politically objectionable. They were both only 25 years of age but already in poor health; one of them had a compensated mitral valve insufficiency, while the other suffered from untreated chronic asthmatic bronchitis.

The guards isolated the one with the recalcitrant cough, afraid he might be suffering from cavitary pulmonary tuberculosis. In the isolation chamber, he met and befriended an older German Catholic bishop. I found out about their long-lasting friendship years later when I was working in Ilia. While covering the clinic on a summer Sunday in 1966, the young deacon showed up at my door, impeccably dressed in a brand new suit and with a fancy car parked at the gate. He had found out where I was employed and drove all the way from Cluj—where he was a medical orderly in a radiology department—to pay me a surprise visit.

I failed to recognize him at first, especially when he introduced himself as a patient. I didn't believe him even after he told me about his fellow with the heart problems, who was now an accountant at a *Cooperativă Agricolă de Producție*, a state farm in his native village, enjoying better health. They both had been released in late 1964, after the amnesty. The bishop had been freed six years earlier, in response to political pressure from West Germany, where he immigrated and resumed his activity, earning a monthly salary of four thousand Deutsche Mark. *{Over two thousand dollars—a very significant amount by Romanian standards.}*

When the bishop discovered that his benefactor—the man who shared his meager prison food portion with him—was finally free, he sent him a German car and six brand new suits as a thank you gift.

What a reward and wonderful gesture of gratefulness!

Prison Food

During my incarceration, I realized that the digestive apparatus was my body's least resistant part. My mother suffered from an intractable gastric ulcer until she was 50, and her brother, *Unchiu' Popa* or Father Ioan Hanzu Jr., went under the knife for a duodenal ulcer before his 52nd birthday. He died in 1942, at the age of 67, after a bleeding episode and ensuing postoperative anemia. It was in prison that I began to understand my family's genetics.

The circulatory system—my body's other weak link—had been exposed, rather recklessly, to tremendous physical exertion in my childhood and adolescence, particularly during World War I. Back then, with all the village men fighting on the front, I was among the youngsters responsible for working in the fields. Most of the farmers' children, high school and college students alike, were forced to engage in physical labor to supplement their meager family income. This often occurred during times reserved for studying, which was much neglected. The pupils were exhausted in morning class during the fall semester, at the time of the harvest, when they worked up to thirty hectares per day.

As a physician, I led an orderly life and enjoyed a balanced diet. I was not fond of sweets, and I preferred to consume fresh fruits and vegetables, especially the homegrown type. Once in prison, however, starting with the months of Securitate detention and culminating with Aiud, my nourishment became inadequate, in terms of both caloric content and nutritional value. This dietary regimen applied strictly to political prisoners and was designed as a potent extermination tool.

The breakfast at Aiud consisted invariably of a small ladle filled with 30 to 50 grams of corn porridge. If it had been mold-free and well cooked, it would have been an acceptable meal, considering the inmates' hunger. Unfortunately, this infamous dish, an economical version of polenta called *terci, turtă de mălai* or simply *turtoi*, became the trademark of the penitentiary because it was so cheap and easy to prepare. Made of poor quality and insufficiently ground corn flour—the type my mother used to feed to the farm animals—it had a semi-liquid consistency, was shaped like a cone, and was barely the size of two baby fists.

Mămăligă, a quality corn mush served in other prisons, was virtually impossible to prepare at Aiud, because the number of portions needed was prohibitively high, around three thousand. The *turtoi* was only cooked on one side, in order to be quickly finished. The opposite side was lukewarm at most, while the inside remained raw. As a result, it played havoc among the inmates, causing a great deal of indigestion and ultimately chronic, frequently lethal, bloody enterocolitis, a severe inflammation of the small and large bowels.

For lunch and dinner, we were served 200 grams of thin, watery soup, made of pickled tomatoes from barrels rejected at the local market. Rare onions had their peel still on, and one had to count the beans, because there were so few, as was the case with the pearl barley sometimes added to the mix. Twice a week, 250 grams of wheat bread or the eighth part of a regular two-kilogram piece, was added to the meals. On a rare occasion we ate bean stew, feeling lucky if that occurred more than twice during a twelve-month period.

Throughout my time at Aiud, our diet contained no animal proteins and no meat, except for the occasional cartilage taken off bones salvaged from the slaughterhouse or pieces of hoofs and beef heads poorly cleaned or downright dirty. A sow's snout or back part was always a source of jokes at the expense of the one who found it in his soup.

Fresh vegetables or fruits remained completely absent; my regular meals included none over seven years. The notable exceptions were onions stolen by kitchen-employed inmates and thrown to us through the cell window, discarded raw potatoes and green tomatoes found accidentally during yard walks, and pieces of garlic and cabbage shared by fellow inmates. Walking with our heads down and eyes fixed on the ground was the regulation, so in essence the jailors made our search for food easier, compensating for the inability to peek at the blue sky. We were so hungry that we ate any scrap of raw, even rotten vegetables we managed to get our hands on. I got lucky only once, when I carried wooden construction materials through the yard and found a few pickles. Such was our craving for food that it provided entertaining incidents like shouting at a flock of crows in an attempt to scare them into dropping the walnuts from their beaks! That, predictably, never happened.

If the kitchen had a list of available food items for review, it would be indicative of the malnourishment forced upon the prisoners. Many perished under the indifferent eyes of the jailors, incriminating them even further. The medical consequences of this dietary abuse can be found in the admission charts of the countless ill, whose records will also point to the absence of proper care. The only people who managed to survive the prison nightmare were those able to digest prison food!

It was just another method of eliminating the weak and unfortunate.

Scurvy

In the spring of 1953, General Alexandru Drăghici, the head of the sinister Ministry of Internal Affairs and the man in charge of all Romanian penitentiaries, visited Aiud for an impromptu inspection. The authorities had already released me from the factory job at the time, due to my progressive illness. While employed in the carpeting department, I had struggled to finish my quota, despite my best attempts not to lose my daily food allowance.

I was suffering from recurrent indigestion and bouts of arterial hypertension, with estimated systolic blood pressures of over 210 millimeter Mercury. I felt very anxious, with an itching sensation over my entire body, and I made serious efforts to stand firmly on my feet. Palpitations bothered me frequently, and in several instances, I felt enduring extrasystoles. Those skipped heartbeats were associated with the unpleasant sensation of acute myocardial pre-infarction, or that of an imminent heart attack. It did not take long to realize that I was experiencing symptoms of left ventricular failure, with precordial chest pains, nonexertional shortness of breath, an enlarged palpable liver the size of my palm, and a sensation of constriction in my throat. Only when I became visibly impaired was I let go from the factory, losing my right to eat wheat bread. Instead of medical care, I received the indigestible corn mush, which became my punishment and torment.

As all this was happening, a study about hypertension that I had read, published in the *Presse Medicale*, a French specialty journal I had subscribed to since 1929, came to mind. University of Leningrad Professor Lang had reached the Pavlovian conclusion that the etiology behind the increased incidence of high blood pressure in the city's population after one year of German blockade was sustained psychological tension and severe malnutrition.

{*In September 1941, within months of Russia's invasion by Nazi Germany, the city of Leningrad was fully encircled and a furious siege began. It lasted nine hundred days. The city's three million people stubbornly refused to surrender despite limited food supplies and lack of heat, electricity, or water. Leningrad's war factories continued to produce and the university remained open, but the death toll reached over six hundred thousand by the time the siege was broken in January 1944.*}

General Drăghici's visit brought many changes with unpleasant consequences for the detainees. The feeding regimen deteriorated even further and overcrowding became the norm—up to forty prisoners were squeezed on bunk beds covered with old, ragged, and dusty mats. An additional "sleeping area" was introduced on the boarded floor for inmates left without a bed. The individual space allocation was reduced to thirty-five centimeters in width, accurately measured by a couple of our engineers. We had to lie on one side at night, and we all could turn to the other side only on command, when one of us would order: *Toți la stânga!* "All turn left!" That maneuver provided temporary relief from the pain caused by the persistent pressure sores and callosity on our hips.

There were about eight hundred ill prisoners at Aiud, people of all backgrounds. Among them was the former Romanian minister of health from 1940, a friendly, joyful man, whom I talked to frequently about the challenges faced by the sick. He was one of the first to be recruited when the need arose for thirty ill people to perform miscellaneous duties in the factory yard. The current director, Captain Dorobanțu, performed a brief inspection and made the arbitrary selection.

Tu ce boală ai, mă? "You, what's your illness?" was his usual screening question.

As I paraded in front of him, he stopped me demanding to know:

Tu ce-ai fost, mă? "What'd you do for a living?"

"I was a doctor," I answered.

Ai supt sângele poporului! Paștile si Dumnezeii.... "You sucked the people's blood, damn you! Move out of the line!" he ordered in a hostile tone, continuing to curse long after I left.

Once among the chosen, I was escorted to the yard and ordered to move wooden construction boards around; some of them were quite heavy and up to fifteen meters in length. We had to lift an entire stack and rearrange it into big piles. I was the one told to count them and to calculate how many cubic meters they would occupy. The heavy cart we had to pull was designed for horses and was loaded with as many boards as the supervising sergeant thought we could handle. Holding a wooden stick in his hand, he hit us on the back, prompting us to move quicker.

Ține-te colonele, mai repede! "Hold on, Colonel, faster!" he kept shouting at one of the older inmates, as soon as he started to struggle.

This activity was strenuous, since the yard was unpaved and very muddy, and the sergeant made no distinction between regular convicts and political detainees. We all had to perform the same task and live by the same rules. At that time, I was ill with lumbago, and I could hardly walk with a straight back. Other than exhausting the prisoners, the entire activity seemed purposeless.

Nevertheless, we were glad to be taken out of our cells even if just for a short, tiring while. And I was happy to recognize at the opposite end of the loaded cart I was pushing a man from Făgăraș, with whom I exchanged a few words.

The lucky prisoners sent to the kitchen to peel vegetables were better off, because they could eat stolen raw cabbage, carrots, and onions. A careful search was the prerequisite for re-entering the cells, so none of the delicatessen could be shared with the rest of us. Until one day—that is—when someone walking behind me placed a piece of cabbage in my hand. Upon discretely turning my head, I recognized Gheorghe Bârsan, the former administrator of the Făgăraș Regional Hospital. He had fled to Yugoslavia, attempting to avoid serving a sentence of one and a half years given at the hospital nationalization trial. For illegally crossing the border, the Yugoslav authorities extradited the man and the Romanian courts re-sentenced him to eight years of imprisonment. Regrettably, Bârsan died of liver failure a year after he was freed, induced by a chronic hepatitis and his inability to maintain a strict diet.

Unsurprisingly, signs consistent with scurvy became evident within two years of my incarceration. If, while awaiting my sentencing at Sibiu, I suffered from recurrent bouts of indigestion, shortly after arriving at Aiud my symptoms became permanent. The uncooked, moldy corn caused chronic inflammation of the lining of my small bowel and then progressed to "fermentation colitis." I started to have loose stools with blood and mucus on a daily basis, associated with diffuse periumbilical tenderness and bowel sounds so loud, one could hear them from across the room. Most of the inmates—and there were up to sixty in a cell—had malodorous belching episodes a couple of hours after meals, followed by diarrheic stools. Not even the night provided relief from those complaints.

The sewer openings serving as toilets were always busy, and the walk to the restroom and back lasted only ten to fifteen minutes. Privacy was nonexistent. Up to twenty inmates had to wait in line at a time, and then stood close to each other—"tete-a-tete"—so one would end up splashing his neighbor if not careful enough. With the observing eye of a clinician, I noticed that virtually none of the prisoners had normal, formed stools. All suffered from cramps and painful defecation, and a few had quite noticeable rectal prolapses, caused by malnutrition, intestinal parasites and the ensuing acute diarrhea. This condition was a further indication of the severity of their digestive disturbance.

Some men had lost so much weight (up to half their initial body weight) that the loose skin hanging from their abdomen and thighs resembled an article of clothing. The degree of this dystrophic transformation was a sensitive predictor of death during the following weeks. Only in pictures of war camp prisoners—such as those of American soldiers in Japan during World War II—had I seen emaciated bodies and walking skeletons like the ones I encountered in the showers of Aiud. The showers were very pleasant but rare and short, and I gradually became the last to get undressed and the last to get clothed, whereas before I got ill I was first.

I would love to have access to my prison medical chart—a privilege I am certain will never be granted—to read my diagnosis. I recalled the Saxons I had treated in 1948 while I was chief of staff at Făgăraș Regional Hospital. They had just returned from forced labor in the uranium mines of Donbas,

Ukraine, where the Russians had deported them during a ruthless campaign in 1945, as part of the German war reparation. Many had generalized dystrophy and "hunger swelling" caused by severe and prolonged protein malnutrition. So, I naturally became alarmed when I observed similar changes in my own body, suggestive that it had reached the maximum limit of its resistance.

From the 74 kilograms I weighed at the time of my arrest, I lost a third over seven years in captivity. I managed to achieve a near-normal body weight of 68 kilograms only after twelve years of keeping a prudent, sparing diet. Every recurrence of gastro-intestinal symptoms was an instant and painful reminder that a deviation from that regimen had taken place. Not even today have I regained the ability to eat boiled cellulose or complex carbohydrates—like potatoes, for example. And I had ample proof of the slow recovery process. When a tailor designed my first suit in 1963, nearly six years after I left prison, my abdominal girth was still six centimetres below the one measured in 1970, another seven years later.

Many former detainees shortened their life span significantly by choosing heavy diets—both in volume and in content—upon their release. Conversely, I have personal knowledge of ex-inmates who are still healthy today primarily because of their restrictive nourishment. As one will conclude, the health consequences of the nutritional abuse in prison lasted well beyond liberation day.

{A surprising, albeit unscientific observation is that among former political detainees who graduated from the Romanian Communist prison system and survived the immediate period, most lived into their 80s and 90s. Drs. Stanciu Stroia and Constantin Diaconescu, Lena Constante, Alexandru Ionescu, Ion Eremia, Cornel Balaj, Fathers Zosim Oancea, Victor Dâmboiu and Alexandru Brotea are only a few names that come to mind. Besides the obvious "natural selection" theory, Lena Constante pointed out another element possibly responsible for that unexpected longevity: the prolonged, imposed lack of dietary excess. The same food restriction that killed many was in fact a sparing regimen and the survivors' fountain of youth. An intriguing thought.}

The official prison doctor labelled my scurvy symptoms repeatedly as "expected," a fact that "I should be aware of and get used to," and thus did not bother to treat them. I was left enduring a chronic, mucosanguinolent enterocolitis, with persistent bloody loose stools and recalcitrant oral bleedings for many years, without any prospects of healing. On the lining of my mouth and especially on my tongue, I developed multiple hemorrhagic pustules, and a relentless one on my left lower lip—where the mucosa was thicker—refused to ever break open. That lesion is still visible today as a permanent reminder of the illness. I was usually able to anticipate the rupture of a bloody lesion because it was preceded by a local stinging sensation. I always informed my cellmates about that symptom, in order to avoid their panic at the sight of a quickly growing boil, big as a nut, breaking spontaneously and bleeding profusely.

{Scurvy is a deficiency disease, resulting from chronic lack of fresh fruits and vegetables in the diet. The vitamin C from these foods is essential for normal formation of collagen, which is a group of fibrous, structural proteins that literally hold the body together. Clinical manifestations require time to develop and follow a significant period of vitamin C depletion. Symptoms include fatigue and anemia; tender muscles and joints; bleeding in the skin and mucous membranes, with swelling of gums and loosening of teeth; digestive disturbances with bloody diarrhea; blood in the urine; delayed wound healing; and an array of other abnormalities. Three to four ounces of daily orange or tomato juice are sufficient to produce healing! Bluish-purple, spongy gum lesions often remain the only traces of the disease years later.}

Hospitalizations

The precise date when I was first hospitalized I do not recall anymore. It must have been during the rough winter of 1953–1954, around mid-February. I was sharing a cell—number 173—in the "Alaska Wing," together with four other physicians, all men of great vigor and character.

One of them was Dr. Octavian Sonea, a native of Beclean, a military doctor and a major in the Romanian Army who was in his early 50s. A former director of the Central Military Medical Laboratory and a respected pathologist and researcher at the Dr. Cantacuzino Institute in Bucharest, he had patients from the royal palace among his loyal patrons. They visited his office regularly for various hematological disorders.

My second cellmate was Dr. Constantin Diaconescu, a military physician as well and an internist by training. He was born in Oltenia, Southern Romania, in a city by the Danube and was a highly intelligent and energetic person. He was eighteen years my junior, and both he and Dr. Sonea somehow managed to regularly exercise (they called it gymnastics) in the incredibly tight space of our cell.

In 1969, I met Dr. Diaconescu again, accidentally on a busy bus ride.

"Hey, Doc, how are you doing?" I yelled, excited to see him and eager to catch his attention.

"Good!" he replied. "I'm preparing for my radiology board exam."

Upon his prison release, after failing to find employment as an internist, he was forced to train for a different specialty. The crowding on the bus made anything beyond a formal discussion impossible. Still, we were both genuinely glad to have had that short encounter.

The news that Dr. Diaconescu had been re-sentenced in 1958 along with a group of others to an additional twenty years behind bars reached me years later. The man allegedly had failed to comply with the rigid instructions ordered by the Securitate the first time around. After he had served eight years, he dared to discuss his experience and paid a hefty price for it. Moreover, he was considered an "anti-Soviet" element, an ill-fated label in those years. Fortunately, the amnesty act of 1964 saved him from completing the entire sentence. That encounter in 1969 was the last time I saw or heard of him.

{Dr. Constantin Diaconescu was still alive in December 2004 at the age of 82, in relatively good physical health and with a mind as clear as ever. He recalled: "All of us in that cell had an unreal life story, so different from the average man. We had faith in our existence; we loved our country and people and were determined to sacrifice the best in us. The years spent in jail were a signature of that love.... Our fellow political prisoners represented the jewels in the crown of the Romanian

soul.... Dr. Stanciu Stroia delighted us with stories from his college years in Cluj and talked about his plans of honoring Cacova's World War I heroes. Years later, we met inadvertently but had to postpone another get-together, since the Securitate was relentlessly on our trails."}

The third colleague was Dr. Gheorghe Scrob, a physician in training from Țara Moților, in the Apuseni Mountains of Northern Romania. A medical student in his last clinical year at the University of Cluj, he had been arrested shortly before his final exams. Recently married, he was informed that his wife had betrayed him. Later, the prison authorities pointed out that she had divorced him as well, hoping to demoralize the man. However, *moțu'* (the mountain man) was tough and stubborn, refusing to allow his jailors the satisfaction of reading his emotions. He remained silent and proud in his suffering.

An assistant professor from the University of Cluj Clinics completed the group, in the midst of which I spent some quality time.

During our debates on medical issues, we often questioned why so many prisoners expired within days of sustaining basic abdominal interventions in the prison infirmary. The surgeons performing those procedures were inmates themselves—both serving ten-year sentences—but they were highly qualified individuals who appeared to possess the perfect techniques. One of them was a skillful university professor and former health minister, while the other surgeon was an experienced attending from Ploiești. We concluded that the poor surgical outcome was not their fault, but rather a consequence of the patients' edematous, water-infiltrated tissues, which did not last and broke open at the suture sites. Most patients succumbed from the resulting generalized peritonitis, an infection of the lining of the abdominal cavity.

I had to undergo a surgical procedure myself in 1964, seven years after my liberation, for a right inguinal hernia, and not even then did my subcutaneous tissues recover normally. As expected, the catgut sutures failed miserably. It was another example—this time in my own body—of the process of dystrophic changes caused by prolonged malnutrition experienced during detention. The same problem did not recur in 1971, however, another seven years later, during the surgical repair of a left inguinal hernia.

Back in February 1954, my scurvy-induced symptoms became more persistent and severe. I had unformed bowel movements after every single meal, and I felt embarrassed having to use the toilet-serving bucket five times a day, because it was emptied so infrequently. Then, one afternoon, following a prolonged episode of enterocolitis, which ended with five foamy and bloody stools, during which I must have lost eight liters of water, I fell into a state of hypovolemic shock and fainted while sitting on the toilet. My roommates, alarmed and encouraged by Dr. Diaconescu, punched the cell door, calling for the officer in charge, who found me lying unconscious on the floor an hour later. I heard, as in a trance, the arguing between the guards and my fellow doctors. They threatened to go on a hunger strike if I was not urgently admitted to the prison hospital for treatment.

The infirmary must not have had a vacant bed at that time because in order to calm my cellmates down, by seven o'clock in the evening, the officer pulled me out and placed me in an empty medical exam room. I laid there semiconsciously for a while, exhausted and unable to move. Once dinner was served I heard Sergeant Ardeleanu, a real rough man nicknamed *zbirul celularului* (the cell section's tyrant), yell visibly annoyed at a guard:

Mă, adu' încă o porție de gris, că ăsta moare dracului până dimineață! "Hey, bring another cereal portion here; we've got one who's otherwise going to fucking die by tomorrow morning."

What an encouragement that was for me!

After slowly eating the small bowl of semolina without milk and gently sweetened, my diarrhea ceased. At around nine o'clock that evening, when the lights went out and the shift changed, the night guard paused briefly by my cell to see how I was feeling. I thought he had a gentler expression on his face, one that I will never forget. That first impression was reinforced when he showed empathy and asked:

Te simți rău? "Are you feeling sick?"

To his unexpected inquiry, which maybe came at the suggestion of the officer who witnessed my fainting, I felt courageous and mumbled a long reply:

Vai, sărman neam românesc, ce am ajuns, să ne stăpânească străinii.... "Oh, poor Romanian people, what have we become, with foreigners our masters...."

He never turned me in for those comments, and I never saw that guard again. The very next morning I was admitted to the infirmary, where I stayed for over two weeks until my condition mildly improved.

A second hospital stay was the result of my refusal to eat the indigestible moldy corn bread for two and a half weeks. I placed all the rotten portions on the window frame, some with five centimeters of *mucegai* (mold) growing on their surface. On the seventeenth day of my hunger strike, I became so weak that around ten o'clock in the morning I almost passed out. My instinct for survival took over in my desolate situation, so I dragged myself to the iron door and sat down in front of it. Propping myself up, I started knocking on the metal with all the strength I had left. Although my previous attempts had failed, the guard responded this time and called the charge officer. Once he inspected the food displayed by the window and recognized the problem, he advised me not to eat any of it....

The next day I was an inpatient again, under the care of the same physician-prisoners, with the only difference being the replacement of Dr. Iriminoiu with a former university lecturer from Iași who—compared to his predecessor—was very attentive and helpful. I spent another two weeks in the infirmary bed, my recovery this time being even more limited.

Back in the main cell section, my roommates were happy to see me alive and aided me further by exchanging their 50 grams of wheat bread for my corn mush in the morning and, at lunchtime, by feeding me from their own bowls with a spoon, as you would feed a child. One should see the bowls we ate from at Aiud—so old and worn out that even the chickens and pigs on my farm would have refused to touch them....

Over the subsequent weeks, my mates continued to provide support by generously serving me the gristles from their soup for a portion of my pearl barley, which I offered in return. This modified dietary regimen decreased the frequency of my stools, but the excrements still contained significant mucus and blood. Nonetheless, I managed to survive that difficult period with God's will and under the constant reminder that half the people my age failed to make it out of Aiud alive!

CHAPTER V—APPEAL

Isolation and Hungarian Uprising—November 1956

My initial sentence for "favoring the crime of plotting against the Romanian state" was six years. Toward the end of the expected last year, I demanded to see the prison director and inquired about my liberation date. His response stunned me. After five and a half uninterrupted years behind bars, I was informed that a petition had been submitted by the prosecutor of the Sibiu Military Tribunal for my sentence to be increased to seven years! It took me a great while to comprehend the situation. The decision had been made in November 1956, right after the complex events that took place in Hungary, about which the prisoners knew nothing at that time.

{In October 1956, Hungary was the stage of a workers' uprising against Stalinist-type oppression. The large anti-Communist riots were swiftly crushed by Soviet tanks and troops. Even though its outcome was a tragic defeat in which thousands were killed, injured, imprisoned, or forced into exile, the revolt pointed to future developments in the Communist Eastern European states.}

After a lengthy process initiated by my brother Mitică Stroia—a former judge relegated to a lowly office clerk position in a brick factory after refusing to approve crooked verdicts dictated by the Communists—an appeal of my conviction was accepted, and the request for a retrial was approved. Then, one early afternoon during November 1956, I was driven to the Aiud railway station, and escorted from the van into a covered train wagon placed right behind the engine. Thirty other political prisoners were transported along with me.

When I got on the train, scheduled to leave for Sibiu within the hour, I recognized a former captain sitting in the middle of a group of convicts. He was the only person in chains, because he had been labelled a "war criminal." I had first met the man at Aiud in December 1953, and I recalled he was in chains back then as well, forced to work in the factory in that condition. One evening, as the chained prisoners were ending their shift, he was hit by a guard with a large, wooden cart shaft, from behind and on the back of his head. The unchained prisoners tried to protect him, but did not have adequate time to react. He was about five meters ahead of me when he tried to enter the cells section, collapsed, and fell into a ditch. He had been hit so ferociously that I decided to pass right beside him and gently touch him with my foot to make certain he was still alive. The features of his face had registered well in my memory ever since.

Even though the guards watched us closely, we recognized each other as we were waiting for the train to depart and managed to sit in the same corner, discreetly starting a conversation. I asked him how he recovered from that vicious blow and wondered if he had any epileptic fits from it. He reassured me that he did not, but said he had been sent to Văcărești prison hospital at a later date to undergo a surgical procedure because of another, unrelated incident. Over the next two minutes, he became my source of desperately needed news; he talked about *puciul unguresc*, the stifled revolt in Hungary as a result of which hordes of prisoners from Oradea, close to the Hungarian border, had been transferred to other facilities. I understood now why so many convicts had been brought to Aiud during the previous month.

Before the train whistled its intention to head off, the prisoners inside our wagon were lined up and handed their sealed files, ordered to hold them up. I was the last one in the row, standing next to the captain in chains. After the train guard inspected my file, spending a few extra seconds glancing at the jumble of notations, he refused to keep me in the wagon. I presumed that a lack of adequate room was the reason I had to travel in a bunk, all alone, isolated from everybody else. *Ce atenție!* How considerate of that train guard! The wagon I was moved to looked like a railway car that had been divided into smaller and larger bunks, with a hallway in the middle for the conductors and guards to pass freely. For the duration of that train ride, I was forced to sit in a cage, a cell smaller then one meter square surrounded by thick iron bars.

Days later, when I returned to Aiud, I was placed in total isolation for thirty days, in a cell adjacent to the guards' room, until I was transported to the next session of the Sibiu Military Tribunal. On the few occasions I had to temporarily leave Aiud, I spent a month alone upon my return. From a psychological standpoint, I tolerated the solitary confinement as well as could be expected, but I was frantically searching for ways to spend all that time. I whistled in a low voice and even tried singing once in a while, careful not to be overheard by the jailors' spying ears. *Fetele de la Sibiu* "The Girls from Sibiu" and *Am și eu numai o fată* "I Only Have a Girl" where my repertoire's favorite tunes. Sometimes I paced around the cell like a bear in a cage; other times I welcomed the isolation and the silence, because I did not have to deal with informers or irate cellmates. I sewed old patches, undid them, and sewed them again. The countless hours of sewing, involving thousands of meters of thread, ensured my rescue from a major depression.

{My grandfather continued to sew almost daily throughout his retirement years, as an activity meant to relax him rather than out of necessity. The makeshift needle he used in prison joined him in his grave, as he requested.}

The return trip to Sibiu took place a month after the first, in mid-December 1956. We arrived there at one o'clock in the morning and were quickly transferred to a police van, riding along with convicts who had been sentenced for petty, non-political crimes. Taking advantage of the guards' carelessness at that early hour, we asked for news, especially for details about the recent events in Hungary.

As soon as we entered the penitentiary, the officer in charge—a former gendarme sergeant from Poplaca, now employed by the military—appeared to recognize me. But upon reviewing my omnipresent "scarecrow" file, he gave orders for my immediate isolation in a basement cell with no bed or light, next to the laundry room. I was lucky to be fed that night, receiving a slice of bread with marmalade only after repeatedly requesting food. A reflection of my harsh treatment was the order to the guards not to talk to me, because I was considered to be "extremely dangerous." What a bandit I must have been!

I remained in Sibiu for three months, for the duration of the retrial, under strict surveillance and—once again—in the company of Iron Guard members. The only significant improvement in that jail was in nutrition, with the wheat bread a true blessing for my debilitating scurvy.

Still puzzled by the manner I was handled, I made an appeal to the prison director for medication and the right to contact my family, after noticing other inmates exercising these privileges. Both requests were bluntly turned down. When I was finally granted an appointment with the prison physician, Dr. Georgescu offered no help and reminded me that my symptoms were a natural result of prolonged incarceration.

"You have to live with them!" he ordered, before he showed me the door.

From the perspective of a physician who has taken the Hippocratic Oath, Dr. Georgescu's refusal to treat seriously ill inmates was an incredible disillusionment, whether those sufferers were political prisoners or otherwise. I soon realized that most doctors employed in the country's vindictive penitentiaries and at the Danube-Black Sea Canal—the construction site turned end-station for many political convicts, nicknamed *canalul morții* (death canal),—were lacking in professional conscience and sense of duty.

[The Oath ascribed to the Greek physician Hippocrates (460–377 B.C.) has been the model for medical ethics for centuries, and it endures in a modern version to this day. The following are excerpts from the original version: "I swear that I will fulfill according to my ability and judgment this oath and this covenant: I will apply dietetic measures for the benefit of the sick according to my ability and judgment. I will keep the sick from harm and injustice. I will never give a deadly drug to anybody, and I will never make a suggestion to this effect. Whatever houses I may visit, I will come for the benefit of the sick, remaining free of all intentional injustice, of all mischief. What I may see or hear in the course of the treatment or even outside of the treatment concerning the life of men, I will keep to myself, holding such

things shameful to be spoken about. If I fulfill this oath and do not violate it, may it be granted to me to enjoy life and art, being honored with fame among all men for all time to come; if I transgress it and swear falsely, may the opposite be my lot." It is most scholars' opinion that Hippocrates was the author of the statement "First, do no harm" as well, but in the context of another writing: "Declare the past, diagnose the present, foretell the future; practice these acts. As to diseases, make a habit of two things—to help, or at least to do no harm."}

Returning to Sibiu after four years, I noticed many changes. The windows had been tightly covered with wooden boards placed in a roof shape and fastened in a slanting way to completely block the outside view; compared to Aiud, they allowed some fresh air to squeeze into the cell, at least. All the doors had been freshly painted, and the old scratches and markings were unidentifiable. Inquiring about remarkable events that occurred in my absence, I was told that two guards had been arrested and convicted after being caught delivering letters from convicts' families.

In addition, I discovered engraved in a brown iron plate hooked to the entry of a cell the words "Major Duma" and underneath, "Sentenced to death." I did not know much about him except that he had been an anti-Communist partisan who took up arms and fought the Securitate in the Semenic Mountains in the Banat region. During his trial at the Sibiu Military Tribunal in a building located next to the prison, the authorities tore a wall down, leaving a hole in it, in order to hide the man from spectators' view. The sign in the cell served as an intimidating reminder of the potential fate awaiting the inmates with pending verdicts.

After many quiet days in solitary, curious next-door inmates sent me a Morse message through discrete taps on the wall. Since I never made any serious attempt to learn the code and was unable to master it during my short-lived tries, I had to answer them somehow. Consequently, I held my hands as a funnel and started whispering through the wall. I told them that I had just returned from Aiud and relayed all of the news I had heard on my way, including that the people of Hungary had unsuccessfully tried to overthrow the Communist regime in October 1956.

At that very moment, the eavesdropping guard opened the door window and inquired:

"What regime are you talking about?"

A real miracle happened then—I was blessed with help in moments like this more than once—and I gave him a heavenly answer:

Regimul alimentar.... "I was talking about a change in the dietary regimen...."

Pleased with my answer, the guard chose not to report me to the officer in charge.

"Why Didn't He Know?"

So here I was, with morale that was not low, but with the painful awareness of my failing memory and intellectual capabilities. While I was being taken for a walk in the prison yard, I thought about the issues that I was going to point out during my appeal. I no longer admitted to the lies contained in the statements from the initial trial, stressing that my confession had been dictated by the Securitate and signed while I was mentally exhausted and physically threatened. In essence, I had been sentenced "in absentia."

At the retrial, after we were notified that the prosecutor had asked for an increase in the duration of my punishment, my attorney's speech struck a different note. We vehemently contested all of the accusations brought against me and denied the validity of the fabricated statements. We insisted that there had been no witnesses at my initial trial. Additionally, I blamed my attorney for not defending me in this manner the first time around!

The first court session was very short, and if the uprising in Hungary had not taken place, I probably would have been a free man that December of 1956. It was evident that the investigation of my case led to no direct connection between the mountain partisans and me. Inspite of all that, my "rehabilitation" and release were delayed for another year.

The prosecutor himself, a magistrate and colonel, declared:

Nu reiese din dosar că a știut.... "The Negoiu file does not clearly show or prove that he knew anything." But then, he added tendentiously: *Dar de ce nu a știut?* "*Why* didn't he know?"

Why did I not know what I did not know? An exercise in the absurd! *Atîta tot!* (That was all!) The sentence that I received was a consequence of the wrong application of an article in the law used against me, and this sentence already had been carried out. Even though the verdict had been based on a juridical error, my lawyer offered no plea, as it appeared fruitless.

Instead of freedom, I had an additional, unjustified, arbitrarily decided, entire year to spend in captivity, as a reward for the work I had performed in the factory and my satisfactory behavior as an inmate!

Family Eviction and Exile

Ignoring the guards' objections, I glanced at my loved ones from the defendants' box and recognized all the members of my immediate family sitting in the courtroom. My mother seemed much older than before—she was 80 years old, after all—and she looked at me but did not make any gesture; her face was carved in stone.

My wife—whom I also saw for the first time after six years without any news—was seated next to her in the middle of the courtroom; she was pale, with a scared look in her eyes and an ostensibly lost expression on her face. Trying to give her courage, I kept looking in her direction. Next, I spotted my daughter Tita at the back of the courtroom; she was standing tall and looked brave and confident.

Even after the appeal was over, the guards did not allow me to talk to my family or to receive a package, at the very least one with needed medication. As I was still standing in the box Tita, in a courageous move, shouted while she was escorted out of the courtroom:

Cere medicamente pentru tensiune, tăticule! "Ask for medications for your high blood pressure, Daddy!"

A doctor herself, she suspected that given the extreme tension I had been forced to live in for so long, my blood pressure could not have been within normal range. And she was right....

I saw Liviu Dușleag for the first time with Tita at the appeal. He was a man at the age of fulfilled adulthood, serious, robust, and with a pleasant face. I met him again in Ilia two years later, when he arrived by motorcycle from Sibiu, probably because he wanted to know me better (he had already met my wife) and, more than that, to inquire about my feelings regarding his old friendship with Tita. He had looked after my daughter since she was a medical student and had proved his commitment.

During all of my years of imprisonment, I constantly thought of my wife and worried about the prospects of her losing her husband. My mother's fate as a young widow—"with honesty and kindness," as my wife liked to say—was not the one I envisioned for Valy. My mother became a single parent with two small children when she turned 26 and remained a widow for another fifty-two years, overcoming enormous difficulties.

Mulțumesc Providenței! Praying in the darkness of my cell, I kept thanking God for helping me maintain my sanity, my precious mental health, my psychological equilibrium, and for the good care I knew my wonderful wife was providing my children. And I felt very fortunate that my son and daughter were able to receive a college education. I sincerely thought that my ostracized family suffered even more than I, the one robbed of liberty.

Immediately following my arrest, Valy had to endure countless episodes of intimidation and persecution, threats and provocations. I discovered upon my return to Făgăraș that my house was checked weekly in my absence, to see how the inhabitants were getting by. The *securiști* or Securitate informers were seeking details about my family's daily existence and were not pleased to conclude that my wife became the breadwinner, sustaining everybody's needs. There were informers recently released from prison who were ordered to interrogate her about alleged contacts she had established with me through intermediaries. Only because of the decision of one of those informers—living on the second level of our house at the time—not to denounce my wife after she had stated that "you intend to exterminate my husband" was she spared a trip to the Securitate office for explanations.

Then, a very unfriendly team from the mayor's office arrived to pick up my Roentgen X-ray machine and ultrasound device, as well as my other medical utensils, including blood pressure monitors, syringes, and medications. My wife could not oppose the confiscation and was told that the small amount of money obtained from the sale of the equipment would count toward "paying rent" for her own house! As another indication of the intent to wipe my family out, the doctors from the ammunition factory in town received everything stolen from my medical office for free; there was no remuneration involved nor were any return conditions imposed in the takeover.

My entire estate, including my horses, cows, and pigs, was soon seized, as well. And my wife was subjected to multiple and unannounced, denigrating and humiliating house searches, under the pretext that "compromising items" had to be found.

What was there to be found, I still wonder, in the house of a peaceful man? I had never been involved in politics, and my attitude had always been that of a true Romanian. I was known as a humble man, and my one-horsepower carriage set me apart from the car-driving physicians in town. I had even given up the large farmlands in Râușor inherited by my wife and donated them to the People's Council in 1948. I believed in fairness and justice, and I had no fear of displaying my democratic views in public meetings. Despite that or maybe because of that, I was constantly pressured to join the Communist party, which I refused repeatedly, given the repulsion I felt toward the Communist doctrine.

The people in town respected and liked Valy, a member of the prestigious Grama family, which included her grandfather, Father Vincențiu Grama, decorated hero in the 1877–1878 Independence War against Turkey. The sad part is that once Doctor Stroia fell into disgrace, most of the previously close family friends chose not to help her and avoided her presence. Fortunately, new friends appeared unexpectedly, and there were individuals of great character who took a courageous stand by refusing to show her their backs. It took genuine heroism for my wife to endure the social disgrace and isolation she was subjected to.

My family was evicted from our house in the summer of 1952, within a year of my arrest and after less than a day's notice. According to my wife, someone called Szasz Ladislau showed up at her door one afternoon and identified himself as the chief of the "Ministry of Buildings and Facilities." He claimed that our house had been nationalized and that it had to be vacated in twenty-four hours or else *mijloace de evacuare forțată* (forceful eviction methods) would be employed. My wife was also informed that she had become "an undesired individual" in the city of Făgăraș, and that she had to move out.

A wealthy aunt, my father-in-law's sister, lived in the vicinity, and she surely would have taken Valy in, and there was also her parents' house in the village of Râușor. But, intimidated and frightened, my wife left town in a hurry and moved to the nearby village of Dridif. There, she rented a small room in a farmer's house, living in extreme modesty for the next five years. Most of our belongings and furniture that did not fit in the oxen-pulled carriage used on the hasty trip had to be divided and stored among family members. Most of those items were recovered years later. Upon her aunt's death, Valy was given permission to return to Făgăraș and move into the inherited, empty property. Shortly thereafter, on May 23, 1955, she lost her mother.

My two humble children, with sound minds and healthy bodies, managed to survive their college years despite facing incredible adversity. They passed all of their exams honorably, and my daughter finished at the top of her graduating medical class in 1958, despite her "unhealthy social origin."

Later I discovered that our house had in fact not been nationalized initially—in accordance with the governmental act that applied to forty-one other buildings in Făgăraș belonging to "exploiters"—but rather after it had been evacuated and considered "abandoned!" The decision to confiscate our house was made by the Făgăraș mayor, who added it to a list of properties owned by citizens who immigrated to America! On that same occasion other homes were forcefully seized, especially those of prominent intellectuals and prestigious professors, like the former president of the Astra Petroleum Society.

An investigation conducted in 1954 by the authorities of Braşov found the ministry chief guilty of abuse of power and dereliction of duty. Making a mockery out of the judicial system, he escaped from serving his sentence.

Unii crează istoria, alţii o scriu şi apoi alţii beneficiază de eroismul luptătorilor, sfidând urmaşii....

Some create the history, some write it, and others take profit in the creators' heroism, defying the descendants—the Romanian saying goes.

I remember how a man from Făgăraş whispered to me once, as we were walking in the prison yard, that my family was living in a small parish, thrown out of our house. But I did not believe him, and that was very fortunate, because the truth would have been demoralizing. The eviction was the most difficult blow to my loved ones, and knowing about it while in prison would have killed me. Their imposed exile is still a very difficult reality to accept.

About three years into my incarceration, the director of the Aiud Penitentiary approached me, trying to find out if I had any news from home or connections to the outside. During our conversation, he inadvertently informed me that both of my children were studying at the university. Maybe the officer's intention had not been to comfort me, but the news had a great calming effect.

During all the subsequent years, I managed not to despair, not even when I was jailed in Făgăraş Castle, only 200 meters away from our house, patiently waiting for a sign from my wife, which never came....

How naïve and how credulous I have always been....

The Russians

In 1945, the Russian soldiers who were part of the Allies Control Commission formed to ensure compliance with the postwar agreements chose not to evict me from my own house. They occupied the building's second floor for six months, after which they moved to a different facility, more adequate for their needs. They even apologized for the intrusion when they left and did not remove a single object; the furniture they used with care still exists in Tita's living room today. My family's excellent relationship with Colonel Rudenko, the Russian commander, is worth mentioning here. He respected my wife and my children and appreciated me as his host and as the local hospital's chief physician.

At the opposite extreme was the conduct of the local authorities. During the winter of 1945, without seeking my approval, they allowed the newly formed Allies Control Commission to set up headquarters in my house. The order even read for our home to be evacuated first! Voicing my strong opposition to the police, I informed them that I would only leave my private property if I were dead.

Aware of my uncompromising attitude, the chief of the commission himself paid me a visit the following afternoon in an effort to ease the tension. Upon noticing the three large upstairs bedrooms with a separate entrance, and after inspecting the medical office with all of its equipment on the first floor, Colonel Rudenko ordered that my family be left in place and the office left untouched. My daughter Tita—who was 12 years old at the time—was entertaining a few of her friends, and perhaps the pleasant family atmosphere is what impressed the colonel, who, as I later found out, had a daughter of similar age.

Three days after the Russians moved upstairs, I started treating the limping colonel with my ultrasound machine for a painful post-traumatic spondylosis he had been plagued by since being shot in the spinal cord during a 1917 World War I campaign. His condition improved greatly thereafter, and the colonel was also grateful for the hospitality extended to his guards. They were served hot tea every night, while standing on duty in front of my house in the freezing cold.

Then, in the spring of 1946, I was called to examine another high-ranking Soviet officer, recently transferred from Constanţa, who was febrile and complaining of excruciating abdominal cramps. I admitted him to our intensive care unit with a diagnosis of paratyphoid fever, and within a month of attentive care, he recovered completely. As a reward, I was invited to attend a formal dinner in the company of Russian officials, who provided an armed escort to ensure my safe arrival home! A year later, upon his return to Făgăraș for an inspection of the local ammunition factory, the colonel called and inquired about my family's well-being.

My experience with our next imposed guest, Colonel Bakaiew, commander of the newly opened Officers School in the classrooms of the local high school Radu Negru, was equally pleasant. He had a sweet tooth, enjoying my wife's homemade baked goods and marmalade, and a picture of him is still in our family album today.

The Russians showed great respect, even veneration, for doctors, especially when they were dressed in white coats. That norm was confirmed to me a couple of days after the last Soviet vacated our house. The Făgăraș Securitate was quick to make a note with white chalk on our front gate, stating that our property was going to house the cafeteria of a Soviet military division. I tried in vain to explain that our gate was not sufficiently wide to accommodate armored vehicles, and that a large yard adjacent to a nearby restaurant was a more suitable location. But my plea had no effect; the police were trying to ensure that I suffered the greatest disturbance possible! Luckily, as soon as the first vehicle barely squeezed through our entrance, one of my patients followed through the door, on time for his appointment.

Observing that I put my lab coat on, one Russian officer asked, *Vraci?* then repeated, "You, doctor?" As soon as I replied *Da!* he ordered the vehicle to leave and the entire moving process ceased. Later that day, two Soviet officials stopped by my office to discuss the incident and left satisfied after consuming one liter of *vișinată* (cherry liquor)....

My first encounter with Soviet troops dates back to the fall of 1944, during the Romanian-Russian counteroffensive against the retreating German armies in Transylvania. Marshal Malinowsky, commander of the Ukrainian Army, set up his temporary headquarters in Sibiu and Săliște, and the Air Force was stationed in Făgăraș. Toward the end of September 1944, a Soviet military doctor brought two soldiers with pulmonary symptoms to my office for an exam and radiographic consultation. Naturally, I served them promptly and with the expected professionalism. Upon their leaving, we saluted cordially, and I offered my medical help in the future if the need would arise.

A colleague of mine, a female doctor who had worked in Basarabia, walked the hallway at that moment and recognized the Russian as the son of the Soviet marshal. She suggested we should treat the foreign official with the outmost attention, which we did once more, when the 30-year-old captain returned with two new patients. I addressed him by his last name, to which he responded, flattered, by asking me how I knew who he was.

"I recognized you from your father's photograph; you resemble him a lot," I answered, having indeed seen Marshal Malinowsky's picture in the local newspaper. After that, we became friends.

I invited him to our house, and I offered him a glass of *țuică* (plum brandy), which must have made a good first impression. An interesting conversation, one that I recall with great pleasure, ensued both in Romanian and in Russian. He told me, among other things, that his father, "Papa Balsoi," had had dinner with Romanian King Michael a few weeks prior, and he promised me a copy of the photograph taken on that occasion. That never happened, unfortunately, because along with the advancing frontline, the Russian troops headed west soon after.

I also had him as a patient and arranged for a confirmation of my—ultimately correct—diagnosis by a distinguished colleague from the University of Cluj, which had its headquarters temporarily relocated in Sibiu during the war. When I inquired about his medical specialty, he replied that he was trained as a general surgeon, having completed a two-year residency in New York City. That was an impressive feat in those days.

The Polish Doctor

The war enabled me to interact and befriend other Slavic neighbors as well. My thoughts return to the prison time and the month of March 1957, when fifty of us were transferred out of Aiud one early morning. We were loaded into a large, black police van, with windows painted dark gray to prevent us from seeing outside. We did not know where we were heading until we arrived at *Cetatea Făgărașului*, a fortified medieval castle transformed into a prison. Today, it serves as a museum, but back in those times, the numerous political arrests led to an overpopulation of the regular correctional facilities.

I had known the fortress well since 1939–1940, when it was used as a military camp for 2,500 Polish refugees. They had their own general physician, who, when faced with challenging cases, often turned to an internist from the Făgăraș Regional Hospital for advice. That is how I ended up providing the Poles with medical consultations as well as radiological services.

I have fond memories of a physician and captain in the Polish Army, Dr. Antoni Firlej, whom I first met in October 1939. His wife and six-year-old daughter, accompanied by her nanny, arrived in Făgăraș with very little luggage, hastily fleeing from the German aerial bombardment of Warsaw.

Dr. Firlej was a decorated member of the 1st Regiment of Cavalry Józef Piłsudski—named after the architect of Poland's re-emergence as a sovereign state in 1918. I was not initially aware of the captain's intentions of leaving Romania to rejoin the Polish Army, which was exiled in France under the command of General Wranghel. A few months later, I facilitated his and his family's departure. On February 2, 1940, he left Făgăraș for Brașov via a taxicab I had hired two days before. He later entered Yugoslavia and eventually found refuge in France. The postcard he mailed me upon his safe arrival in the port of Split, Yugoslavia, I still have today.

{With the Blitzkrieg or "lightning-war" of September 1939, Germany invaded Poland at a time when Romania had declared its neutrality. Poland's political and military leadership and essential elements of its government managed to escape via Romania, where they were granted temporary refuge. Romania also allowed the provisional safe deposit of Poland's treasury in its National Bank, despite Germany's escalating threats and pressure. A few months later, the Poles reassembled in Paris and organized a governing structure in exile.... A silver cigarette holder with the Polish Army logo on the outside and golden lining on the inside was a gift from Dr. Firlej to my grandfather and one of his most prized possessions. It had been previ-

ously given to the captain by a group of Polish officers for outstanding service to his regiment. An inscription engraved in Romanian and dated February 1, 1940, reads: "D-lui Dr. St. Stroia, pentru inima Dv. Bună"(To Dr. Stanciu Stroia, for your good heart). It was passed on to me upon entering medical school.}

Făgăraș Castle

As soon as we entered through the gate of the fortress, I smelled the fresh air of Făgăraș. It was the incentive to keep on going, to survive, in addition to the knowledge that my captivity had to be coming to an end. Once the police van stopped, I was the last to descend from it and was instructed to walk with my back toward the guardsmen, which was quite awkward. I assumed that the purpose of that maneuver was to avoid being recognized by the local jailors. This was undoubtedly in accordance with my file and my returning "home" after a hiatus of six years.

Next, I was carefully escorted to the first tower of the castle, up in the northwest corner, looking toward the Făgăraș Orthodox Church. The choice for my accommodation could not have been better because a month later, on Good Friday, I was able to hear the religious procession and recognize the voice of Father Traian Ciocănelea, as the congregation walked around the church. Once every few minutes, when our positions were aligned, and the evening breeze worked a little magic, I enjoyed the chorus chant *Cristos A Înviat!* (Christ Has Risen!). One can only imagine the feeling of elation I experienced that night.

I entered my castle cell with no luggage, other than one extra set of underwear. Other inmates had received boxes of items from their families, and some even carried prescription drugs. Noticing that, I cheered myself up with the hope that at least a package of medication would finally be granted.

Shortly after I settled in, the sergeant in charge climbed the stairs to the tower at a fast pace. He recognized me as soon as he entered the room:

Ce, ai sosit deja domnule Director? "What? You arrived already, Mister Director?" he asked visibly surprised.

Within a minute, he appointed me—alas!—chief of the cell, and I soon discovered that it carried the benefit of a double morning portion of "coffee" (in reality an artificial substitute or a mash). Nevertheless, the diet was what pleased me most in Făgăraş: 250 grams of relatively fresh wheat bread every day meant 500 to 600 calories of easily digestible nutrient. Gone was the execrable moldy corn porridge, and here was a chance for my health to recover. Even though the windows here were also covered with wooden boards to block any fleeting look outside, the ventilation was significantly better because the cells were larger.

Some of the restrictions were similar to those at Aiud. During our daily ten-minute walk in the paved courtyard, we were not allowed to speak to each other or to look up toward the towers and the sky; we had to walk with our eyes fixed on the dirty ground. The guards were carefully monitored as well, which ensured compliance with those rules. The surveillance was performed by the officer on duty and by another jail employee, an informer who watched the guards from the second floor of the prison building.

The cells reserved for chastisement were in the cellar of the castle. Built in medieval times, those crypts were half-buried in the ground, short, narrow, and uneven, with solid iron bars serving as doors. They appeared suitable for savage beasts, and the entire site had a barbaric appearance. Fortunately, those spaces were seldom used.

{Făgăraş Castle was first mentioned in 1310, built on the former site of a 12th century wooden fortress. Placed in the center of a feudal estate, the fort was rebuilt and enlarged between the fifteenth and seventeenth centuries, to serve as protection against Tartar and Turkish invasions. Constructed of red brick, with massive walls, tall roofs, five towers, and four corner bastions, it consisted of eighty rooms on three levels, an exterior fortification wall, and a surrounding water-filled defense canal. The citadel, accessible only through a bridge, served as residence to Iancu de Hunedoara (1455) and Michael the Brave (1599–1600), and included Maria Theresa (1740–1780) as one of many owners. By the end of the eighteenth century, the fortress was turned into a military garrison and in 1948 was seized by the Communists, who misused it as a dreadful political prison. According to historian

Ioan Ciupea, nearly 5,000 individuals were detained here in the 1950s. Since the early 1960s, the castle has housed the Museum of Făgăraș County.}

After a few days at Făgăraș, I requested to see the director of the penitentiary, who had the reputation of being a bit more understanding. At my demand for medication, he replied bluntly that receiving anything from my family was out of the question, and if he were in my situation, the same regimen would apply to him. What democracy, I thought!

Despite that failed attempt, the period spent at Făgăraș Castle was the only one in seven years of detention during which life felt manageable and the privations bearable. Maybe the passing years led to a resigned acceptance of the prison routine, but a major reason was the absence of spies within the cells and knowing that I *had* to be released soon. After enduring 2,200 days of my sentence, there was a feeling of certainty that I *had* to be set free by the end of the year. It was a morale-boosting thought and something I reminded myself of every day. I had no other job but to calculate in my mind all the days I had left to spend in jail and to ask to be received by the prosecutor when he visited the penitentiary to review the inmates' files. Especially since the October 1956 events in Hungary, the Communist regime and implicitly the prison authorities appeared to have softened.

Overall, my physical strength improved, but the tormenting scurvy led to another trip to the infirmary. The nurse in charge (no doctor was in sight) was in fact a midwife by training, whom I had hired at Făgăraș Regional Hospital in 1947. My immediate concern was that she would seek revenge, in retaliation for an incident that occurred while I was doing rounds in the tuberculosis section. I found her still in bed that morning, sleeping on the job after—without doubt—a busy night shift, so I lifted the blanket from her eyes and said loudly and jovially: *Bună dimineața!* "Good morning!" Aside from the obvious embarrassment, there was no reprimand. My fear proved groundless as the nurse was attentive, even making an effort to withhold unpleasant news about my family's fate from reaching my ears.

As a further proof of the improved conditions, a day before I left the castle I was given a brand new set of prison clothing, including a striped hat. I was even given permission to keep my old ones. That was the first time that had happened since my arrival at Aiud.

By the end of May 1957, when I saw the iris with its stunning blue flowers blooming in a corner of the prison yard and was reminded of the seventh springtime in captivity, I whispered, unable to look up to heaven:

Dumnezeule, câți ani până ce voi vedea irisul înflorit în libertate? "God, how many more years will pass until I will see these flowers through the eyes of a free man?"

Back to Aiud

Then, on a summer morning in 1957, twenty-five castle inmates dressed in new garments, were rounded up and delivered by a well-guarded police bus to the railway station. Without access to a calendar, keeping track of the exact date was challenging. I sensed that it was mid-June by observing the landscape and recognizing the seasonal flowers lining the platform. As usual, none of the detainees was informed of the purpose or direction of the travel. You could almost smell the hope amidst the deadly silence on that platform.

Flanked by armed guards, we were protected from the curious eyes of the morning commuters, patiently waiting for their rides to Brașov and Sibiu. Effectively hidden behind the bodies of our jailors all the way from the police bus to the wagon, we were placed in the compartments immediately behind the engine. The prison car was attached to several regular passenger wagons. With all the precautions, a few people managed to spot me within our group, and I heard them whisper:

Uite-l mă pe doctoru' Stroia! "Look, there's Doctor Stroia!"

I was in a good mood and found it difficult to abstain from greeting the bystanders or a few station workers I recognized. No exchange of words or signs took place, however, as the strict surveillance and the guns proved too much of a deterrent. Once again, I traveled isolated in a separate bunk, with covered windows and insufficient room on the narrow bench, so I had to lie down on the dirty floor.

As the train approached Sibiu, which I knew from the ticket collector's announcement, I felt overwhelmed by regrets that despite spending three months in Făgăraş, I was unable to get in touch with my wife. In a straight line, our house was a bare 200 meters away from the fortress's entrance. At the time I was still unaware of my empty residence and my family's forced exile.

When we passed Sibiu without descending, I started to worry. I noticed the train's effort in climbing a hill, and I sensed we were heading toward Hula Săcelului. Curious, I climbed on top of the bars of the covered windows, stretching my neck to catch an outside glimpse through a crack. The window was on the left side of the train, and all I could see were green leaves atop tall trees. Minutes later, I discovered that we were passing through the Cacova train station without stopping.

That is when I finally realized I was going back to Aiud. I watched dejectedly as we passed Vinţul de Jos, then Simeria, where some of the prisoners got off the train, probably headed for a construction site, and I thought that the railway men's shouting of the stations' names became less clear. Overcome by fatigue, I dozed off, only to be rudely awakened by the engine's sudden stop. I climbed to the window again and noticed a sign that read "Deva." That was to become a familiar name upon my release from prison, when I went to work in the nearby rural clinic of Ilia....

But for now, I was transported from Deva to Aiud by means of another dark police van, sent back to the prison the Ministry of Internal Affairs considered fit for recalcitrant convicts.

Having to undergo another thirty days of solitary confinement, I was placed in a cell with twenty empty beds, without mattresses or sheets.

CHAPTER VI—RELEASE

Last Day—December 6, 1957

From the end of June 1957 on, I shared the cell with three quiet and collected Macedonians from Dobrogea, peasants from the dry plains of Southeastern Romania, bordering the Black Sea. They were natives of Greece who had moved to Romania, duped by the government's promise of fertile farmlands. Their stubborn refusal to give up the newly acquired and barely cultivable land and to join the inefficient state-owned farms—the so-called *C.A.P.* or *Cooperative Agricole de Producție* (collective agricultural cooperatives)—landed them in jail.

We were getting along very well, and the men's peacefulness transferred to me as well. By October 1957, I felt even more relaxed because—based on my multiple calculations—my liberation day was fast approaching. That is, if the authorities respected the Prisoners' Act with its "Conditional Time Law," which stipulated that every working day in prison would be subtracted from the sentence at the rate of one-and-a-half days. I was so impatient that I had already struck a deal with the Macedonians to hand them my new set of striped clothing and old boots. They were going to be of no use to a free man.

According to the results of my math, verified hundreds of times, I had exceeded the number of days of my sentence by 150 because I included my conditional time in that equation. I had worked approximately a year and a half in the prison factory, with periods of interruption, until my scurvy and hypertension disqualified me. Those additional 150 days felt heavy as lead, but paled in comparison to the fate of other political detainees, who were simply not released after serving their time.

During a haircut in October 1957, I asked the charge officer to allow the barber to keep my hair a little bit longer. I was going to leave soon—I confidently explained—and I would make the prison authorities look like fools if I graduated with a shaved head; my baldnesss was going to put a dent in their reputation. The officer smiled, meaningfully, but denied my plea.

As I returned to my cell, walking down the hallway, the last in a row of inmates, a whispering voice coming from behind my back said softly:

Pleci în curând! "You're going to leave for Făgăraș soon!"

I could not see who the voice belonged to, perhaps a kinder guard, because that well-intended someone disappeared like a ghost as soon as I turned my head around. Maybe it was just a hallucination, but the immediate effect was incredible, encouraging me at a point where my patience was running thin. I made another request for an audience with the prosecutor the very next morning, and a few more throughout the subsequent weeks. By November 1957, I was finally allowed to meet with the official. He interrupted me as soon as I attempted to present my case:

Ai răbdare! "Be patient!" he ordered.

As I stormed out of his office, I felt determined to stage a protest, even if I realized I was still a political inmate whose noise-making would not only be futile, but hazardous. Against all wisdom, I was ready to go on a hunger strike. Fortunately, there were more and more indications, albeit subtle, that my freedom hour was near.

When the day of December 6, 1957, arrived, it was time to celebrate Saint Nicholas—the wonderful Christian Orthodox holiday, honored in festivities throughout the villages of Transylvania. At seven o'clock that morning, the change of guards and the prisoner count took place uneventfully. After our breakfast was served, I received a cup of fake coffee with three pieces of sugar. I thought about the meaning of the holiday, heralding the arrival of Christmas, and I announced in a loud voice:

Sfinte Nicolae, eu astăzi plec! "Saint Nicholas, I'm leaving today!"

I felt rested after a good night's sleep. Reviewing my detailed plan for the day, I was contemplating what else to do during my last hours in captivity. A few minutes later, the officer on duty cracked the small service door and asked, while looking at us, one at a time:

"Hey, what's your name? And yours?"

Unhappy with the answers he received, he shouted impatiently:

Care ești Stroia? "Which one of you is Stroia?"

When I told him it was me, he ordered the guard to open the solid iron door. I can still clearly hear the sound made by the key that day, as it forcefully turned in the door lock. In those seconds, before the cell door was completely open, I handed my new clothes to the three Macedonians, according to our agreement. I switched the boots with one man, the pants and the jacket with another, and my coat with the third one. I kept my shirt and underpants and grabed my old, worn-out outfit.

Ce faci mă? "What do you think you're doing?" the stunned officer asked me, watching me undress and get dressed again.

Plec! "I'm leaving," I said boldly, buttoning my pants.

De unde știi? "How can you be so sure?" he continued, nodding his head in disapproval. "You'll see how you're going to tremble in those tatters."

The officer's warning was justified, because it was the beginning of a cold December, my seventh winter in confinement....

I shook hands with the nice Macedonians and grabbed my luggage, a few pieces of old clothing, with the other hand. Everything else I had I was wearing at that time, and it can be found today in the little bag in Cacova.

When I left the cell that morning, I walked happily between the two escorting jailors. Five rooms down the hallway, I noticed a young prisoner taken out of solitary and ordered to face the wall. Most of the inmates kept in isolation were young, under 40, while I was 53 years old at that time. I did not recognize the man, but he whispered a sigh of relief as I walked by and told me softly, "I feel better now." Prisoners removed from cells individually were more likely to be sent to punishment than the ones joining a group.

We were both content, even if for different reasons, and that was obvious to everyone. Walking down the steps to the first floor of the main building, I made brief eye contact and discreetly greeted a student I knew from

Sâmbăta de Sus. The joyful expression on my face must have been evident; his mimic showed he understood my situation.

Somehow, I was in no doubt that my sentence was ending. My transferred mate, conversely, could not have been certain of the fate that awaited him. As he followed me leisurely, he recounted that he was a factory worker in his late 30s and a native of Sighișoara, the picturesque medieval town in central Transylvania. A few minutes later, we arrived at the prison's barbershop. The barber—a convict himself—shaved me with outmost care this time. He asked me, after he rubbed my face with soap and foam for over ten minutes, if I would like the shaving done against the direction of hair growth as well! It was just another sign that I was being prepared for freedom.

All clouds of doubt dissipated as we were led to the facility's utility room, where the prisoners' belongings and civilian clothes were stored. When the guards returned my personal items, after seven years of safeguarding, I noticed that my wedding ring was missing. I was certain that someone at the Făgăraș Securitate had stolen it, likely during the search that Second Lieutenant Tache, a former patient of mine, performed on me with such zeal. I soon realized that my handkerchief was gone as well, and how I liked that fine handkerchief! They had covered my eyes with it when I was taken to one of my interrogations. Once it was removed from my face and I was thrown down the basement, I never saw it again. Nevertheless, my precious pocket watch and other items I carried with me at the time of my arrest had carefully followed me from Făgăraș to Sibiu and eventually to Aiud.

Dressed in my smelly and dusty old suit, I was led to the prison's third gate, the main iron gate, large, imposing, and frightening. I recalled the guard's prophecy when I first passed through it: "You will never walk out through here as a free man!" Leaving the second gate behind, I entered the administration building, where I was sat on a chair next to a table in an empty office. I was unable to continue the short talk with my colleague, who was ready to confess the reason behind his incarceration, because we were separated, each in a different room. Minutes later, a guard brought me a plate with 250 grams of fresh bread, 50 grams of marmalade, and 50 grams of *slănină* (bacon), the first I had tasted in so many years. I savored the meal, eating unhurriedly. Feeling satiated was a sensation that I had forgotten.

After an hour of sitting in that chair, I overheard another guard ordering the man from Sighișoara to follow him, which meant that the traveling documents required for leaving Aiud had been completed. He was either transferred to another penitentiary or sent to work at a construction site or state farm. I made that assumption based on information I had from other inmates, knowing that numerous political prisoners received additional "administrative punishment" after completion of their initial sentence, and in most cases that involved forced labor camps. The dry southern plains of Bărăgan were a favored destination.

I chased away the thoughts of uncertainty that were blurring my mind and kept waiting patiently.

"Rebirth Certificate" for a "Re-educated Element of Society"

It must have been noon when a different guard escorted me to another, more spacious office, where a Securitate captain greeted me politely. He appeared in good spirits, was quite pleasant, and looked at me with a certain kindness. His gentleness was quite different compared to what I was accustomed to in prison, where the rude officers' mere presence provoked negative emotions. The nice captain had come all the way from the Bucharest headquarters of the Ministry of Internal Affairs, accompanied by a major, to inspect and release selected prisoners. He held my file firmly in his hands and invited me courteously to sit down, the first humane gesture I had witnessed coming from a Securitate officer.

Based on his accent and way of speaking, I judged him to be a native of Transylvania. Quite voluble, he mentioned that he had been promoted to a position in the capital because he intervened on behalf of a Romanian worker imprisoned in Arad, a western Transylvanian city with a large Hungarian population. That individual was denied his ration of bread when he refused to request it in Hungarian! The one detail that still escapes my memory is the nice captain's name.

For the length of four hours, I was respectfully asked questions—not interrogated, as I had been in the past—about the statements and notations in my file. On three separate occasions, roughly every hour or so, the captain left me alone in the room for a few minutes, only to return with more involved questions requiring detailed answers. It was clear that he was trying to convince himself of the truth and validity of the accusations in my file but was having significant doubts. He also wanted to find out if I had behaved well during my prison time.

I never lost my morale and never despaired in the seven years of captivity. What gave me confidence that day was the captain's curiosity about my medical specialty and my methods of treating certain illnesses. He appeared particularly interested in liver diseases, maybe because someone in his family suffered from such problems. He put my memory to a strenuous test and that is when I realized—with some pride and satisfaction—that I had not lost *all* of my medical knowledge!

To the captain's last few questions, I answered courageously, with outmost sincerity and an open heart, and I was pleased to notice that my attitude did not upset him. I even mentioned the appeal and the increased sentence at the prosecutor's initiative. He appeared to have studied my file well and understood my circumstances. Displaying genuine concern, he went so far as to inquire about the quality of life in prison.

God was on my side when this particular Romanian was chosen to question me prior to leaving prison. He concluded from the lack of evidence in my file that the authorities committed an abuse of power. Agreeing with my lawyer's opinion, he stated that an article of the law according to which I was sentenced had been misinterpreted. However, he could not openly condemn those who had manipulated the facts and fabricated my accusations, nor could he criticize the sentence, of course.

The captain spoke to me about my current situation: I was going to be free in just a few minutes, largely because of his recommendations. He stated that I should be considered a "re-educated element of society," shook my hand, and gave me my *bilet de liberare*, my prison release note or "rebirth certificate," as I like to call it. It became my "second diploma," earned after successful completion, or rather survival, of my "second university." It was my ticket to freedom and bore the number 15238, which meant that there had been more than 15,000 people sentenced and released from Aiud Penitentiary before me up to that date. Aside from detailed personal data, such as the reason for my arrest and the dates of my imprisonment, the document ended with a note granting me the right to work in any private or state-owned institution.

At last, the captain cautioned me that I needed to present myself to the Făgăraș Securitate headquarters in ten days. Then he ordered me to sign a typed statement agreeing that I would not disclose to anybody what I had seen and experienced in prison. Otherwise—the document warned—my offense would be punished with another ten to fifteen years of detention.

This type of intimidating language served as a powerful deterrent and a persuasive invitation to passivity for ex-political convicts. For the courageous ones, there was no lack of evidence that the Communists followed through with their threats. A former cellmate who was incarcerated for another decade after complaining about his ordeal to people who, in turn, denounced him, was a painful example. His fate represented a needed reminder of the validity of the captain's caution. My friend was eventually set free in 1964, after a governmental decree granted amnesty to all survivors of Romania's political prisons. At least, in his case, the additional confinement tine counted toward retirement.

As I was leaving his office, the captain said in a soft voice: *Afară se cântă un alt cântec....* "There's another song outside...."

Care? "Which one is that?" I asked, naïve as always in political matters. *Deșteaptă-te Române?* "Wake up, Romanian?"

Nu! the captain replied. *Este: Românul nu piere!* "It is: Romanians won't die!"

{"Wake up, Romanian" was a reference to the patriotic, freedom song composed by Anton Pann with lyrics by Andrei Mureșanu. Called the "Romanian Marseillaise," the hymn was popular during the 1877–1878 Independence War against Turkey. It was banned under Communism and spontaneously re-adopted

during the 1989 Anti-Communist Revolution. Currently, it serves as the official Romanian national anthem.}

Home and Family

When I finally passed through the last gate and stepped onto the street as a free man, the on-duty sergeant noticed the absence of an escorting guard. He congratulated me in a loud voice, and then felt compelled to remind me:

Ai avut mare noroc! "You were very lucky!" Then, as if he clearly understood my circumstance, he added: "You must have been well behaved!"

Was I the fortunate one for having my freedom robbed for seven years, rather than receiving a customary—in situations similar to mine—one-year sentence with suspension? The answer seemed rather obvious. The political inmates involved in any form of protest were reprimanded and received labels such as "disobedient" or "unable to be re-educated." This led to additional years in jail, courtesy of the prison administration. God had been on my side, however, and I considered myself lucky not to have collected bonus time, considering that I gave my jailors plenty of opportunities. I endured solitary confinements as a result of behavior judged to be inadequate, but none of the incidents earned negative marks in my file. Those episodes still haunt me during sleepless nights, which any man of my age (not to say old) experiences sometimes.

It was four o'clock in the afternoon, and I had a strange feeling standing on the other side of the prison gate. I must have appeared confused, as the main entrance guard reminded me about the train leaving for Sibiu at five, traveling via Teiuş. He pointed in the right direction and urged me to hurry because the train was scheduled to arrive within fifteen minutes.

The railway station was a short walking distance from the prison compound. After a couple of minutes of tense waiting, my freedom locomotive arrived with a squeaky noise. The wagons were old, rusty and dirty, and several officers with long coats and inexpressive faces got off in no hurry. I asked a traveler if the soldiers were Russians from the Red Army; he reassured me that they were Romanians.

{The Soviet military occupation of Romania commenced in 1944. The repatriation of these forces took place in August 1958, whereas in other Eastern European countries it was completed as late as the early 1990s. The rationale behind the early troop withdrawal was the absence of threats to Soviet imperialism from a friendly government and a subdued population. Romania was also securely enveloped by Communist neighbors and shared a long border with the Soviet Union.}

Without hesitation, I got onto the train, carrying just one item: the small hempen bag, in which my family had sent me underwear in the winter of 1952. I entered the first booth and sat down carefully on the only free seat, squeezed between other travellers. With my frail appearance in crumpled and oversized clothing, the very short haircut, and the skinny and pale face, I quickly became the object of stares of the people in the compartment. The bad-smelling outfit from years of warehouse storage identified me as a recent jail graduate. Most, if not all, passengers must have been aware of the prison facility housed in Aiud. Some were blunt in their curiosity, gazing uninterruptedly while others showed more discretion, cautiously inspecting me from the corners of their eyes. But nobody dared speaking. Naturally, given the awkward situation, I did not start any conversations either. Then, one of the travellers gained enough courage to break the silence and ask me—to everyone's relief—if I had just been released from prison. I avoided confirming his worst suspicion and excused myself, moving to the hallway of the wagon. There, I came face to face with an individual from Făgăraş who recognized me instantly. He spread the news by announcing to everybody:

A fost eliberat doctoru'! "The doctor has been freed!"

Upon my safe arrival in Sibiu at one o'clock in the morning, I knocked at my brother's window and announced: *A sosit Stanciu!* "Stanciu has arrived!" in response to his concerned *Cine bate?* "Who is it?"

Regaining his composure and reassuring himself that he was not dreaming, my brother provided me with much wanted news about my wife and children. For seven long years, I had not received a single direct piece of information about their fate. It was perhaps better that I was not aware of their share of hardship, convinced they were still living in the spacious house we designed and built in 1938. I would have lost my mind and faith in life had I known that they were driven out of our home and forced to live in exile for the past five years. Adding insult to injury, I soon discovered that our home had been demolished on orders from the Communist city officials.

After a night of talking, I left for Cacova (renamed Fântânele in the interim), a short twenty-two kilometers from Sibiu, to see my ailing mother. At 81 years of age, she was suffering from debilitating heart failure and had completely lost her faith in our reunion. *Fie iertat Stanciu* "God forgive Stanciu" was what she had just written in a letter addressed to my wife.... My mother died three months later, on March 23, 1958.

My next stop was Cluj, my children's city of residence. As I was riding the train, I recalled the dignified presence at my appeal of Tita, a young beautiful woman with a self-confident look. She appeared unchanged when I saw her again, waiting in the right corner of the railway platform, on that first trip back to Cluj.

In my absence, Zeno had married Stela Băcilă, a pediatrician he had met through his sister. She and my son lived in a one-room rented apartment owned by Mrs. Alice Czitrom. I called her early in the morning from Sibiu, a day after my return; she had just gotten out of the shower when she picked up the phone. I wondered how I should introduce myself to her; spontaneous, as I have always been, I announced in a happy voice:

A sosit socrul tău, Fetițo! "Your father-in-law is here, my girl!"

The first time I saw my wife again, on December 7, 1957, the state of her health was poor. The degree of hypertension and heart disease induced by the uncontrolled hyperthyroidism she had been plagued with since 1935 concerned me tremendously. At the root of her problems had been the intense physical exertions she was subjected to in my absence, the constant tension she was forced to live in, the lack of available subspecialty care, and her own noncompliance with the indicated regimens. I could not help but wonder how much of this would have been avoided if I had been by her side all those years....

Her uncompensated low output heart failure progressed because effective medications against hyperthyroidism were unavailable. Given the emergent situation, while I was still working in Ilia and my daughter was starting a pediatric practice in Jibou, we decided to admit my wife to the Parhon Endocrinology Institute in Bucharest in 1960. There, she reluctantly agreed to undergo thyroidectomy, the complete removal of her thyroid gland, a challenging procedure in those days. It turned out to be a wise choice because she tolerated the surgery well, and her cardiac function improved immediately afterward. That fragile balance lasted only until 1967, however, when an influenza episode led to a relapse.

For the next eight years, her disease advanced steadily despite proper care, but never became incapacitating. And that proved to be her blessing.

Consequences of Imprisonment

Nu mor caii când vor cîinii! "Horses won't die when dogs think it's time!"

With those words, declared in a loud voice for everyone to hear, Gheorghe Ganea, an engineer and the city's former prefect, greeted me on the platform of the Făgăraș railway station. We shook hands, but I did not reply to his statement. The harsh reality is that upon my return to Făgăraș, I was an ill, debilitated individual incapable of work requiring sustained mental effort. I was back to life now; a free man with the right to hold a job, but— I kept asking myself—what was the real cost of my prison experience?

As a result of my severe and prolonged scurvy, I must have lost fifty percent of my nerve cells through irremediable atrophy, an insult from which I never recovered. Only a detailed postmortem pathological exam could demonstrate the extent of injuries sustained by a scurvy-affected brain. Many intellectuals I met in Aiud, especially those experiencing generalized dystrophic symptoms, lost their short- and long-term memory. Knowing that I was a physician, they would ask me if this loss was reversible. Of course I had to encourage them, even if they told me, for instance, that they could not remember the names of their own grandchildren.

The memory problem became serious for me as well, and this was hard to accept because I knew very well that a nerve cell would never recover. Even today, if I want to memorize a name or an address, I have to write it down several times and keep it constantly under my eyes for a few days. I have lost my full capacity for memorizing something new—a poem or a prayer, for example—and I have never regained the ability to analyze or compose, to master new skills, or to acquire new knowledge. All I have left is the memory from the distant past and the power of the routine. That is what keeps me functioning with relative efficiency in my profession and daily life.

On top of the scurvy-inflicted damage, the hypertension that emerged in 1953 became a systemic, well-organized illness with severe repercussions. My family physician from Cantacuzino Hospital, Dr. Grigore Beligan, deserves a lot of credit for the skill and tactfulness with which he treated me as an inpatient in the autumn of 1978.

After all I had been through, I was left thinking: *Puțin a rămas din această viață, trăită în cinste, munca și omenie!* "Stanciu, have a little more patience! Little is left of this life, lived in honesty, work, and kindness...."

Ilia

Only after three months of recovery did I have the courage to apply for a position appropriate for a person with minimal medical training. But at the Făgăraș Health Department, I was categorically rejected. The thought of applying for the job I held before I was arrested never crossed my mind because I would not have been able to perform such an immense amount of work. However, I was found unfit to occupy any position in the district, not even a part-time job in a rural or factory clinic.

Support from any of my old colleagues was absent. Notwithstanding that I protected their interests as president-elect of the Regional Medical Association, the physicians of Făgăraș received me with open hostility. Was it the fear of my authority and previous professional erudition, or were they simply avoiding contact with a former convict? A typical example proved to be a former collaborator I trusted faithfully, who, in response to my (only ever) request for a symbolic loan, refused by saying he planned to use the funds to improve one of his garages instead. The most dishonest attitude was that of a doctor from the ammunition factory who embezzled my Roentgen and ultrasound machines; recovering those devices became the most daunting task.

În această lume, nimic nu este desăvîrșit! In this life, nothing is flawless!

In contrast, the county's population—regardless of nationality—was not merely polite but almost ceremonious, bowing with respect and raising hats when it encountered me. That excessive attention became overwhelming and embarrassing at times. The hospital employees did not shun me either, seeking my company in social situations.

However, I continued to remain jobless and was virtually penniless. Still in search of employment, I visited nearby Brașov County, where I found equally negative answers and closed doors. My wife was unable to work because of her hyperthyroidism and uncompensated heart failure, so we were in great need of money, especially for repayment of debts accumulated in my absence, when she had been left with hardly any means of subsistence.

Over time, many area residents started to inquire about my whereabouts, even asking for medical assistance; they remembered the many successful years I had spent at their service. Then, one day in late March 1958, a group of peasants from the nearby villages of Viștea de Jos, Viștea de Sus, Feldioara, and Ucea showed up at my door, led by the local mayor, with a petition signed by eight hundred of them. They requested my acceptance for employment in their clinic, recently vacated because of the death of the local doctor under dubious circumstances. The offer sounded very attractive, as the area was located a mere twenty-five kilometers south of Făgăraș. Nevertheless, the plan failed to materialize the moment the regional Securitate officer—whose permission I was legally bound to obtain—advised me to refuse the position. Noticing my hesitation and aware of my popularity, he added an open-ended question:

"Do you know how the doc out there died after he was arrested by the Securitate?"

Taken by surprise, I answered cautiously: "I don't know."

A reply failed to follow. The expression on the man's face was self-explanatory.

In all truth, the officer did me a great favor, allowing me to avoid suspicious situations leading to more trouble. The incident served as a reminder of the document I signed upon my release from prison.

Eventually I was redirected to the Ministry of Health, where I was told to search for jobs in under-served areas of the country, like the Northern territories of Maramureș and Moldova. That is how I arrived at the Ilia Clinic in the Hunedoara District at the end of 1958, as a consultant physician in internal medicine. I worked there for ten years before retiring in December 1968.

Excited about the new opportunity and eager to have a good start, I purchased the latest edition of the most widely used internal medicine textbook, a total of six volumes, confident of my ability to bring my knowledge base up to date. It turned out to be an impossible undertaking; any serious attempt to study gave me a severe and stubborn headache. Once I began to see patients, I started to suffer from sudden-onset dizzy spells, leading to frequent cancellations of appointments. I had to lock myself in the office for twenty to thirty minutes and attempt to lie down in order to recover. Luckily, I was not very busy at first, but this became more of a problem when my patient volume increased to forty a day.

My fellow physicians in Ilia respected my medical credentials and trusted my expertise; some had even heard my name mentioned during Professor Hațieganu's university lectures. Starting with the district chief of staff, everybody received me well and offered generous help throughout my ten years there. However, I was not the same Doctor Stroia from prior to detention. My colleagues had a difficult time understanding that I was not capable of the same intellectual effort of the past. My scurvy-ravaged brain was simply incapable of more. None of them knew—at least that is what I thought—about my seven years' absence from practice.

As the Romanian saying goes, *În tot răul e și un bine* "There is some good in every evil." Ilia allowed me to recover my family life and reclaim my professional pride. Slowly but surely, over many years, my physical well-being improved where it was still possible, where the deep scurvy scars were not irreversible. My improved capacity for effort resulted in an increased workload. I started examining inpatients at the end of my clinic hours and responded to consultations from general practitioners as well, trying to be correct and conscientious. By the end of the eighth year in Ilia, I was elected honorary director of the clinic and represented our group in conferences organized by the larger Medical Center of Timișoara. I was even offered the opportunity to oversee the internal medicine department in the nearby city of Ghelar, which I had to politely refuse because of time constraints.

With my colleagues, I maintained a strictly professional relationship. No social interaction or house visits ever took place. After all, those were the directives I had received from the Securitate and had to comply with upon my release. Occasionally, as I was hearing about ex-political detainees being frivolously fired from their jobs, some well-meaning individuals were compelled to remind me:

Fii atent, doctore! "Be careful, Doc!"

But what else was I supposed to do?

Compared to my peers and the city's officials and citizens, the attitudes of the Communist district prime-secretary and the Securitate officers were at the opposite pole. Their aversion toward me was unconcealed, ranging from labels like "cheat" and "bandit" to restrictions against treating local Communist leaders.

Nu aduce anul cât aduce ceasul! "Sometimes an hour brings more than a year." That is precisely what occured one evening in 1963, when the "Damocles Sword" was finally raised from above my neck. The prime-secretary himself requested an appointment at his house, at the suggestion of the other concerned local physicians. His 18-year-old son had returned from a high school graduation party, which included a lot of *țuică* consumption, and had failed to wake up after twenty-four hours of deep sleep. With an unconscious son, he was requesting the opinion of the *escroc bătrân* (old crook), asking for treatment and a fair prognosis. Aided by my knowledge of toxicology acquired during long night shifts at the university emergency room and following a thorough exam, I reassured the prime-secretary that despite the lack of guarantees in medicine, his son would wake up rather than suffer a post-comatose death. Forty-eight hours of a toxic sleep later, the young man returned to life.

From that moment on I became the savior, and the prime-secretary, my biggest and most vociferous fan. My presence was acknowledged from a distance, and he made sure to shake my hand and congratulate me over again on every social occasion. The help offered to his offspring paid further dividends: Shortly thereafter, on June 8, 1966, I obtained my final political and judicial rehabilitation, as a resuslt of the decision of the Ilia Regional Tribunal.

Este complet reeducat! "He is entirely re-educated!" proclaimed the judge. "He can reclaim his place in society as if he had never committed a crime," he concluded.

Fericiți cei săraci cu duhul! "Happy shall be the poor in spirit," says the Orthodox Church.

I recall the last day in Ilia with great pleasure and professional satisfaction. Opening the doors to my office for the very last time on December 31, 1968, at three o'clock in the afternoon, and seeing another thirty patients eager to be examined, I addressed them cordially:

La spartul târgului, cine mai dorește în cabinet? "Now that the show is almost over, does anyone else desire to step into my office?"

I completed another three retirement proposals that afternoon, always accepted by the Ministry of Labor because of their judicious documentation. And I kept receiving thank you letters from my Ilia patients for many years after my retirement....

Next Generations

It was not easy to leave Ilia; it was a difficult good-bye from my colleagues and staff, both from the hospital and the clinic, to whom I still remain so indebted. Nevertheless, I had a feeling of comfort when I left for Bucharest, and my psychological tonus was greatly enhanced by my wife's support, by the love and attention generously given by my children and their spouses, and especially by the presence of my three grandchildren: Ligia Stroia, born in 1960; Alina Duşleag, in 1965; and Dan Duşleag, in 1966. I viewed them all as clear signs of the vitality of my descendants.

In the summer of 1963, while my daughter Tita was visiting us in Ilia, where she found it peaceful enough to study for her board certification, the young Dr. Liviu Duşleag paid us a second visit. Valy knew him from the time he dated my daughter while they were both in medical school. She had never shared any details with me, as we avoided discussing anything related to those miserable years. At the time, Valy was tormented by her heart failure and was recovering from her thyroidectomy, while I was still in a dystrophic state.

It did not take a lengthy discussion to understand the scope of Liviu's visit. With complete trust in his honesty, seriousness, and noble intentions, I gave him my blessing for the wedding which was organized two months later, in the house of his brother-in-law, Dr. Nicolae Cristian, a surgeon from Sibiu, in a discreet, strictly familial environment.

My decision to retire at 64 years of age, after thirty-four years of work and seven of imposed hiatus, and to move to the capital rather than to Sibiu, closer to my native Cacova, was made at the Duşleags' insistence, but was well pondered over. The assurance of help in case of illness, but especially the joy of being surrounded by my grandchildren and watching them grow, weighed heavily in my choice. My wife—the absolute grandmother—had no second thoughts.

The summer, spring, and almost every winter vacation we continued to spend entirely in our family house in Cacova, a nature's paradise for the little ones.

{The gardens surrounding the property were filled with blooming, brightly colored flowers, and every fruit one can imagine was growing under my grandfather's skillful hands, there to be taken and eaten: a variety of apples, pears, prunes, cherries, strawberries, and raspberries—to name a few.}

With the years passing by, I had to reflect on the recent comment my well-developed 13-year-old grandson Dan made, as we were embarking on another bus trip together:

Tatamare, ai îmbătrînit! Acum te împing eu sus! "Grandpa, you're getting old! You used to be the one to push me up; looks like the roles have been reversed!"

Heroes' Grave and Monument

In the summer of 1970, during a hiking excursion on Cacova's surrounding mountains, I reached the Augur Plateau on Merezi Hill, a site with historical significance at an altitude of roughly 1,000 meters. The names of the area originate from the Latin "Augur," which means foreteller of events, and "Meridies," signifying midday, or the place over which the sun shines at noon. The hill with its plateau overlooks the village, and the tall pine trees were visible from our own front yard. In 1916, seventy-five Romanian soldiers belonging to the 2nd Vâlcea Regiment from Olt district paid the ultimate sacrifice on that ground. They were fighting a battalion of German soldiers during World War I at the time of Transylvania's quest for reunification with Romania.

Naturally, I stopped for a moment to reflect in front of the common grave of those heroes, who resisted a superior enemy both in numbers and in arms for over two weeks, aided by the local peasants. As I was standing there, trying to imagine the fierce bayonet battle that took place half a century ago and ended with the brave Romanian soldiers—including their commander, Sublieutenant Vasile Godeanu—being encircled, attacked from behind, shot in the head, and thrown in a ditch, I was suddenly overwhelmed by feelings of responsibility.

The Germans took no prisoners that day, and the only survivors of the massacre were a few soldiers protected by the thick hornbeam woods surrounding the plateau. The commander's brother, Gavrilă Godeanu, survived as well; he was intentionally shot in the back rather than the head and was released to report the outcome of the frightening battle. Seriously wounded, he managed to return to his retreating regiment and handed his fallen brother's gear, which contained a last letter addressed to his family. The sole survivor of the six Godeanu siblings, Professor Florica Nisipeanu of Brașov, passed the bloodstained note—a document of immense historical and emotional value—to me, many years later. I donated it to the Central Military Museum in Bucharest where it belonged and where it is displayed today.

As soon as the hostilities ceased and at the order of the Hungarian authorities, the population of Cacova—consisting solely of women and children, with the husbands and fathers deployed to the front—buried the soldiers' bodies in their own trenches and the holes in the ground made by explosives. Some of the participants, most well over 80 years old, are still alive to recount that tale.

Seven years later, at the initiative of my mother's brother, Father Ioan Hanzu Jr., the remnants of the fallen heroes were exhumed and a common grave was dedicated during a proper Christian Orthodox burial ceremony. A large cedar cross was set at the grave's head, and the area was encircled with a wooden gate. Pine trees were planted and large construction stones were hauled to the plateau to be used in the erection of a local monument. The Father's limited budget, consisting mainly of his own meager pension, did not allow him to see the project accomplished. Nevertheless, he organized a yearly pilgrimage headed by the village's children to Merezi Hill to commemorate the heroes for as long as he lived. He died in 1942.

What was displayed in front of my eyes that day in 1970 saddened and revolted me beyond limit. Cows were resting on the grave under the shadows of the trees, there was no gate left, and the vertical pillar was all that remained of the cross. Some stones were dispersed throughout the area, but most of them were missing. The conifer trees were either diseased or dried out, and a few had some irresponsible citizen's signature encrusted on the bark. Simply put, the total lack of respect and piety for Transylvania's freedom fighters was disturbing.

My spontaneous reaction was to collect all the stones I could find and pile them up on top of the grave, so that everyone could see a sign that something sacred was being protected. As I pulled my sleeves up and went to work, Father Hanzu Jr.'s plea emerged vividly from my memory:

Nu te îndepărta de sat, nu îl părăsi.... "Don't distance yourself from the village, don't abandon it...."

Heading down a mountain path on my way back home, I arrived at the point where the village borders the bottom of the hill, and I stopped to catch my breath and clear my thoughts. Then, I knocked on the gate of the first house, that of my childhood friend Coman Popa, a godchild of my mother's.

Excited to welcome an unexpected guest, he greeted me jovially: "Where're you coming from, godfather?"

"From Augur...," I replied, visibly troubled.

Not allowing me to continue with my story, he said—face turning serious—in a sarcastic voice: *Și-ți place?* "And you like it?"

I told him how affected I was, but he would not hear it.

Ce rușine! "What a disgrace, how shameful!" he raged. "It took the lives of those boys and others like them for you to have the chance to study and become a doctor; we all would be still living under Hungarian rule today, if it weren't for them! People forgot how it felt when we were not even allowed to speak our own language...."

{Following two years of neutrality, Romania entered World War I in 1916 on the side of the Allies (France, Britain and Russia), in an effort to recover the Austrian-Hungarian-occupied Transylvania, Banat, and Bucovina. After a heavy initial defeat courtesy of the Central Powers (notably Germany), Romania's fortunes changed; she pursued the retreating enemy and accomplished the reunification with Transylvania in 1918, ratifying Austria-Hungary's demise.}

My guilty conscience reacted to my old friend's words and intensified my indignation at my—only apparent, of course—indifference.

His wife quickly joined in the conversation:

"In 1936, Father Hanzu Jr. was going to build a real mausoleum on that gravesite, with an electrical light on top which was going to be visible all the way from Sibiu.... What happened to all that?" she asked rhetorically.

I left the farmer's house that evening with a heavy heart and painful thoughts. Falling asleep was not an option, and during such a sleepless moment, I took the decision to undertake everything in my power to honor the forgotten heroes.

Back in Bucharest, forming an ad hoc committee with three other fellows came as a logical next step in an attempt to collect the necessary funds. Teodor Iacob, Gheorghe Gruia, and Ioan Popa were all natives of Cacova, now successful and resourceful young professionals in the capital. Starting in the winter of 1971 and ending in the summer of 1975, through personal donations of money and construction material, it all became a reality. A few of my monthly pensions, ten bags of cement, twenty-four iron pipes (painted by my grandchildren), twelve reinforced concrete pillars, a bronze plate with an inscription, forty conifers, and numerous flowers are what it took for the project to be completed.

The fallen soldiers were honored with *Mormântul Eroilor*, (The Heroes' Grave), a burial site to commemorate their heroic deeds. After many hours of volunteer work from virtually every villager, I had finally found my inner piece.... Or, at least, so I thought....

That tranquillity lasted only until a few days later, when it disappeared during an end-of-the-year school festivity to which I had been invited. As I was sitting in the audience enjoying the children's celebration, Emilia Răulea, an elderly woman, there in the company of her granddaughter, took the stand unexpectedly. With tears rolling from her eyes, she turned toward me and addressed me with the following words:

"So, Doctor. You seem to care for the boys from Olt, but what about our *own* war heroes, do you feel for them?"

That apostrophizing hit me instantly and as hard as a cannon blow! And it was a second one, mind you! The first, handed by my childhood friend, I had survived. I had redeemed myself; I was acquitted, expiated, forgiven....

Overcome by the scene, I recalled that the woman had lost her husband during World War I, only to see her only son perish in World War II. And I relived images witnessed one evening in July 1914, when I heard the church's bells deafening ring *ca de mort*, as if somebody had died. I soon discovered that Emilia Răulea's husband and his comrade, Coman Miclăuș, were ringing their own death bells as the draft had been declared and they were both called to arms.... None of them returned alive....

The idea of a monument erected somewhere in the village had been in my mind for years, and the roots grew only stronger every time I looked toward Merezi Hill, a mere 300 meters—in a straight line—distance from our family yard. However, resources for such an endeavor were scarce. Out of almost 150 former citizens of Cacova dispersed throughout the country, only half honored my plea for financial help.

Going back to work and research, I was granted an appointment at the Military Arts Studio in Bucharest, where Colonel Marius Butunoiu, a trained sculptor, received me with a lot of understanding. His continuous guidance proved invaluable over the following year.

Iară n-ai bani doctore? "No money again, Doc?" he used to joke with me, using that line instead of hello.

N-am nici măcar idei! "Not only that, I'm lacking ideas as well!" I would reply.

My persistence eventually paid off. For a small fee, sculptor Pavel Mercea designed an artistic bas-relief depicting a bayonet battle, much like the one that took place on Merezi Hill. Architect Dan Aurel from the Bucharest Architecture Institute designed the project for the monument free of cost. The director of the Central Military Museum donated a bronze statue by Horea Giroșanu depicting the head of a Romanian soldier; the Simeria Factory provided the marble pieces; the Sibiu Independența Factory produced the metal plaques encrusted with the names of the village men who died during World War I and World War II; and the whole structure was assembled with the sweat of the soldiers from the Sibiu Garrison. My grandchildren volunteered once again for the job of painting the surrounding iron bars. Without much debate, Zăvoi was the memorial's chosen site. It was truly the most appropriate location, alongside the road exiting the village, which was frequented by tourists hiking toward the mountains.

It took years of perseverance, of queries and letters, multiple trips, audiences, and pleas to the local Communist authorities, notes asking for support written to *Flacăra* (The Flame) and *Magazin Istoric* (The Historical

Magazine), and personal loans totaling ten thousand lei before the monument was finished in October 1976 and officially dedicated in December 1978. *{Two thousand lei was the average Romanian salary in the late 1970s.}*

Despite my status as "private person," my straightforwardness and lack of diplomacy, and the convoluted maneuvers required to subdue the Communist bureaucracy, the project was a success. There were many rejections along the way, humiliations by authorities aware of my past, and a last-minute deletion from the speaker list for the dedication ceremony. However, as the witty mayor of neighboring Săliște, Toma Lupaș, was forced to acknowledge:

Bătrânu' pensionar nu glumește! "The old man is not kidding!"

Since 1979, on every Memorial Day, the village children with their teachers and parents pay tribute to Cacova's war heroes at the site of the monument in the mayor's presence. I am confident that *Monumentul Eroilor*, (The Heroes' Monument), a solid structure of an impressive artistic quality, will survive over centuries. *Spuneți generațiilor viitoare, că noi am făcut jertfa supremă....* "Tell the next generations that we have paid the ultimate sacrifice...." reads the inscription on the monument's façade.

One evening in 1979, as I was listening to national radio, an army general was discussing the memorable World War I battles of Oituz and Mărășești in 1917, where the Romanian soldiers proved the famous saying: *Pe aici nu se trece!* "There is no way through!" The next morning, I mailed a memorandum to the Ministry of Military Affairs, politely reminding them that the slogan mentioned on the program was first put in practice in 1916 in the battle of Merezi Hill by Cacova in the Sibiu District. *This* was the scene of the first fierce encounter between the liberating Romanian Army and the German invaders. To my great satisfaction, the minister agreed to delegate a military historian to investigate my claim, and that is how Colonel Dr. Victor Atanasiu, professor and chair of the history department at the Bucharest Military Academy, got involved. Following interviews with survivors and meticulous studies of unearthed documents, a history book was published in 1982 under the title *The Battle of Sibiu-Câineni: September 1916.*

My preoccupation with Romania's recent history and my labor in its service turned out to be fruitful, a fact for which I am very thankful. Respect needs to be fostered in every Romanian heart toward the heroes of our nation. We should worship them in return for the freedom they so selflessly offered us.

{After years of practicing medicine and the time spent in prison, retirement brought my grandfather well-earned peace and the chance to pursue his passion: history. The previous subchapter was included at the end of his prison memoir as it depicts the type of man he was: selfless and a true patriot.}

Thank You!

In the end—because I have finished over one hundred pages of my notebook—I am grateful to God for allowing me to enter into the 82nd year of my life. I was born on August 10, 1904! From now on, I have to consider every day as a gift from above, and all I can hope for is a decent, Christian death—if I deserve it.

I apologize for the mistakes I have made as a result of which my family had to suffer. And I am thankful to my wife, for showing so much devotion and for being such a wonderful mother. I think of her, who left me in 1975 after a long suffering but a painless death, as the Orthodox Church wishes for the faithful. *Un sfârșit creștinesc, fără durere, cum dorește Biserica credincioșilor....*

I also want to express my gratitude to my good children, Zeno and Tita, and their spouses, Stela and Liviu, for the support and comfort they have always given me.

One day, my grandchildren, Ligia, Alina, and Dan, will find out everything that is written in these notebooks. They are only to be read after my passing.

Stanciu Stroia
Bucharest, Romania, written between 1979 and 1986

"When God created the world,
He also created sorrow, suffering and trouble;
And He laid them on a big stone and the stone broke;
And He laid them on a big tree and the tree withered;
And finally He laid them on man and man carried them.
And so will you, my brother, carry your sufferings."

Father Gheorghe Calciu-Dumitreasa

Sibiu Courthouse, former residence of the Sibiu Military Tribunal, stage of political show trials in the 1950s.

View from within the Sibiu Penitentiary, located behind the Sibiu Courthouse. The prison building was vacated in 1970.

Main entrance to the Sibiu Penitentiary. The metal door leads to a stairway connecting three floors. Steel gates on every floor provide access to the actual cell section.

Inside a basement cell of the Sibiu Penitentiary, located deep into the ground, cold, unlit and with unfinished brickwalls.

Entrance sign to the Aiud Penitentiary, still an active prison (for regular convicts) as of September 2004.

External fence with barbwire and sentry box at Aiud Penitentiary.

Aerial view of the Aiud Penitentiary, from a nearby hill. The white building in the foreground is the prison factory. Our request to enter the compound was denied.

The Aiud Railway Station, a few hundred feet away from the penitentiary.

This postcard mailed on December 9, 1952 from Aiud Penitentiary, was the only piece of correspondence allowed between Dr. Stanciu Stroia and his family in seven years.

Copy of Dr. Stanciu Stroia's inmate file at Aiud, dated May 31, 1955. Despite a seven years sentence for a "political crime," his past and present political affiliations are listed as: none ("apolitic").

Stanciu Stroia's prison release document, which he also called "rebirth certificate" and "second diploma." Dated December 6, 1957, it was his ticket to freedom.

"The Ordeal" is a temple of grief erected in 1992 by the Association of Former Political Detainees. It is made of seven pairs of six meters tall united crosses, representing the martyrs' unity in death, supporting the larger cross of destiny. The round openings symbolize God's eyes.

NEÎNFRÎNTI AU RĂMAS SUB
ACEASTĂ GLIE MARTIRII
CĂZUTI ÎN TEMNITA AIUDULUI
PE BARICADA LUPTEI ÎMPOTRIVA
COMUNISMULUI. EI S-AU JERTFIT
PENTRU HRISTOS DEMNITATE ȘI
LIBERTATE NATIONALĂ.
MEMORIEI LOR
ASOCIATIA FOSTILOR DETINUTI
POLITICI ANTICOMUNIȘTI
HUNEDOARA

"Unsubdued rest the martyrs fallen on the barricades of the anti-Communist fight. They sacrificed themselves in the name of Christ, national demnity and liberty. This is in their memory."

Fagaras Castle, a medieval fortress misused as a prison by the Communist regime in the 1950s.

This five meters tall marble cross was erected in 1995 next to the Sambata Monastery by the Association of Former Political Detainees. It commemorates the Fagaras Mountains anti-Communist fighters. Dr. Stanciu Stroia's name is listed in the center.

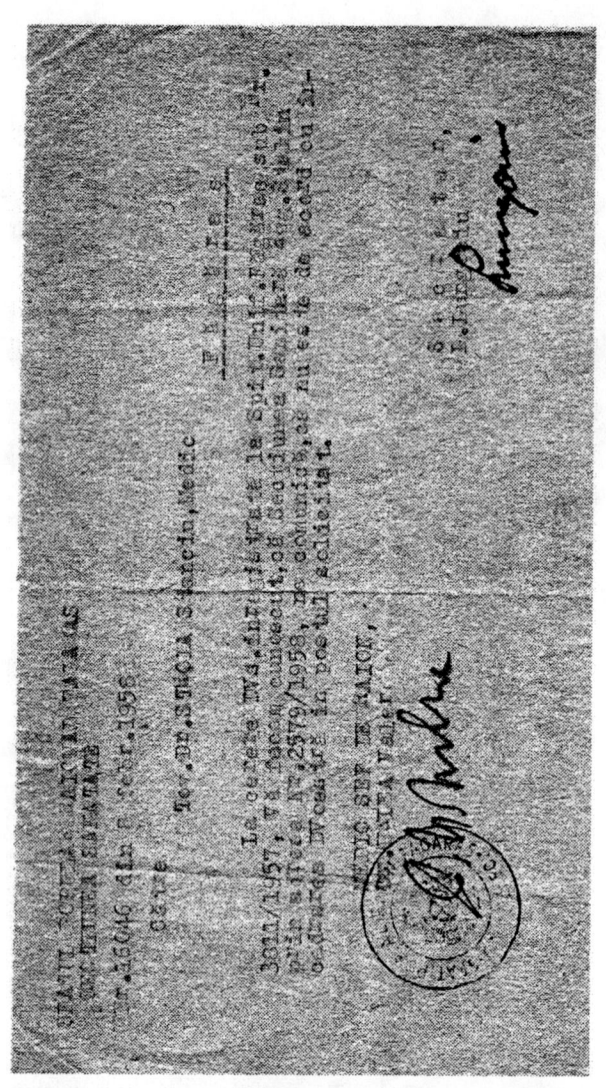

Employment denial letter from Fagaras District People's Council, dated February 8, 1958:
"Comrade Dr. Stanciu Stroia,
In response to your application submitted to Fagaras Hospital under Nr. 3811/1957, we inform you that the Health Department of Stalin Region has denied your request for employment in the solicited position, through the decision Nr. 2579/1958."

Dr. Stanciu Stroia, before (1951) and after (1958) imprisonment.

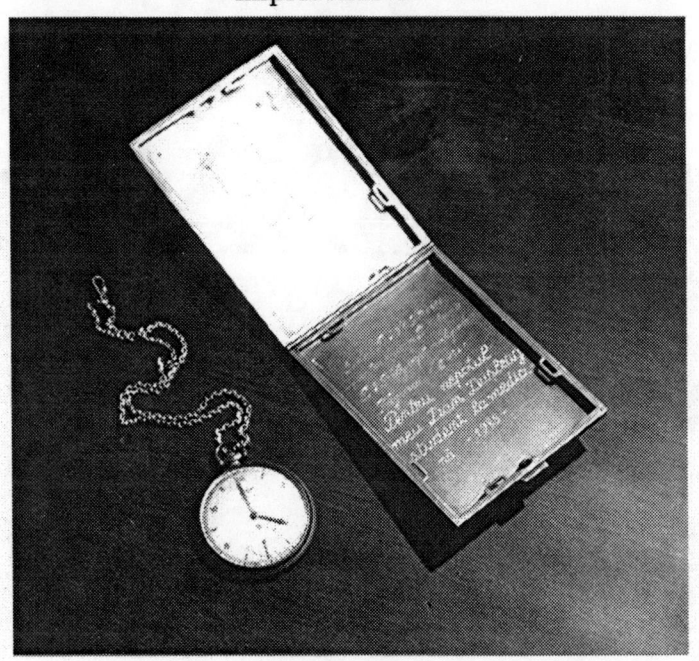

The Tissot Swiss pocket watch and Dr. Antoni Firlej's Polish cigarette holder.

Zeno Stroia and Stela Bacila on their wedding day in July 1956, a year prior to Stanciu Stroia's release from prison.

A father reunited with both children after many years. Cluj, Easter 1959.

Stanciu Stroia with his first grandchild Ligia Stroia, in 1966.

A happy, loving grandfather, with Alina and Dan Dusleag. Ilia, summer of 1966.

Stanciu Stroia with grandson Dan Dusleag, unseparable during vacations. On a walk in Pucioasa, December 1973.

Stanciu Stroia's daughter Lucia Dusleag, with husband Liviu, son Dan and daughter Alina. Bucharest, 1971.

REPUBLICA SOCIALISTA ROMANIA
Tribunalul Popular raional Ilia
      regiunea Hunedoara   Copie:
Dosar nr. 494/1966.

            S E N T I N Ț A   P E N A L A   Nr. 170/1966.-

            Ședința publică din 8 iunie 1966.
            Președinte   : Kalanyog Francisc, judecător.
            Asesor popular : Marig Cornel
                           : Bîrsoianu Remus
            Secretar   : Pele Maria
            Procuror   : Meteș Nicolae, procuror șef.
    Pe rol e fiind judecarea cererii de reabilitare introdusă la aceas
instanță de către numitul Stroia Stanciu.-

                - 3 -
Tribunalul Militar Sibiu.-
Fără cheltuieli de judecată.-
Cu recurs în termen de 10 zile de la pronunțare.-
Dată și citită în ședință publică din 8 iunie 1966.-
Președinte   Ases. populari   Secretar
ss Falanyog Francisc   ss Marig C.   ss Pele M.
                      ss Bîrsoianu R.
==

                Tribunalul Popular al Raionului Ilia
                Prezenta copie fiind conformă cu originalul ei se legalize
de noi fiind definitivă prin nerecurare.-
                Ilia la data de   23 iunie 1966
    secretar
    Alexandru Cioară

Legalized copy of the political and judicial rehabilitation document of Dr. Stanciu Stroia, dated June 8, 1966, nine years after his prison release.

The Heroes' Grave on the Merezi plateau, near Cacova, the site where seventy-five Romanian soldiers paid the ultimate sacrifice in 1916, during World War I.

The Heroes' Monument in Cacova, honoring the local men who fought and died during World Wars I and II.
Both structures were erected at the initiative, through the effort and with the funds collected by Dr. Stanciu Stroia.

Poster on a wall in downtown Bucharest in December 1989, depicting a man demanding liberty, only to have his mouth covered and his life threatened by the hammer and sickle, Communism's eternal symbols.

Dan Dusleag on the streets of Bucharest during the December 1989 anti-Communist revolution, holding his grandfather's 1930 Romanian flag in the right hand, and another—with the Communist emblem cut out in the center—in the left.

Consiliul Național pentru Studierea Arhivelor Securității

Colegiul
Gheorghe Onișoru, *Președinte*
Mihai Gheorghe, *Vicepreședinte*
Constantin Buchet, *Secretar*
Florian Chirițescu
Ladislau-Antoniu Csendes
Mircea Dinescu
Viorel-Mircea Nicolescu
Horia-Roman Patapievici
Andrei-Gabriel Pleșu
Aurel Pricu
Claudiu-Octavian Secașiu

Nr. 394 din 14.03.2002

Dnei LUCIA DUSLEAG

Stimată Doamnă,

    Vă aducem la cunoștință faptul că am primit cerea dumneavoastră de acces la dosarul domnului STROIA STANCIU.
    Până la preluarea integrală a arhivelor fostei Securități de la deținătorii actuali (S.R.I., S.I.E., S.A.M.), Colegiul Consiliului a demarat formalitățile de verificare solicitate prin cererea dumneavoastră.
    După primirea răspunsurilor de la cei trei deținători de fonduri de arhivă, provenind de la fosta Securitate, vă vom face cunoscut rezultatul cercetărilor.

Cu stimă,

PREȘEDINTE,
Conf. univ. dr. Gheorghe ONIȘORU

Reply from the "National Council for the Study of the Securitate Archives" in response to our family's 2002 request for access to Dr. Stanciu Stroia's previously classified file. The personal folder contained detailed documentation of his monitoring well into his retirement years.

EPILOGUE

Beyond my Father's Memories

My father wrote his memories a quarter of a century after his nearly seven years of detention in the terrible prisons of Sibiu, Jilava, Aiud and Făgăraș. Remembering the circumstances of arrest and details of imprisonment became an obsession for him throughout the years following his release.

For a long period of time, he remained hesitant to document the horrors he experienced in detention, knowing that the shadowy Securitate continued to monitor him. While reading what my father's hand had written, I was constantly under the impression that he felt an invisible presence looking over his shoulder. He revised his notes multiple times, wrote some additions, but in the end made no essential changes. And a lot of details not registered in his narrative are alive in our memory.

Through his remarkable personality, his stoicism in facing the harshness of Communist jails—so difficult to endure for the free spirit he was—and for the way in which he chose to live his years of freedom, *Tatamare*, (Grandpa), left an immense mark on his family. The decision to put his thoughts on paper was encouraged by his son-in-law, Dr. Liviu Dușleag, and the desire to publish them belongs to his grandson, Dr. Dan Dușleag, who worships the memory of his grandfather above anything else.

I attempted to organize the Romanian manuscript and accurately transcribe what my father had meant, respecting his style of writing in the process. As I fulfilled this mission, I relived parts of my own life, from the days in my native town of Făgăraș to Cacova, my father's village of birth so dear to him. I felt pain and grief but also joy brought by the moments of fulfillment that followed those dreadful years....

Toward the end of World War II, pieces of news and rumors from the social and political scene bombarded my adolescent ears. The atmosphere they portrayed was one of gloom. I vividly recall the evening in late 1947 when King Michael's forced abdication was announced on the radio. The reports—always wrapped in caution and mystery—of a student refugee from Basarabia whose father had been deported by the Soviets to Siberia, emerged afterward. I gradually started to understand his suffering and acknowledge his fear that the hordes from the East would overrun us all....

The world we were living in was shifting at an alarming speed toward another reality. I sensed a web of ill intentions engulfing my family. It soon became clear that our life in the ivory tower could not be sustained for much longer. We were forced to subsist in a lie. I remember the embarrassment I felt when, after twenty-four hours of intense studying, I landed second in a national school contest on the topic of "Soviet culture, the most advanced culture in the world." I was disturbed by the ridiculousness of the situation, knowing that my family was being persecuted as I was standing on that podium. Despite that performance, the imposed memorizing of meaningless phrases from Stalin or Lenin's school booklets was beyond my ability. Somehow, those readings always managed to surface in my nightmares.

Eventually, the inevitable took place. My father, the undesirable character, was ushered from the scene, and our family was left to endure whatever destiny still had in its plans. My 18-year-old mind recorded with extreme fidelity the events which followed my father's arrest and our forced exile. From the very beginning of the Communist dictatorship, his social status and esteemed personality had made him a *persona non grata*. This had not been the case with other families, able to continue their lives undisturbed by the change in regime and without having to openly declare their devotion to it.

I knew the three young men, my brother's colleagues, whom my father had helped unconditionally with my mother's, my grandmother's and my consent. I had always been happy to greet them during Christmas time, when they went from house to house singing carols. A delicate young man and talented poet in love at the time with a girlfriend of mine, Nicolae Mazilu was someone I admired in particular.

All of us understood the consequences of our act the moment we closed the door behind the men that fateful evening. Our concerns intensified after my father's first summoned trip to the Securitate headquarters. I recall his moments of hesitation followed by despair resulting from that encounter, when he appeared increasingly capable of a reckless gesture. The image of the tiny glass bottle filled with a deadly white powder remains vivid in my memory.

After my father's disappearance, we were forced to leave Făgăraș within twenty-four hours. We headed in a random direction even though, through the authorities' "goodwill," the evacuation time was extended to forty-eight hours. In Dridif, we were received with a kindheartedness that never faded over the years in the home of the Opriș family. We took refuge in their modest two-room farmhouse located right off the national road, seven kilometers south of Făgăraș. Aside from our hosts, the local notary, supportive as well, was the only other person we knew in town. By comparison, my father's former colleagues avoided us systematically, imprudent as it was to maintain a relationship with an outlawed family. There were a few exceptions, which I am happy to mention here together with the gratitude I still owe them.

My maternal grandfather's sister, dear aunt Simfora Purice, plagued by illness and living of her late husband's modest pension, showed toward us the compassion and generosity of an admirable soul.

Dr. Coriolan Pereni, a Făgăraș surgeon and former collaborator of my father was discreet but bighearted in his help. I felt protected by him and his family, and I continue to keep them in my prayers today.

Maria Ciora, the tall and slender teacher with expressive eyes and a perennial smile, was a bundle of energy. With a toddler held tightly in her arms, she rushed on the national road covering the few hundred meters distance from her house the evening we arrived. She did not know my mother, but offered her unconditional help in a spontaneous gesture of kindness, respect, and understanding.

Bebe Urdea, my brother's good old friend, was often the real rescuer. I recall him arriving from Făgăraş on his speedy bike with "substantial messages" from his parents, Mr. and Mrs. Captain Capătă, and from his aunt, consisting invariably of basic food items. With all the gratefulness, I wish I could hold this wonderful boy and his family in my arms once more.

After years of assisting with our household activities in Făgăraş and becoming an integral part of our family, Frosina and Joji Borzaş continued to visit us. On every return to my hometown, it was their house I chose to sleep at, before visiting relatives the next morning, especially those resting in peace under the white crosses of Făgăraş and Râuşor cemeteries.

My subsequent acceptance at the University of Cluj Medical School took place against all odds, with the aid of Clara Levi, the daughter of Făgăraş's Rabin, and Nicolae Popescu-Doreanu, the minister of education, who intervened on my behalf—the offspring of a political convict with the right academic credentials, but wrong social background. Later on, the university administrator, Petre Opriţoiu's firm refusal to accept the repeated proposals for my expulsion, allowed me to continue my studies.

My college years in Cluj were full of bitterness brought on by the thoughts of the father that I loved, who was in great suffering. I felt profound sadness mixed with fear of the uncertainty. During those years, my mother and grandmother desperately tried to cover my education expenses. I had no other financial help and was denied a scholarship. Cash required to eat at the school cafeteria was sparse and I lived off little packages scraped together and sent from home. And students are always so hungry....

The families of engineers Ioan Nedelcu and Gheorghe Brebenaru, Eliza and Ioan Rusu, Mrs. Gaia Litan, and my friend Viola Chihaia all became my adoptive parents and welcomed me in the warmth of their homes.

After years of frightening events and deprivations, my dear grandmother Letiţia Grama, fighting a chronic illness while sustaining my likewise sick mother, passed away in the spring of 1954.

I often wonder what my mother would have done, ailing and isolated in a strange village, without the solicitude of all the above mentioned human beings. Even if life's whirl has long taken them from this world, I remember them all with the deepest appreciation, one that also belongs to the few I might have forgotten, given memory's inherent deficiencies. These friends may not be among us now, but their descendants should be blessed for their parents' risk-defying behavior. Thanks to them, our family survived the years of my father's absence.

After his return to life, my father did for Cacova everything in his power during that dark period of our recent history. While fighting with today's hardships, the village priest Aurel Hărşan and his few parishioners are striving to keep the spiritual fire of that community alive, from which the forefathers and the heirs of Doctor Stroia inherit their vigor.

In the end, I confess that my soul never harbored feelings of resentment; it only sheltered the hope, strong as a conviction, that the intrinsic values in all of us will eventually bear fruit, compensating for the suffering of the past. I am slowly approaching the judgment day with a clear conscience, and I am pleased that my children have taken the initiative to restore the memory of my father, thereby passing his thoughts to his descendants.

Together with my children and the family of my brother, Zeno Stroia, we view these pages as homage to Dr. Stanciu Stroia and to that of my late husband, Dr. Liviu Duşleag.

Lucia Duşleag
Toronto, Canada, March 2005

LISTS OF POLITICAL DETAINEES

In Memoriam

The first in a series of three lists of political detainees includes more than eight hundred names of individuals from **Făgăraş County** and surrounding villages, arranged in alphabetical order, who were not afraid to say "NO!" to the Soviet occupation and Communist takeover of Romania. When challenged by history, these incorruptible spirits had the courage to speak out. The result was their arrest, imprisonment, or death at the hands of the Securitate during the state-sponsored purge that continued from 1945 to 1964.

The list is published for the first time in these pages, courtesy of History Professor Ioan Ciupea from the National Museum of Transylvanian History in Cluj, a specialist in the Romanian anti-Communist resistance. According to Professor Ciupea, the list consists of people representing the entire political spectrum of interwar Romania, as well as many individuals with no political activities or affiliations, such as Dr. Stanciu Stroia. The only experience common to this heterogenous group was the struggle more than half a century ago to oppose the imposing of the Communist plague on the Romanian nation.

Out of Romania's population of eighteen million people in 1945, half a million were imprisoned or deported during the Red Holocaust. That represented one incarcerated individual for every thirty-six "free" people, a relative notion for those living under dictatorship. Almost three percent of Romania's inhabitants were political detainees in the 1950s.

The reader should keep in mind that the eight hundred names of prisoners listed on the next pages are only the *known* ones, from *one* county out of Romania's forty-one. Făgăraş County consists of seventy communities, which means that each village had more than ten arrested subjects. Out of Râuşor (Valeria Stroia's birthplace) alone, a tiny rural community numbering 767 souls and 170 houses in 1956, thirty families (almost one in six) had loved ones who were detained. Unmentioned in the total number are the countless relatives and friends of the imprisoned who suffered various persecutions short of incarceration. This sad but proud record places Transylvania's Făgăraş County and its brave inhabitants at the center of the Romanian anti-Communist resistance.

The first list, which undoubtedly will suffer additions in the future, includes the name of Dr. Stanciu Stroia, as well as those of several people found in the pages of his memoir: Ioan Mogoş, Nicolaie Mazilu, and Silviu Socol, the three young men he helped; Emil Ţeposu, the urology professor who committed suicide rather than collaborate with the Securitate; Lae Greavu, the protagonist of the "Frightening Encounter" episode; Ion Roşca, the youngster from Râuşor; Gheorghe Bârsan, the Făgăraş Hospital administrator; Father Zosim Oancea, the leader of the improvised prison church; Gheorghe Bica, the witty peasant; the seven farmers, members of the "abortive group;" and Drs. Remus Doctor, Lucian Stanciu, and Vasile Munteanu.

Former partisans and authors Victor Ioan Pica, Virgil Mateiaş, and Gheorghe Urdea-Slătinaru, writer and freedom fighter Paul Goma, and former dissident Doina Cornea are on the list as well. Two dozen Hungarian, German, Jewish, and Slavic names can be identified, as can multiple situations of father-son concomitant imprisonment. Sixty-one women (representing nearly eight percent of the names) and three U.S.-born Romanians who returned to their families' country of origin after World War II complete the record. The latter group includes Jean Pop, a native of Detroit shot to death by the Securitate.

The list also includes a few distinguished individuals from counties surrounding Făgăraş. One is Ioan Stroia, born in 1902 in Cacova, who was a distant relative with considerable physical resemblance to Dr. Stanciu Stroia. A graduate of the Bucharest Commercial Academy, he managed the Sibiu branch of the Romanian National Bank and was an active member in the National Liberal Party. For his democratic views, he was incarcerated between 1952 and 1954 within the walls of Valea Neagră, Borzești, and Onești prisons. A similar fate awaited Mircea Dordea of Sibiu, an acquaintance of Dr. Stanciu Stroia, who was a successful attorney and a registered member of the other important interwar democratic organization, the National Peasant Party. During the same period, he was jailed at the Danube-Black Sea Canal, Borzești, and Onești. Both individuals were victims of the atrocious Communist campaign to eradicate the political opposition in post-World War II Romania.

Clergymen were also major targets of the Communist purge, and the first list of political detainees is not short of remarkable examples. In order to pay a small tribute to this courageous group, a brief parenthesis is necessary. It will tell the stories of two men and their fates, of which my family and I had direct knowledge.

Father Victor Dâmboiu was born in 1923 in Râușor, Făgăraș County, and was the godson of Dr. Stanciu Stroia. An Orthodox priest in the villages of Șinca Noua and Drăguș, he was arrested for blessing, providing advice, and accepting confessions from the region's anti-Communist mountain fighters. Together with other villagers, he supplied the partisans with food by leaving his cellar door unlocked and failing to report the missing items. That one of his brothers defected to the United States shortly after World War II complicated Father Dâmboiu's prospects. Following the familiar accusation of "plotting against the security of the Romanian state," he was arrested in 1957 and sentenced to ten years, of which he served seven in the prisons of Jilava, Galați, Făgăraș Castle, Pitești, Codlea, and Poarta Albă.

Released after the amnesty act of 1964, he returned to preaching in his native village of Râușor. When he was briefly authorized to leave the country in 1985 to visit his brother in Los Angeles, Father Dâmboiu began writing his prison memoirs on the ten-hour flight. It was the first time he recorded his thoughts on paper. Courtesy of Joe Dâmboiu, his brother, who has safeguarded the unpublished notes until today, I offer the reader a short excerpt:

"Planning my visit to the United States was not without difficulty. I had to be first interrogated by a Securitate man, a lieutenant by the name of Ioan Raț—at least that is how he introduced himself. I explained to him that I was an old man now, and that my brother Joe, his wife Paulina, and their daughter Elena just wanted to see me. After lengthy discussions, he promised he would approve my trip but warned that if I were not to come back, he would send an agent to kill me. That threat upset me tremendously, since defecting to America had never been in my thoughts. How could I have left my wife at an old age when we both needed each other? She had once waited almost eight years for me to return....

I thanked God and the Virgin Mary for granting me the happiness of seeing my brother and his family, after they had protected my wife and children while I was in prison and fed me when I was starving.... That happened while I was detained at Codlea Penitentiary. The period spent there was a torment; however, in order to avoid worse conditions, I never complained. I had been isolated in the same cell for over six months. It was early winter and the cell was unheated. I was not allowed to lie in bed during the day and had to stand up or sit on a hard wooden chair. When my swollen knees made walking impossible, I had to lie down on the bare cement. It was about five o'clock one morning. I was hungry and cold. Resting my head on the frozen heating pipe, I started to cry. 'Virgin Mary, I'm hungry and cold.' I began repeating those words a dozen times. My cry gradually turned into a baby's wail....

Then, all of a sudden, the little cell door window opened, and I saw the face of a militiaman. I had never seen that face before. He asked me what my profession was. 'I am a priest,' I replied. Then he asked me if I was hungry. 'Yes,' I answered. At once, he brought me a large slice of bread and told me to eat it all or give him back the leftover. 'You should not keep a piece of bread larger than your daily ration in the cell,' he cautioned.... Unexpectedly, I heard the sound of burning gas. Within half an hour, the cell heater was hot....

The new guard must have felt pity when he witnessed my suffering. For the entire two weeks he was on duty, I was fed and kept warm. God must have sent him my way and without his help, I might not have survived that day.... I thanked the Virgin Mary and ever since, I started to firmly believe in Her might....

I have learned the diabolic system of Communist punishment. The free world needs to know about it, too...."

Father Victor Dâmboiu passed away in 2003 at the age of 80. Next to his name, I am taking the liberty of adding another worthy Transylvanian clergy, an Orthodox priest as well and a native of an area bordering Făgăraş County.

Born in Mateiaş, Braşov County, in 1892, Father Alexandru Brotea was a Romanian Army veteran of World War I. Following decades of work in Rupea, he was accused by a parishioner in 1949 of "preaching against the Communist regime" and was imprisoned without a trial or a formal sentence. After a brief release from Gherla Penitentiary, he was swiftly re-incarcerated. Such had been his physical transformation during his prison time that upon his return home in 1953, his wife failed to recognize him. She mistook him for a burglar when he knocked at her door late at night. Having dropped in weight to one hundred pounds, he was a shadow of the man he had been. Nevertheless, his having been an athlete in his youth and his optimistic personality helped him survive.

Despite avoiding discussing the details of his nightmare, Father Brotea told his grandchildren one particular prison story. It happened while he was doing forced labor at the Danube-Black Sea Canal. Physically weak and mentally depressed, he was overcome by despair one early morning. However, when he walked toward the work site, he witnessed an incredibly beautiful sunrise. He read it as a divine sign that he should not lose his hope and faith in life.

Father Brotea was one of the fortunate survivors of the Danube-Black Sea Canal and lived to be 88. He died in Bucharest in 1980, and a few of his descendants immigrated to the United States in the early 1990s.

Besides the above recognizable names are the countless *nameless*, lost or temporarily forgotten, but *by no means powerless* individuals. Given the absence or disappearance of adequate official records, obtaining an *exact* account of the number and names of political prisoners during Romania's Communist reign is an impossible task. Similarly, the circumstances of arrest and subsequent ordeal have often remained registered only in the victims' memory. An enormous regret will thus persist for as long as all persecuted individuals are not correctly identified. Because, in the end, they all made their contribuition to the demise of Communism.

The names in the following list are not fictitious. Each person's place of birth or origin is noted in parenthesis. A few of the entries are incomplete (e.g., first name or city of origin is unknown) or inaccurate (two versions of the last name are given). An addendum in italics denotes that the individual was killed or died in prison. There are sixty-one such examples: Fifteen people were shot to death, forty-three died during detention, and one committed suicide.

The sources consulted by historian Ioan Ciupea in compiling this impressive record are acknowledged in the Romanian bibliography section with the † symbol.

Adămoiu Iacob, Adămoiu Nicolae (Sâmbăta de Sus), Albu Ieronim (Crihalma), Aldea Andrei (Berivoi), Aldea Octavian (Șinca Veche), Aldeailie Gheorghe (Netotu/Gura Văii), Alecu Gheorghe (Perșani), Andreiaș Ilie (Hârseni), Anghel Dumitru (Vaida Recea), Anghel Gheorghe (Americanu, Arpașu), Anghel Liviu (Feldioara), Apost A. Petru (Noul Român), Aron Clemente (Făgăraș), Aron Gheorghe (Râușor), Aron Ioan (Noul Român), Aroneasa Ion, Aroneasa Romul (Retiș/Cincu, *died in Gherla prison*), Aroneasa Otilia (Cincu/Brașov), Arsu Gheorghe (Râușor, *shot to death*), Badea Ion (Vad, *died in prison*), Balaban Ioan, Balaban Ilie, Balaban Octavian, Balaban Vasile (Toderița), Balaban Iancu (Toderița/Brașov), Balea Ion (Sărata), Balea Octavian (Luța), Balint Traian (Felmer), Banciu Aurel (Cârțișoara), Banciu Ilie (Cârțișoara/Iași/Brașov), Banciu Vasile (Noul Român), Barbu Eugen (Făgăraș), Barbu Gheorghe, Barbu Ion (Felmer), Barbu Ionel (Ileni), Barbu Iosif (Săsciori), Barbu Nica (Hurez), Barbu Toma (Ileni), Bardan Lazăr (Hurez), Baltă Moise (Rucăr/București), Băcilă Victor, Bălan Ioan (Făgăraș), Bălan Filimon (Șinca Veche), Bălan Teodor (Hârseni, *died in prison*), Bălescu Nichita (Viștea de Sus), Băluț Ioan (Calbor), Bănescu Nicolae (Șercaia/

București), Bărbat Alexandru (Ucea de Sus/Cluj/Brașov), Bărcuțean Ion, Bărcuțean Moise (Felmer), Bărdaș Candit, Bărdaș Ioan (Scorei), Bărdaș Ilarie (Râușor), Bârsan Alexe, Bârsan Puiu (Șinca Veche), Bârsan Gheorghe (Făgăraș), Bârsan Ion (Retiș), Bârsan Victor (Sâmbăta de Sus), Bebelea Ilie (Șercaia), Beleanu Nicolae (Cincu), Beleaua Aurel, Beleaua Cornel, Beleaua Elena, Beleaua Emilian, Beleaua Ghedeon, Beleaua Gheorghe, Beleaua Ioan, Beleaua Maria, Beleaua Matei (Berivoii Mici), Beleuță Valeriu (Mândra/Poiana Mărului), Beltram Iosif (Sebeș), Belu Cristea Lucian (Daneș/Voila), Bențe Constantin (București/Făgăraș), Bențea Aurel, Bențea Clement, Bențea Iosif (Hurez), Bera Gheorghe (Mândra), Bercea Rafira (Mândra/București), Berderaș Gheorghe (Crihalma), Berger Ioan (Bruiu/ Botoșani), Betea Nicolae (Făgăraș/București), Biliboacă Liviu (Voila), Blebea Cornel (Șinca Nouă), Blebea Emilian (Cuciulata/Brașov), Blebea Elena, Blebea Toma (Ileni), Bica Gheorghe (Cincul Mare/Voivodenii Mari/ Brașov), Birkner Andreas (Cincșor/Bratei), Boamfă Gheorghe, Boamfă Ion, Boamfă Sabin (Părău), Bobeș Constantin (Ucea de Jos), Boboia Gheorghe (Veneția de Jos), Boca Arsenie (Mănăstirea Sâmbăta), Boceanu Dumitru (Făgăraș), Boerescu Mircea (Radovanu-Ilfov/Făgăraș), Bogdan Gheorghe (Arpașu de Jos), Boier Dumitru (Perșani), Boier Iacob (Ohaba), Boier Ioan (Grid), Boier Victoria (Făgăraș), Boieru Ambrozie, Boieru Aurel (Vlad), Boieru Constantin (Toderița), Boieru Eftimie (Șona), Boieru Gheorghe (Șinca Veche), Boieru Ilie (Făgăraș), Bolovan Gheorghe (Sâmbăta de Jos), Bontea Grigore (Hălmeag/Sinaia), Borzea Gheorghe, Borzea Nicolae, Borzea Olimpiu, Borzea Pavel (Viștea de Jos), Boșteanu Nicolae (Viștea/ Brașov), Boșteanu Traian (Făgăraș, *died at the Danube-Black Sea Canal*), Boțoman Victor (Fântâna/Satu Nou/Brașov), Bozonea Ioan (Feldioara/Cluj), Brescan Ioan (Sâmbăta de Jos/Făgăraș), Broscățan Alexandru (Lisa), Brotea Alexandru (Mateiaș/Rupea-Brașov/București), Brudea Petre (Șoarș/ Petrești-Alba), Brumbea M. Romul (Făgăraș, *died at the Danube-Black Sea Canal*), Bucelea Ion, Bucelea Leon, Bucelea Gh. Vasile, Bucelea V. Vasile (Viștea de Jos, *died in prison*), Bucur Adam (Făgăraș), Bucur Dionisie (Crihalma), Budac Ioan (*died in Aiud prison*), Budac Remus (Cârța), Budac Vasile (Cârțișoara), Bulgăre Gheorghe (Iași/București), Buracu Coriolan, Buracu Mihai (Făgăraș/Caransebeș), Burlacu Nicolae (Făgăraș), Bursu Ioan

(Ucea de Sus), Buta Iacob, Buta Ion (Părău), Buta Gheorghe, Buzeche Ioan (Șona), Catană Ion (Lisa/Turnu Severin), Căbuz Gheorghe (Voivodeni), Călin Gheorghe, Călin Iacob (Ohaba), Călin Mihai (Șona), Călin Paraschiva (Șercăița), Căpățână Constantin (Porumbacu de Sus), Câcit Ioan (Cuculata), Câlția Corneliu, Câlția Doru, Câlția Moise (Șona), Câlția Vasile (Felmer), Cândea Ioan (Scorei, *shot to death*), Cânduleț Liviu or Silviu (Cârțișoara), Cârje Octavian (Olteț), Cârlig Ion, Cârlig Mihai (Basarabia/Hălmeag), Ceapă, Cerbu Andrei, Cerbu Ioan, Cerbu Valer (Părău), Cerbu Ieronim (Șercaia), Chichernea Ion (Grid), Chiujdea Ioan (Berivoii Mici, *died in Jilava prison*), Chiujdea Maria (Berivoii Mici), Ciobanu (Voivodeni), Ciocan Augustin, Ciocan Petru (Șercăița), Ciocea Florea (Făgăraș), Cioloboc (Făgăraș), Ciora (Făgăraș, *died in prison*), Cismaș Constantin (Porumbacu de Sus, *shot to death*), Ciulei Dumitru (Fântâna/Hârseni), Ciurilă Gheorghe, Ciurilă Ion (Grid), Clem Aron (Cuciulata), Clonța Eugen (Beclean/București), Coantă Damaschin (Comăna de Jos/București), Cocan Octavian (Sâmbăta de Sus/Făgăraș), Cocoradă Vasile (Boholț), Codrea Vichente (Drăguș), Coman Ioan (Ileni), Coman Ion (Berivoi), Coman Mircea (Făgăraș, *died in prison*), Comanici Alexandru, Comanici Alexe (Dridif), Comanici Dumitru, Comanici Nicolae (Veneția de Jos, *died in prison*), Comanici Octavian (Ludișor), Comanici Traian (Veneția de Jos/Constanța, *died in Văcărești prison*), Comănar Mircea, Comănar Octavian, Comănar Titus, Comănar Victor (four brothers from Făgăraș), Comardicea Gheorghe (Perșani), Comaromi Ioan, Comaroni Cornel (Ohaba), Comșa Constantin (Cincu), Comșa Dumitru (Cincu/Dumbrăveni), Comșa Aretia or Harieta (Copăcel/București), Comșa Gheorghe (Săsciori), Comșa Ioan (Galați), Comșa Nicolae (Sâmbăta de Sus), Comșa Virgil (U.S.A./Comăna), Comșulea Alexandru, Comșulea Aron, Comșulea Nicolae, Comșulea Tănase (Răușor/Cluj), Comșulea Vichente (Răușor), Cordea Gheorghe (Gura Văii), Cornea Doina (Ileni/Brașov/Cluj), Cornea Dorel, Cornea Dumitru (Ileni, *died in prison*), Cornea Gheorghe (Veneția de Jos/Târgu Mureș), Cornea Iacob (Făgăraș), Cornea Ioan (Ileni), Cornea Marcel (Șinca Veche, *shot to death*), Cornea Maria (Ileni), Cornea A. Valeria, Cornilă Șerban (Lisa), Corșatea Iacob, Corșatea Ilie, Corșatea Traian, Corșatea Virgil (Ileni), Cosgarea Emil (Făgăraș), Cosgarea Emil (Vlad), Cosma Partenie (Șona/Răușor), Cosma

Valeria (Șona/Râușor), Cotoros Matei (Hârseni), Crețu Tănase (Părău), Cristea Nicolae (Făgăraș), Cristea Petru (Pojorta), Cristea Vasile (Calbor), Cristian Aurel, Cristian Ion (Netotu), Cristian Ion (Viștea de Sus), Cristian I. Nicolae (Netotu), Cristian Marcel (Pojorta), Crișan Elena (Șinca Veche), Crișan Eugen (Făgăraș), Crișan Octavian (Șinca Veche), Cruțiu Cornel (Crihalma), Damian Ion (Sâmbăta de Jos), Dan Ioan (Mândra), Danciu Vasile (Noul Român), Dascălu Cornel (Arpașu de Jos), Dateș Nicolae (Netotu), David Ioan (Sărata/Scorei, *shot to death*), Dăneț Emilian (Vlad), Dâmboiu Victor (Râușor/Drăguș), Deac Cornel (Victoria), Dobrea Dumitru, Dobrea Spiridon (Sâmbăta de Sus), Dobrescu Aurel (Alba/Făgăraș/București), Dobrin Cornel (Bucium), Dobrin Ion, Dobrin Maria (Ohaba), Dobrin Victor (Arpașu de Jos), Doctor Remus (Brașov/Cluj/București), Dordea Mircea (Sibiu), Dragoș Gheorghe (Toderița/Râușor), Drăghici Horia (Făgăraș/București), Drăghici Mihai (Ludișor), Drăghici Sabin (Grid, *died in Gherla prison*), Drugă Gheorghe (Pojorta), Drugă Nicolae (Ludișor), Drugă Victor (Pojorta), Dumitru Constantin (Făgăraș), Duminică Ion (Aluniș/Olt/Făgăraș), Dușa Dumitru Junior (Toderița), Dușa Dumitru Senior (Toderița), Enache Nicolae (Cilibia/Făgăraș), Eșanu Alexe (Sâmbăta de Jos/Sibiu), Eșanu Hariton (Sâmbăta de Sus), Faina Elena, Faina Maria (Mărgineni), Făgărașan Iuliu (Ludișor), Făgărașan Savu (Drăguș), Fărcaș Ioan (Ileni), Fătu Aurel (Comana de Jos/Rupea), Fătu Victor (Ludișor/Brașov), Fățan Ion (Șomartin/Cluj), Fâciu Iancu, Fâciu Nicolae (Șercăița, *died in Gherla prison*), Fenechiu Ion (Șinca Nouă), Feriu Nicolae (Feldioara), Florea Dănila (Iași), Florea Gheorghe (Sâmbăta de Sus), Florea Ioan (Toderița), Florea Ioan (Iași), Florea Matei (Iași), Florea Victor (Sâmbăta de Sus), Florescu Octavian (Făgăraș), Flucuș Gheorghe, Flucuș Ion (Șinca Nouă), Fogoroș Gherasim, Fogoroș Liviu (Rucăr), Fogoroș Romulus (Drăguș), Frățilă Aurel (Viștea de Sus), Frâncu Alexandru (Porumbacu de Jos), Frâncu Nicolae (Porumbacu de Sus), Fulicea Alexandru (Mărgineni/Brașov), Fulicea Ion (Mărgineni, *died in Gherla prison*), Fulicea Tereza, Fulicea Victor, Fulicea Victoria (Mărgineni), Fulicea Virgil (Vaida Recea/Blaj/Cluj), Gabor Ioan (Toderița), Ganea Ion (Pojorta), Gavrilă Alexandru (Lisa), Gavrilă Ana, Gavrilă Gheorghe, Gavrilă Ion (Netotu), Gavrilă Ion (Cincu), Gavrilă Nicolae (Cincu), Gânscă Elisie (Făgăraș), Geamănu Victor

(Rucăr), Georgescu Ioan (Scorei/Blaj/Cisnădie), Gheran (București/ Victoria), Gherghel Gheorghe (Toarcla/Sibiu), Gheța Matei (București/ Făgăraș), Ghețea Vasile (Arpașu de Sus), Ghindea Ion (Viștea de Sus/ Drăguș, *died in prison*), Ghindea Nicolae (Ucea de Sus/Valea Chioarului), Ghindea Zaharia (Crihalma), Ghioarță Alexe (Mândra/București), Ghioarță Ioan (Mândra), Ghizdavu Dumitru, Ghizdavu Gheorghe, Ghizdavu Maria, Ghizdavu Simion (Ileni), Ghizdavu Iosif (Ileni/Sighișoara), Ghizdavu Simion (Ileni/Blaj), Giurcă Ioan (Făgăraș), Gligor Anica, Gligor Maria, Gligor Mircea (Sebeș), Glăjar Ioan (Ucea de Jos/Sibiu), Glăjar Ioan (Ucea/ Făgăraș), Goilă Ecaterina, Goilă Nicolae (Șinca Veche), Goma Paul (Basarabia/Făgăraș/Sibiu/București/Paris-France), Gorun Gheorghe (Viștea de Jos), Gorun Valeriu (Făgăraș), Govoran Gheorghe (Făgăraș), Göllner Ana, Göllner Georg, Göllner Susana (Jibert), Grama Matei (Toderița), Grancea Ioan (Sebeș), Grapă Antonie (Viștea de Sus), Gräef Mihai (Șoarș, *died in prison*), Greavu David, Greavu Ion (Lisa), Greavu Ion (Breaza), Greavu Ioniță (Noul Român), Greavu Lae/Nicolae (Olteț/Victoria), Grecu Dănilă (*died in prison*), Grecu Ioan (Copăcel), Grecu Ioan, Grecu Nicolae (Șoarș), Grigore Liviu (Veneția de Jos/Brașov), Grițu Gheorghe (Porumbacu de Sus), Grosu Gheorghe Gherasim (Hârseni/Constanța), Grosu Vasile (Ileni/Timișoara), Grovu David (Lisa), Grovu D. Emilian (Cârțișoara, *died in Aiud prison*), Grovu Maria (born Cârțan, Cârțișoara), Gubernat Rusalim (Comăna de Jos), Gugescu Nicolae (Odobești/Făgăraș), Guiman Avisalom, Guiman C. Gheorghe (Poiana Mărului), Guraliuc Vasile (Voloca/Cernăuți/ Victoria), Gurlea Ioan (Ucea de Jos), Gușeilă Gheorghe (Pojorta), Gușeilă Nicolae (Făgăraș), Györfy Dionisie (Sâmbăta de Sus/Petroșani, *died in Gherla prison*), Halmaghi I. Ioan (Arpașu de Sus), Halmaghi Emil (Bărcut), Halmaghi Gheorghe (Sâmbăta de Jos/Cârțișoara), Halmaghi Ioan (Veneția), Halmaghi I. Ioan (U.S.A./Lisa/Arpașu de Sus), Halmaghi Iosif (Hoghiz), Hampu Gheorghe (Scorei), Hanu Gheorghe, Hanu Toader, Hanu Victor (Gura Văii), Hașu Andrei (Pojorta, *shot to death*), Hașu Alexandru, Hașu Eugenia, Hașu Gheorghe (*died in Jilava prison*), Hașu Laurian (*died in Jilava prison*), Hașu Mărioara, Hașu Victoria (Trâmbițașu), Hașu Virgil (Breaza), Hașu Zenobia (Pojorta), Hațieganu Ion (Veza-Alba/Făgăraș, *died in Brașov prison*), Hârciogea Gheorghe (Hârseni), Helerea Ioan (Șomartin), Herseni

Aurel, Herseni Ilarie, Herseni Iosif (Hârseni, *died in Făgăraș Castle*), Herseni Traian (Iași/București), Horvath Denes (Grânari), Iancu Atanase (Rucăr), Iarca Ioan, Iarca Pavel (Făgăraș), Iaru Gheorghe, Iaru A. Ion, Iaru Matei, Iaru Traian (Netotu), Idomir Gheorghe, Idomir Maria, Idomir Ștefan (Ohaba), Ieșanu Ion (Sâmbăta de Sus), Ignat Viorel (Cincu), Ilioiu Ion Junior, Ilioiu Ion Senior (Sâmbăta de Sus), Ilina Eufrosina, Ilina Ioan (Cârța), Ioan Ilie (Voivodenii Mari), Ioanid Nicolae (Făgăraș), Ionașcu Moise (Șona/Făgăraș), Ionescu I. Cornel (Buzău/Făgăraș), Iordan Ion (Sebeș), Itoafă Gheorghe (Părău), Ivan Ion (Iași/București), Ivan Gheorghe (Iași, *died in prison*), Judele Valeriu (Veneția), Juncu Elena, Juncu Iacob (Râușor, *died in prison*), Ksutak Grigore (Făgăraș), Kondor or Kandor (Comăna), Lascu Ion (Cincu, *died in prison*), Lațcu or Lascu Ioan (Sibiu/Făgăraș), Lazăr Mara (Arpașu/Grid), Lazea Laurian, Lazea Vasile (Netotu), Leancu Aurel, Leancu Ion (Hurez/Merghindeal), Leabu Gheorghe (Gura Văii), Leluțiu Aurel (Olteț/Blaj), Leluțiu Ion (Olteț), Leluțiu Viorel (Rucăr), Literat Radu, Literat Valeriu, (Luța/Făgăraș), Ludu Mircea (Luța), Ludu Sorin (Făgăraș), Logrea Gheorghe (Rucăr), Luca Matei, Lungoci Dumitru (Recea), Lungoci Nicolae (Dridif), Lungoci N. Nicolae (Cergău-Alba/Bărcut), Lupi Ioan (Cârța), Lupu Aurel (Iași), Lupu Ion (Cincu), Lupu Zahiu (Iași), Macavei Cornel (Făgăraș), Maga Mihai, Maga Virgil (Berivoi), Maier Nicolae (Făgăraș), Major Ștefan (Mândra/Cluj), Malene Elisabeta, Malene Gheorghe (Porumbacu de Jos), Malene Ion (Boholț), Manciulea Petru, Manciulea Rusalim (Părău/Victoria), Manolescu Aristide (București/Șercaia), Manta Ioan (Hârseni), Manta Ioan (Copăcel/Cluj), Marcu Vichente (Râușor), Mare Sabin (Firiza/Făgăraș, *shot to death*), Mareș Ion (Iași), Mareș (Colun), Marhau Ion (Făgăraș), Marhau Nicolae (Galați), Marin Ion (Breaza), Matei Ion (Făgăraș), Matei Vasile (Ucea de Sus), Mateiaș Iosif, Mateiaș Virgil (Mândra/Făgăraș), Mateica Alios (Bucovina/Arpașu de Jos), Matieșanu Elena, Matieșanu Gheorghe (Viștea de Jos), Mazilu Nicolaie (Leu/Craiova/Făgăraș/Timișoara, *shot to death*), Măețiu Vichente (Feldioara, *died in Făgăraș Castle*), Măgureanu Vasile (Arpașu de Jos, *died in Gherla prison*), Mălin Nicolae (Ohaba), Mățău Victor (Perșani), Mândrea Titus, Mândrea Victor (Sâmbăta de Jos), Mânea Gavrilă (Copăcel), Mârza Pavel (Galtiu/Făgăraș), Metea Gavrilă, Metea Gheorghe (Ileni), Metea Octavian

(Ileni/Timișoara), Metea Remus, Metea Romulus (Făgăraș), Metea Toma (Râușor), Metea Victor (Ileni, *died in Jilava prison*), Micu Aurel, Micu Gheorghe (Săvăstreni), Mihai Aurel (Craiova/Făgăraș), Mihai Ieronim, Mihai Ion (Bărcut), Mihalache Constantin (Vaslui/Făgăraș), Mihăilă Gheorghe, Mihăilă Matei (Pojorta), Mija Cornel, Mija Vasile (Toderița), Milea Ioan (Vad, *died in Gherla prison*), Milea Ioan (Ileni), Milea Valer (Ileni), Miloșan Pandele (Dejani), Mitrea Vasile (București/Recea), Mitruț Ion (Râușor), Moga Matei (Bucium), Mogoș Ioan (Toderița, *shot to death*), Mogoș Marin (Cincu, *died in prison*), Moian Vasile (Viscri/Jibert), Moldovan Aurel, Moldovan Ariton (Pojorta), Moldovan Dumitru (Lisa, *died in prison*), Moldovan Ion (Vaida Recea), Moldovan Gheorghe Octavian (Șinca Veche), Moldovan Valeriu (Șinca Veche), Monea Ioan (Olteț), Monea Horațiu, Monea Traian (Veneția, *died in prison*), Moraru Gavrilă, Moraru Iancu (Ohaba), Moraru Ion (Fântâna), Moraru Nicolae, Moraru Traian (Ohaba), Moraru Traian (Făgăraș), Mosora (Colun), Motoc Aurel, Motoc Ioan (Săsciori), Motoc Ioan (Iași), Motoc Nicolae (Săsciori), Motoc Nicolae (Iași), Muntean Ion, Muntean Maria (Cincu), Muntean Vasile (Cincșor), Munteanu Gheorghe (Lisa), Munteanu Ioan, Munteanu Maria (Cincu), Munteanu Ion, Munteanu Iosif (Făgăraș), Munteanu Nicolae (Șinca Veche/București), Munteanu Petre (Făgăraș/București), Munteanu Octavian, Munteanu Vasile, Munteanu Vichente (Lisa), Mureșan Domnica, Mureșan Gheorghe, Mureșan Vasile (Dăișoara), Nanu Virgil (Arpaș), Nanu (Părău), Nastea Ilie (Șinca Nouă), Năftănăilă Ioan (Breaza), Neacșu Alexandru, Neacșu Aurel, Neacșu Nicolae (Fântâna), Neagoe Vasile (Viștea de Jos), Neagu Gheorghe (Sâmbăta de Sus), Neamțu Emil (Hurez), Neamțu Iulian (Hurez/Făgăraș), Negrea Simion (Pojorta), Nicapopii Victoria (Lisa), Nicoară Liviu (Rucăr), Niculici Ion (Cincu), Nistor Gheorghe (Porumbacu de Jos/Sibiu), Nistor Victor (Netotu), Nistor Vlase (Dejani), Noară Ioan (Tăbăcuț), Noară Gheorghe, Noară Nicolae (Părău), Norel Vichente (Toderița), Novac Gelu, (Făgăraș, *shot to death*), Novac Gema (Făgăraș), Novac Ioan (Berivoii Mici, *died in Jilava prison*), Novac Mihai (Șona/Făgăraș), Novac Aurel, Novac Aurelia, Novac Petru (Berivoi), Nuțu Dumitru, Nuțu Ioan, Nuțu Leonte (Perșani), Oană Clemente, Oană Ion (Cută), Oană Lascu, Oană Serafim, Oană Sofron (Părău), Oancea Ion, Oancea Nicolae, Oancea Victor, Oancea

Virgil (Breaza), Oancea Zosim (Alma/Sibiu/Sibiel-Sibiu district), Olea Aron (Mărgineni), Opriș Dumitru (Hurez), Opriș Gheorghe, Opriș Ioan, Opriș Nicolae (Dridif), Opriș (Făgăraș), Orlandea Ion (Cârțișoara), Ostăcioaia Gheorghe (Dolhasca/Breaza), Ovesea Gheorghe, Ovesea Ion (Veneția de Sus), Paler Nicolae, Paler Savu, Paler Silvia, Paler Șerban Ioan (Lisa), Pandele Ion (Calbor), Pandrea Clemente, Pandrea Vincențiu (Mărgineni/Cluj), Pandrea Vasile (Mărgineni), Pandrea Dumitru (Ucea de Sus), Pampu Gheorghe (Arpașu de Sus), Pascu Gheorghe, Pascu Ioan (Toarcla), Pasencu Dumitru (Ucea de Sus), Paștina Gheorghe (Porumbacu de Jos), Patrichi Vasile (Galați/Făgăraș), Păcurariu Serafim (Părău), Păiș Gheorghe (Toderița), Peptea Dănila, Peptea Gheorghe, Peptea Traian (Iași), Peptea Gheorghe (Vaida Recea), Pârvu Gheorghe, Petrașcu Gheorghe, Petrașcu Nicolae, Petrașcu Vasile (Sâmbăta de Sus), Petrișor Ion, Petrișor Nicolae (Recea), Pica Ioan Victor (Făgăraș), Pică Gh. Ion, Pică Valer (Râușor), Pieptea Ion (Iași), Pirău Toma (Ileni, *shot to death*), Pirău Toma (Râușor), Polexe Ion (Breaza), Pop Gavrilă (Lisa), Pop Gheorghe, Pop Ion (Râușor), Pop Jean (Detroit, U.S.A./Lisa, *shot to death*), Pop Oara (Lisa), Pop Valeriu (Copăcel), Pop Zaheu Junior, Pop Zaheu Senior (Râușor), Popa Aldi Ioan (Comăna de Jos/Făgăraș), Popa Emil (Făgăraș), Popa Gheorghe (Breaza), Popa Gheorghe (Șinca Veche/Suceava), Popa Gheorghe (Grid), Popa Grigore (Mândra), Popa Ioan (Arpașu de Sus), Popa Ioan (Vad/Sebeș Alba), Popa Iosif (Berivoii Mici), Popa Irodion (Grid), Popa Liviu (Făgăraș), Popa Moise (Lisa), Popa Nicolae (Netotu), Popa Nicolae (Netotu/București), Popa Nicolae (Șoarș), Popa Gh. Nicolae (București/Mărgineni), Popa Nistor (Comăna de Jos), Popa Octavian (Făgăraș), Popa Octavian (Făgăraș/București), Popa Pompei (Custelnic/Ucea), Popa Remus (Șinca Nouă/Constanța), Popa Romulus (Șinca Nouă/Luduș), Popa Ștefan (Hârseni/Sebeș), Popa Traian (Șinca Nouă/Sibiu), Popa Vichente (Drăguș), Popa Victor (Breaza), Popa Victoria (born Cordea, Netotu/Lisa), Popaiov Ioan, Popaiov Octavian (Sâmbăta de Sus), Poparad Andrei, Poparad Ion (Recea), Poparad Ion (Drăguș), Poparad Nicolae (Recea), Popescu Remus (Basarabia/Lisa), Popione Gheorghe, Popione Traian (Șinca Veche), Pralea Gh. Ioan (Breaza), Preda Ion, Pridon Ioan (Părău), Prună Gheorghe, Prună Roman (Șercaia), Puia Gheorghe, Purice Ion (Șoarș), Rad Ion (Lisa), Radeș

Gheorghe, Radeș Virgil (Berivoii Mici), Radocea Emil, Radocea Vichente, Radocea Virgil (Bucium), Radocea Nicolae, Radocea Virgil, Radocea Victoria, Radocea Viorica (Veneția de Jos), Raita Gheorghe (Șona), Raita Ioan (Săsciori), Ramba D. Gheorghe (Șotcan), Ramba I. Gheorghe, Ramba Z. Gheorghe (Voivodenii Mici), Ramba I. Ioan (Voila), Rațiu Eugen (Mândra), Rădulescu Albert (Porumbacu de Jos), Rădulef Victor (Berivoii Mari), Rânea V. Andrei (Hârseni), Rânea Emilian (Copăcel), Receanu Liviu (Dejani), Rogozea Solomon, Rogozea Viorel (Drăguș), Rohat Nicolae (Vaida Recea), Roibu Pavel (Mândra/Beclean), Roman Aurel (Ohaba), Roman Elisabeta (Mândra), Roman Gheorghe (Ohaba), Roman Gheorghe (Netotu), Roman Maria (Ohaba), Rosondai Avram (Hălmeag), Roșală Gheorghe (Părău/București), Roșală Iosif (Comăna de Jos), Roșca Constantin, Roșca Ion, Roșca Matei, Roșca Miron, Roșca Victor (Râușor), Roșca Gheorghe (Copăcel), Roșca Viorel (Făgăraș), Rosoiu Zenovia (Sâmbăta de Sus/Săsciori), Rozorea Virginia (Veneția de Jos/București), Rucăreanu Gheorghe (Pojorta), Rus Alexandru (Lisa), Sasebeș Ioan (Părău), Sasu Alexandru, Sasu Ioan (Hurez), Săbăduș Petru (Sânmărtin-Cluj/Făgăraș, *died in Gherla prison*), Scârneci Gheorghe (Jibert), Schitea Ioan (Avrig/Făgăraș), Schindler Andrei, Schindler Mihai (Șoars), Schlatner Eginald (Făgăraș), Schmidt Adolf (Făgăraș), Schmidt Gizela (Bocșa Montană/Făgăraș), Schuster Martin (Bruiu), Scorei Iuliu (Făgăraș), Serafim Elisie (Sărata, *died in Văcărești prison*), Silea Ion (Porumbacu de Sus), Sima Ion, Sima Victor (Mândra), Socaciu David, Socaciu Traian (Mândra), Socol Alexandru, Socol Aurel, Socol Eugenia, Socol Silviu (Berivoi, *shot to death*), Socol Virgil (Berivoii Mari), Sofonea Axente, Sofonea Gheorghe, Sofonea Remus (Drăguș, *shot to death*), Sofonea Solomon, Sofonea Vasile, Sofonea Victoria, Sofonea Viorica (Drăguș), Stan Ilie (Măciuca-Vâlcea/Făgăraș), Stanciu Ion, Stanciu Pompiliu (Viștea de Jos), Stanciu Nicolae (Viștea/Timișoara), Stanciu Viorel-Lucian, (Viștea de Jos, *died in prison*), Stanislav Axente (Lisa), Stephani Ioan (Ticușu Vechi), Stinghe Gheorghe (Brașov/Făgăraș), Stiniguță Alexandru (Făgăraș/Brașov), Stoia Ioan (Berivoii Mari/Baia Mare), Stoica Aurel (Veneția de Jos/Turda), Stoica Octavian (Arpașu de Jos/Sibiu), Stoica Pavel (Cârțișoara/Sibiu), Stoica Victor (Ticușu Nou/Veneția de Jos), Stoica Ion, Stoica Nicolae (Veneția de Jos), Stoica Pavel,

Stoica Victor, Stoica Virgil (Sărata), Stoichiță Ioan (Porumbacu de Jos/ Sibiu), Strâmbu Aurel (Făgăraș), Strâmbu Coriolan (Vad/Făgăraș), Strâmbu Eugen (Vad/Ploiești), Strâmbu Ștefan (Șinca Veche/Arad), Strâmbu Ion, Strâmbu Maria, Strâmbu Nicolae (Șinca Veche), Streza Gheorghe (Dridif/ Brașov), Streza Ioan (Copăcel), Streza Ilie (Copăcel), Streza Vasile, Streza Victor, Stroia Ioan (Cacova-Sibiu), **Stroia Stanciu (Cacova-Sibiu/Făgăraș/ Ilia/București)**, Stuparu Laurențiu (Făgăraș), Suciu Ionică (Făgăraș), Suciu Gheorghe, Suciu Nicolae (Cincu), Surdu Vasile (Olteț), Szabo Cocan Rozalia (Făgăraș/Breaza-Prahova), Szocs Gustav (Făgăraș/Sibiu), Șandru Victor (Viștea de Jos), Șerban Aurel (Copăcel/București), Șerban Cornel, Șerban Gheorghe (Lisa), Șerban Gheorghe (Voila), Șerban Ioan (Făgăraș/Voila), Șerban Maria (Lisa), Șerbănuță Emilia, Șerbănuță Petre (Șercăița), Șofariu Ion, Șofariu Nicolae (Viștea de Jos), Șofariu Victor (Olteț), Șofletea David (Recea), Șoltea Ion (Perșani), Șotcan Virgil (Șoarș), Știrbu Tiberiu (București/Ucea), Șulea Iacob (Părău), Șuler Virgil (Berivoii Mici), Șuvăilă Cornel, Șuvăilă Ilie (Berivoii Mici), Șuvăilă Gheorghe (Berivoii Mici, *shot to death*), Taflan Vasile (Făgăraș), Teodorescu Gheorghe (Cincșor), Teodoru Valeriu (Făgăraș/București), Toader Ion Junior, Toader Ion Senior (Colun), Toader Gheorghe (Galați, *died in Gherla prison*), Toma Ioan (Toderița), Tomuta Octavian (Făgăraș/București), Trandafir Nicolae (Arpașul de Jos), Trâmbițaș Ion (Netotu, *died in prison*), Trâmbițaș Nicolae, Trâmbițaș Cornelia (Beclean), Tretiu Pavel (Șinca Nouă), Trifan Constantin (Buzău/ Făgăraș), Trif Elena (Jidvei-Alba/Șercăița), Țenghea Ioan (Făgăraș/Victoria), Țeposu Aurel (Sărata/Constanța), Țeposu Emil (Comăna/Cluj, *comitted suicide in 1948*), Țeposu Ion (Sărata/Porumbacu), Țepuș Iosif (Ohaba), Țețu Aurel, Țețu Ioan (Săsciori), Țețu Aurel (Hurez), Țețu Constantin (București/ Berivoii Mari), Țețu Dorel, Țețu Ion (Hurez), Țețu (Corbi), Țipu Ștefan (Hurez), Udroiu Constantin (București/Victoria), Urdea Firon (Șona), Urdea-Slătinaru Gheorghe, Urdea-Slătinaru Silvia (Părău), Urs Nicolae, Urs Samoilă (Șinca Veche), Ursu Corneliu Mircea (Făgăraș), Ursu Ioan (Noul Săsesc/Dridif), Ursu Romulus (Făgăraș, *died in Văcărești prison*), Ursu Romulus Victor (Făgăraș, *died in prison*), Ursu Traian (Rucăr/Făgăraș), Ursu Victor (Bucium/Cluj), Vanga Gheorghe (Hurez), Vasilescu Ion (Argetoaia/ Făgăraș), Vanga Traian (Hurez), Vasu Mircea (Făgăraș/Brașov), Vasu Viorel

(Arpașu/Uricani), Văcaru Iosif, Văcaru Vasile (Lisa), Vlad Cornel, Vlad Octavian, Vlad Valer (Toderița), Vlad Victor (Ucea de Sus/Cermei), Văcaru Alexandru, Văcaru Vasile (Lisa), Vâjeu Carmina, Vâjeu Zoe (Făgăraș), Vâja Ion (Făgăraș), Vijoli Aurel (Făgăraș/București), Vijoli Ioan (Netotu/ Făgăraș), Vintilă Gheorghe (Hălmeag/Brașov), Voilă Viorel (Ucea de Sus), Voilean Dragomir (Șoarș/Făgăraș), Voineag Aurel (Porumbacu de Sus/ Zărnești), Voineag Ioan, Voineag Vasile (Porumbacu de Sus), Vulcu Constantin, Vulcu Ion, Vulcu Virgil (Breaza), Vulcu Vlad (Viștea de Sus), Wagner Michael, Wagner Nicolae (Jibert), Wagner (Făgăraș), Wonner Friederick (Cârța), Zaharia Iacob (Hurez), Zamer Iohann (Bruiu), Zară Ilie, Zară Maria, Zară Nicolae (Mândra), Zăgan Ioan (Făgăraș), Zăgan Ioan (Vaida Recea), Zăgan Vichente (Beclean), Zdrăilă Gheorghina, Zdrăilă Petru (Șercăița), Zikeli Ioan (Bruiu) and many, many others....

In addition to the above list, Ioan Ciupea—together with Professor Florentin Olteanu, Dr. Andrea Dobeș-Fürtős, and Robert Fürtős—has been researching the recent history of the **Făgăraș Castle**, the imposing medieval fortress misused as a Communist prison during the period of September 1950 to February 1960. Throughout that decade, nearly 5,000 political detainees (including Dr. Stanciu Stroia) were housed there. Many were Romanian Army members and civil servants from the former, pre-Communist justice and police institutions, hence the nickname *Închisoarea Polițiștilor,* ("policemen prison") given to the facility. Făgăraș Castle became the graveyard of Romanian democracy.

At least 165 political detainees found their death within the castle's walls. Their names are presented for the first time to the readers of this book:

Achim Victor, Aldea Alexandru, Anghel Ilie, Anghel Vasile, Arghir Constantin, Axente Dumitru, Bălan Nicolae, Bălosu Romul, Băncila-Picu Nicolae, Bărbulescu Dumitru, Bărdescu Titus, Berleanu Ioan, Blujdescu Nicolae, Bora Sever, Botezatu Teodor, Ceapă Panait, Cernăianu Florentin, Chirilă Ștefan, Chișinschi Sergiu, Ciobanu Petre, Ciorăscu Tache, Cârdei Ștefan, Cocea Scarlat, Cocora Ștefan, Codica Dobrea, Colomițchi Ioan,

Constantinescu Alexandru, Constantinescu Dumitru, Constantinescu Gheorghe, Constantinescu Ioan, Constantinescu Telemac, Costescu Haralambie, Crăciun Dumitru, Crețu Constantin, Cristescu Florian, Danciu Iosif, Diaconescu Bondoc-Teodor, Dracea Iacob, Dragomirescu Anghel, Drăgoi Nicolae, Duca I. Constantin, Duma Aurel, Dumitrescu Ioan, Dumitrescu Teodor, Dumitriu Haralambie, Dure Ilie, Fehervari Matei, Florea Emilian, Florescu Mircea, Frâncu Aurel, Gheorghiu Casian, Gheorghiu Ioan, Gheorghiu Nicolae, Ghișoiu Ioan, Golstein Isac, Grosu Vasile, Groza Ioan, Gute Ioan, Haiduc Ioan, Henzel Simion, Hera Ioan, Herlea Liviu, Herseni Iosif, Horeanu Constantin, Husărescu Zaharia, Iancu Dumitru, Iancu Gheorghe, Iani Vasile, Ioan Constantin, Ionescu Gheorghe, Ionescu Simion, Ionescu Victor, Ioniță Ilie, Ioniță Petre, Iordan Ștefan, Leoveanu Emanoil, Liteanu Gheorghe, Lucaciuc Constantin, Lupuțiu Aurel, Maghiar Augustin, Mailatescu Florian, Malamuceanu Gheorghe, Manolescu Alexandru, Manolescu Ferand, Matyas Iosif, Măețiu Vichente, Michiu Dobre, Mihăilescu Ștefan, Modoc Vasile, Moraru Dumitru, Moravec Nicolae, Motaș Gheorghe, Murgău Liviu, Muscu Nicolae, Năsărâmbă Gheorghe, Neacșu Constantin, Nedelcu Dumitru, Nicolau Filip, Nuță Dumitru, Olărașu Gheorghe, Orendi Ioan, Pangrațiu Aurel, Para Dumitru, Păpușoi Teodosie, Pâinișoara Ilie, Pârvulescu Iulian, Perghel Constantin, Periețeanu Alexandru, Petricioiu Florea, Pintilie Ilie, Pipernea Bucur, Pisoschi Petru, Popescu Gheorghe, Popescu Marin, Popescu Marius, Popescu Teodor, Popescu Vasile, Popescu Victor, Popovici Ștefan, Porumboiu Mihail, Predescu Gheorghe, Prodan Dumitru, Rațiu Alexandru, Rădulescu Dumitru, Rădulescu Ioan, Rățescu Ioan, Recea Ioan, Reinhardt Iosif, Râmniceanu Titi, Rodivoevici Gheorghe, Rotaru Minu, Rotaru Teodor, Rotman Iancu, Sfetcovici Teodor, Sfetescu Tudor, Silvășan Pantilimon, Simion Gheorghe, Son Aurel, Spanoche Sandu, Spuderca Nicolae, Stipor Aurelian, Suflețelu Emil, Susan Ioan, Ștefănescu Anton, Ștefu Traian, Tabără Nicolae, Teodorescu Alexandru, Timoftei Nicolae, Todirașcu Gheorghe, Tofan Gheorghe, Toma Gheorghe, Triteanu Ioan, Trișcu Alexandru, Turculeț Dumitru, Țibuleac Traian, Țiclete Pavel, Țipa Gheorghe, Țârea Gheorghe, Udrea Ștefan, Vasilescu Dumitru, Vintilă Dumitru, Vițianu Iacob, Zerves Iosif, Zenici Mihai, Zorzor Vasile.

When the Făgăraș Castle was abandoned in 1960, 460 detainees were transferred to **Gherla Penitentiary,** where 40 more perished until the amnesty act of 1964. Another 300 former castle occupants died in prisons throughout the country and the Soviet gulags they were relocated to in 1960. These patriots may have lost their lives, but their generous sacrifice was not in vain; it is remembered and cherished. Here are the names of the victims from Gherla:

Anagnastopol Nicolae, Ananiu Gheorghe, Andronic Benone, Anghelescu Radu, Ariton Virgil, Bălan Teodor, Bejan Viaceslav, Bobonea Ioan, Braha Aurel, Brândușescu Cristache, Cărăruș Vasile, Cernat Constantin, Coropiță Marin, Eftimie Vasile, Florea Alexandru, Gheorghiu Dumitru, Grigore Marin, Iagolnița Emil, Ioja Ioan, Ionescu Dinicu, Ivănescu Petre, Lenguceanu Alexis, Leon Nicolae, Maimuca Constantin, Mateescu Alexandru, Nemeș Ioan, Petcov Teodor, Pihăl Ioan, Popescu Nicolae, Potorac Vasile, Râșnoveanu Nicolae, Roșioru Panait, Slavu Ilie, Ștefănescu Nicolae, Todor Toma, Varabiev Nicolae, Voinicu Petre.

The life paths of many other people at odds with the Communist regime intersected with mine while I was growing up in **Bucharest.** I can only enumerate the names I can still recall from my childhood memory, along with some details of their fate, as further proof of the indiscriminate Communist terror.

Aunt Ana Boițeanu, wife of Spiru Boițeanu, the former administrator of the Royal Fishery and brother of a retired Royal Army general, is the first name that comes to my mind. She belonged to the previous, now deposed "high society," which was connected to the exiled royal family so incessantly targeted by the Communists. Forced to share her private apartment with another family, Ana was denounced by her new neighbors for making "inadmissible anti-Communist remarks" during a women's tea party. A listening device carefully implanted in her telephone receiver provided further proof of her "plotting against the Communist regime." Listening to Radio Free Europe proved to be the ultimate crime and the final straw.

She was 53 years old at the time of her arrest and was sentenced to four years of political imprisonment, which she served at Jilava between 1959 and 1963. A bright and elegant woman, Ana Boițeanu became an integral part of our family life after she was freed. She passed away in 1984 at the age of 78.

While in prison, Ana befriended Elena Rafael, a former chemist at Cantacuzino Institute who had been apprehended after she performed laboratory analysis on ill and injured anti-Communist partisans, including legendary freedom fighter Elisabeta Rizea. Elena spent six years at Jilava and Aiud, between 1956 and 1962. She died in 1987.

Also worth mentioning is the story of Alexandru Ionescu, who endured almost eighteen years of incarceration, spanning his entire adult life. After he was arrested and released in the late 1940s, he was re-detained from 1952 to 1958 following an accusation of "plotting against the security of the Romanian state." Allowed a couple of months of freedom in mid-1958, Ionescu was jailed again between 1958 and 1964 as a result of his perceived "anti-Soviet attitude." A former resident of nearly a dozen different prisons, including Bucharest-Rahovei, Jilava, Aiud, Gherla, Botoșani, and Câmpulung-Moldovenesc, Alexandru Ionescu somehow managed to survive and still be in reasonable health in 2004, at the age of 87.

Finally, I remember witty Achile Milas, a Romanian of Greek ancestry, whose inoffensive political jokes during a bridge game with acquaintances landed him in jail for more than two years, and Nicolae Mitulescu, a geologist, good family friend, and superb photographer, who suffered a similar fate....

Scenarios such as those continued throughout that age of horror....

As descendants of Dr. Stanciu Stroia and all listed or forgotten anti-Communists, we have the moral obligation to perpetuate their memory and learn from their harsh destiny.

May this never happen again!

BIBLIOGRAPHY WITH EXCERPTS

In English

References were obtained from the following bibliography as well as from many articles, both printed and in electronic format (e.g., from The World Encyclopedia and Wikipedia/The Free Encyclopedia). A few titles were included as an open invitation for the reader to review them. No attempt has been made to cite all sources consulted, since such a list would be unfeasible.

Andreescu, Ştefan. *A Little-Known Issue in the History of Romania: The Armed Anti-Communist Resistance.* Bucharest, Romania: Editura Academiei Române, 1994.
Antal, Dan. *Out of Romania.* London: Faber and Faber Ltd, 1994.
Black, Jeremy. *World History.* Bath, England: Parragon Publishing, 2003.
Boia, Lucian. *Romania: Borderland of Europe.* London: Reaktion Books Ltd, 2001.
Bragin, Irina Eremia. *Subterranean Towers: A Father-Daughter Story.* Lincoln, NE: iUniverse, Inc. 2004.
Burford, Tim. *Hicking Guide to Romania.* Old Saybrook, CT: The Globe Pequot Press Inc., 1996.
Cayne Bernard S. & Lechner, Doris E. *Webster's Dictionary: The New Lexicon of the English Language.* New York: Lexicon Publications, Inc., 1990.
Chin, Mel, Huerta, Benito & Lippard, Lucy R. *Inescapable Histories.* Mid-America Arts Alliance, 1997.
Clark, Charles Upson. *United Romania.* New York: Dodd & Mead, 1932.
Codrescu, Andrei. *The Disappearance of the Outside.* Reading, MA: Addison-Wesley Publishing Company, Inc., 1991.

Codrescu, Andrei. *The Hole in the Flag: A Romanian Exile's Story of Return and Revolution.* New York: William Morrow and Company, Inc., 1991.

Constante, Lena. *The Silent Escape: Three Thousand Days in Romanian Prisons.* Berkeley & Los Angeles: University of California Press, 1995.

Deletant, Dennis. *Communist Terror in Romania: Gheorghiu-Dej and the Police State, 1948–1965.* New York: St. Martin's Press, 2000.

Drakulic, Slavenka. *How We Survived Communism and Even Laughed.* New York: HarperPerennial, 1993.

Fitzpatrick, Sheila. *Everyday Stalinism: Ordinary Life in Extraordinary Times.* New York: Oxford University Press, 1999.

Georgescu, Adriana. *In the Beginning Was the End.* București, România: Memoria Cultural Foundation/The Aspera Educational Foundation, 2003.

Gerolymatos, Andre. *The Balkan Wars.* New York: Basic Books, 2002.

Grun, Bernard. *The Timetables of History: The New Third Revised Edition.* New York: Simon & Schuster/Touchstone, 1991.

Hitchins, Keith. *A Nation Affirmed: The Romanian National Movement in Transylvania, 1860–1914.* Bucharest, Romania: The Encyclopaedic Publishing House, 1999.

Hitchins, Keith. *Rumania: 1866–1947 (Oxford History of Modern Europe).* New York: Oxford University Press, 1994.

Hochschild, Adam. *The Unquiet Ghost: Russians Remember Stalin.* New York: First Mariner Books, 2003.

Hupchick, Dennis. *The Balkans: From Constantinople to Communism.* New York: Palgrave MacMillan, 2002.

Hupchick, Dennis P. & Cox, Harold E. *The Palgrave Concise Historical Atlas of Eastern Europe.* New York: Palgrave, 2001.

Kaplan, Robert D. *Balkan Ghosts: A Journey through History.* New York: St. Martin's Press, 1993.

Keefe, Eugene K. *Romania: A Country Study.* Washington, D.C.: U.S. Government Printing Office, 1979.

Kellogg, Frederick. *The Road to Romanian Independence.* West Lafayette, IN: Purdue University Press, 1995.

Khlevniuk, Oleg V. & Conquest, Robert. *The History of the Gulag: From Collectivization to the Great Terror.* New Haven & London: Yale University Press, 2004.

Klein, Shelley. *The Most Evil Dictators in History.* New York: Barnes & Noble, Inc., 2004.

Klepper, Nicolae. *Romania: An Illustrated History.* New York: Hippocrene Books, Inc., 2002.

Klepper, Nicolae. *Taste of Romania.* New York: Hippocrene Books, Inc., 1997.

Kligman, Gail. *The Politics of Duplicity: Controlling Reproduction in Ceaușescu's Romania.* Los Angeles: University of California Press, 1998.

Lerner, Harry Jonas. *Romania in Pictures: Visual Geography Series.* Minneapolis: Lerner Publications Co., 1993

Miller, Francis Trevelyan. *The Complete History of World War II.* Armed Services Memorial Edition, 1945.

Miroiu, Mihai. *Romanian Dictionary & Phrasebook.* New York: Hippocrene Books Inc., 2002.

Murphy, Dervla. *Transylvania & Beyond.* Woodstock, N.Y.: The Overlook Press, 1993.

Nelson, W.E., Behrman, R.E., Kliegman, R.M. & Arvin, A.M. *Nelson Textbook of Pediatrics, 15th Edition.* Philadelphia, PA: W.B. Saunders Company, 1996.

Octavian, Tudor & Georgescu, Mihai Petru. *Interbellum Bucharest: Victoria Avenue.* Bucharest, Romania: Noi Media Print, 2004.

Orwell, George. *Animal Farm.* Introduction by C. M. Woodhouse. New York: Signet Classic, 1972.

Orwell, George. *1984.* Afterword by Erich Fromm. New York: Signet Classic, 1992.

Pacepa, Ion Mihai. *Red Horizons: The True Story of Nicolae & Elena Ceaușescu's Crimes, Lifestyle, and Corruption.* Washington D.C.: Regnery Gateway, 1990.

Rady, Martyn. *Romania in Turmoil.* London: I.B.Tauris & Co Ltd Publishers, 1992.

Richardson, Dan & Burford, Tim. *Romania: The Rough Guide.* London: Rough Guides Ltd, 1995.

Rotshild, Joseph. *East Central Europe between the Two World Wars, vol. IX.* Seattle: University of Washington Press, 1974.

Tismăneanu, Vladimir. *Stalinism for All Seasons: A Political History of Romanian Communism.* Berkeley & Los Angeles: University of California Press, 2003.

Toma E., Iorga F., Toropal C., Munteanu D. & Decea L. *Romania.* Bucharest, Romania: Ministry of Public Information, 2001.

Walters, Garrison E. *The Other Europe: Eastern Europe to 1945.* New York: Syracuse University Press, 1998.

Williams, Nicola. *Romania & Moldova: From Tarzan's Birthplace to Ovid's Grave.* Hawthorn, Australia: Lonely Planet Publications, 1998.

Wood, Neal. *Tyranny in America: Capitalism and National Decay.* London/ New York: Verso, 2004.

In Romanian

Antohe, Ion. *Răstigniri în România după Ialta.* București, România: Editura Albatros, 1995. 1

Atanasiu, Victor. *Bătălia din Zona Sibiu-Câneni: Septembrie 1916.* București, România: Editura Militară, 1982. 2

Bărbulescu, M., Deletant, D., Hitchins, K., Papacostea, S. & Teodor, P. *Istoria României.* București, România: Editura Enciclopedică, 1998.

Blănaru-Flamură, V. *804 Zile și Nopți in Lanțurile Morții: O Trecere Sângeroasă prin Temnițele Infernului Comunist ca Osândit la Pedeapsa Capitală.* București, România: Editura Sepco S.R.L.

Bota, Ioan & Ionițoiu, Cicerone. *Martiri și Mărturisitori ai Bisericii din România (1948–1989): Biserica Romano-Catolică, Biserica Greco-Catolică.* România: Editura Patmos, 1998. †

Cesianu, Constantin. *Salvat Din Infern.* București, România: Editura Humanitas, 1992.

Ciupea, Ioan, Olteanu, Florentin, Dobeș-Fürtös, Andrea & Fürtös, Robert. *Cetatea Făgărașului: Închisoarea Polițiștilor (1950–1960)*. România, due for publication in 2005. 3

Ciupea, Ioan & Virgiliu Țârău. *Universitari Clujeni în Viața Politică*. România, due for publication in 2006. 4

Constantiniu, Florin. *O Istorie Sinceră a Poporului Român*. București, România: Univers Enciclopedic, 2002.

Dumbrăveanu, Gheorghe. *Piața Universității*. București, România: Imprimeria Coresi, 1991.

Eșan, Ioan. *Vulturii Carpaților: Rezistența Armată Anticomunistă din Munții Făgăraș, 1948–1958*. Făgăraș, România: Editura RAR, 1993. †

Gavrilă-Ogoranu, Ion. *Brazii Se Frîng, Dar Nu Se Îndoiesc Vol I-III*. Timișoara, România: Editura Marineasa, 1995 and 1997. 5 †

Gavrilă-Ogoranu, Ion. *Brazii Se Frîng, Dar Nu Se Îndoiesc Vol IV: Documente din Arhiva Securității*. Făgăraș, România: Editura Mesagerul de Făgăraș, 2004. 5

Georgescu, Adriana. *La Început A Fost Sfârșitul: Dictatura Roșie la București*. București, România: Editura Humanitas, 1992.

Gheorghe, Christache & Tucă, Florian. *Altarele Eroilor Neamului: Monumente si Însemne Memoriale în Aria de Trăire Românească*. București, România: Editura Europa Nova, 1994. 6

Grigorescu, Ioan. *Bine ați Venit în Infern*. București, România: Editura Nemira & Co., 1994.

Hanzu, Ioan Jr. & Mogoș, Simion & Brote, Nicolae & Hărșan, Aurel. *Cartea de Aur a Satului Cacova/Fântânele*. Sibiu, Romania: Parohia Ortodoxă Romănă, 1998. 7

Hațieganu, Iuliu și colaboratori. *Douăzeci de Ani de Activitate Românească in Clinica Medicală I din Cluj: 1919–1940*. Sibiu, România: Tipografia "Cartea Românească din Cluj," 1941. 8

Ionițoiu, Cicerone. *Cartea de Aur a Rezistenței Românești Împotriva Comunismului: Vol I-III*. București, România: Imprimeria Hrisovul/ Microhart, 1995, 1996, 1998. 9

Ionițoiu, Cicerone. *Rezistența Armată Anticomunistă din Munții României: 1946–1958.* București, România: Editura Gîndirea Românească, 1993.

Ionițoiu, Cicerone. *Victimele Terorii Comuniste: Arestați, Torturați, Întemnițați, Uciși.* București, România: Editura Mașina de Scris, 2000–2004. †

Levițchi, Leon. *Dicționar Român-Englez Editia a II-a.* Bucuresti, România: Editura Științifică, 1965.

Manea, Vasile & Ionițoiu, Cicerone. *Martiri și Mărturisitori ai Bisericii din România (1948–1989): Biserica Ortodoxă.* România: Editura Patmos, 1998. †

Marin, Florea. *Iuliu Hațieganu: Monografie.* Cluj-Napoca, România: Editura Medicală Universitară "Iuliu Hațieganu", 1999. 10

Mateiaș, Virgil. *Anii de Groază din România Comunistă-Mărturii. Existența Tragică-Însemnări. Testament.* România: fără editură, după 1990. †

Nandriș-Cudla, Anița. *20 de Ani în Siberia: Destin Bucovinean.* București, România: Humanitas, 1991.

Oancea, Zosim. *Închisorile Unui Preot Ortodox.* București, România: Editura Christiana, 2004. 11

Păcurariu, Mircea. *Cărturari Sibieni de Altădată.* Cluj-Napoca, România: Editura Dacia, 2002. 12

Pica, Victor Ioan. *Libertatea are Chipul lui Dumnezeu.* Sebeș-Petrești, România: Editura Arhipelag, 1993. 13 †

Radina, Remus. *Testamentul din Morgă.* București, România: Editura Tinerama, 1991.

Steinhardt, N. *Jurnalul Fericirii.* Cluj-Napoca, România: Editura Dacia, 1992.

Știrbu, Ion. *Moara de Vise: Însemnări din Viața unui Dascăl.* București, România: Editura Viitorul Românesc, 2002.

Tucă, Florian & Cociu, Mircea & Chirea F. *Bărbați ai Datoriei 1877–1878: Mic Dicționar.* București, România: Editura Militară, 1979.

Urdea-Slătinaru, Gheorghe. *Între Speranță și Moarte.* București, România: Memoria-Revista Gândirii Arestate nr. 9, 1993, p. 79–85. †

Excerpts

The following pages include thirteen brief quotations, translated from Romanian, that contain references to Dr. Stanciu Stroia. They are from eleven books in print and two soon-to-be-published, all of which are listed in the above Romanian bibliography.

1 Former political detainee Ion Antohe describes the following prison scene involving Dr. Stanciu Stroia, on pages 335–336 of his memoir titled *Crucifying in Romania after the Yalta Treaty*:
"Among the convicts working at the Aiud factory [in 1954] were two intellectuals from Transylvania, of similar age, both around [fifty]. They were frequently seen together and had the distinguished appearance of two Roman senators.

One of them was Dr. Stanciu Stroia, an internist from Făgăraș, who enjoyed a good reputation, especially among his former patients. A kindhearted personality, he was friendly toward everybody, and always found the patience to listen with genuine concern to the sufferings of confessing inmates. The other man was Engineer Mircea Ionescu from Brașov. They belonged to the same batch of prisoners and had known each other for a long time. Their involved conversations carried on even during lunch breaks.

One day, I noticed Dr. Stroia looking quite dejected. I suspected that something terrible had happened. As I joined him at the lunch table, he explained—without me asking—the reason for his sorrow. The previous night, his good old friend, the engineer, had died of a heart attack. [It was June 21, 1954.] Every prisoner who had known the man was very affected by the news, given that Ionescu's kindness had won him only friends. A day of mourning followed for all of us...."

2 Colonel Dr. Victor Atanasiu, author of the World War I historical book entitled *The Battle of Sibiu-Cîineni: September 1916*, generously acknowledged in his foreword, on pages 9–10:

"I wish to thank through these pages [...] Doctor Stanciu Stroia, through whose initiative this book came to life."

Chapter III, on page 89, includes the following paragraph:

"One of the eyewitnesses, Stanciu Stroia, recalls that the Merezi Hill was located 8–900 meters East of his house: 'For two weeks I witnessed those heroic events [...] One evening, around 21 or 22 hours, on August 25th, as I was visiting the town hall inquiring about the progress of the war, I overheard the notary receiving a telephone order to evacuate the local population westward. Quickly running home, I delivered the big announcement [...] The Hungarian gendarmes were trying to enforce the citizens' evacuation of their homes, but nobody left the village. People sneaked through their yards bordering the mountains, and climbed along the river edges to the high plains, where every family owned a small cabin. The doors to the village houses were left wide open, with plenty of food inside for the Romanian soldiers expected to occupy the town soon."

3 Ioan Ciupea, Florentin Olteanu, Andreea Dobeș-Fürtös and Robert Fürtös, historians specialized in the Romanian anti-Communist resistance, describe in the soon-to-be-published book titled *Făgăraș Fortress: The Policemen Prison (1950–1960),* the remarkable life and personality of Dr. Stanciu Stroia. The details of the text were not available at the time of this publication.

Professor Florentin Olteanu, president of the Negru Vodă Foundation in Făgăraș, also conducted an impromptu experiment among local high school students in December 2004, regarding events that took place half a century ago. When asked what she knew about Dr. Stanciu Stroia, Gabriela Nițurat, an eleventh grader, responded, "He was a humble man, one you could easily talk to, one you could trust. He was among the best doctors in town, who understood and helped his patients, even if that meant a house call in the middle of the night." Mrs. Sanda Oanță, a retired teacher interviewed as well, concluded, "He was a good man, a good doctor, and a good Romanian."

Bibliography with Excerpts 249

4 Together with Virgiliu Țârău, Professor Ioan Ciupea is currently working on another project titled *University of Cluj Faculty in the Political Life*, which will present Dr. Stanciu Stroia's story in a chapter dedicated to the victims of the Communist repression. Valuable data newly obtained from the Securitate Archives in Bucharest is included in this volume, which is due for publication in 2006.

5 Ion Gavrilă-Ogoranu, a former partisan who fought in the Făgăraș Mountains and survived the Securitate's manhunt, lists Dr. Stanciu Stroia among the individuals, partisans and supporters, implicated in the anti-communist resistance. The author includes Dr. Stroia's photograph on page 355 (volume II) and on page 25 (volume IV) of the book titled: *Pine Trees Break, They Do Not Bend.*

The caption in the photo section of volume II urges the following:
"Nobody should be left unmentioned [...] Every [anti-Communist] needs to be dedicated a few lines, brought back into our memory, as it is the only chance he has left in this world."

The cover of volume IV depicts a commemorative marble cross with Dr. Stanciu Stroia's name engraved in the center. The Association of Former Political Detainees erected the memorial in 1995 next to the Sâmbăta Monastery, in Făgăraș County.

6 In their historical dictionary entitled *Sanctuaries of the Nation's Heroes: Monuments and Memorials in the Romanian Living Space*, Drs. Florian Tuca and Christache Gheorghe write on pages 146–147:

"The Monument of local World Wars I and II heroes has been erected in the center of the locality of [Fântânele, Sibiu County] at the initiative of Dr. Stanciu Stroia, with the contribution of the local population and the support of the National Ministry of Defense."

7 In *The Golden Book of the Village of Cacova/Fântânele*, Father Aurel Hărșan notes on page 110:
"Among the many papers donated to the parochial library [...] one letter-document [...] denotes the love, devotion and effort, the author [Dr.

Stanciu Stroia] of the imposing Heroes' Monument in Zăvoi and the Heroes' Grave in Augur, has put forth in the realization of these projects."

A photograph of Dr. Stroia is printed on page 137, and a testimonial by engineer Ilie Hanzu can be read on page 96:

"This community has always held in high esteem the church and the school [...] and has yielded outstanding personalities like that of Doctor Stanciu Stroia [...] whom we owe the creation of the monuments in Zăvoi and Augur."

8 In the volume titled *Twenty Years of Romanian Activity in the Cluj Medical Clinic I: 1919–1940*, Dr. Stanciu Stroia is listed on page 280, with a photograph on page 286, as science faculty and collaborator in Dr. Iuliu Hatieganu's clinic between 1928 and 1930:

"[...] contributing to the progress of Romanian medicine and science and the improved living conditions of Transylvania's peasants [...]"

9 Writer Cicerone Ionițoiu, the tireless researcher of Romania's anti-Communist movement, includes Dr. Stanciu Stroia's name in his remarkably comprehensive work *The Golden Book of Romania's Anti-Communist Resistance*. He makes the following note in volume III, on page 288:

"Stanciu Stroia, born on August 10, [1904], in Cacova, Sibiu County; former assistant professor of Medicine at the University of Cluj/Sibiu; internist in Făgăraș; arrested in 1951 and sentenced in 1952 to seven years for aiding partisans; detained in Făgăraș-Sibiu-Jilava-Aiud-Făgăraș-Aiud; released in [1957]."

10 In *Iuliu Hațieganu: Monograph*, Dr. Florea Marin, a member of the Romanian Academy, remarks on pages 352, 357, and 361:

"Professor I. Hațieganu chose his collaborators with outmost care; he selected them based on strict professional criteria, from former talented pupils and, seldom, if recommended by others. [...] He instilled into them the highest professional, scientific and ethical values. [...] When the professor judged that a young doctor's training was complete, he summoned him to his office, congratulated him on his performance, thanked him for his collaboration and suggested to him the founding of his own internal medicine department in a regional hospital. [...] Many trainees became specialists of the same calibre as their university professors [...] practicing in the great cities of Transylvania and beyond [...] Simultaneously, the apprentices influenced the venerable master to such a degree, that he acknowledged to them how much he owed them, without whom he never would have achieved anything. [...] Among the devoted collaborators of the great professor and his internal medicine clinic [...] was Dr. Stanciu Stroia, an attending from Făgăraș, between the years of 1928–1930."

11 In *Prisons of an Orthodox Priest*, Father Zosim Oancea recalls on pages 144 and 145 his first encounter with Dr. Stanciu Stroia within the prison walls of Aiud:

"I was soon returned to the second pavilion, in a larger room with bunker beds, different from the small cells I was accustomed to at Zarca.

'Welcome, Father!'

'Thanks, but....'

'Don't you recognize me?'

'I know your face, but I can't recall your name...'

'I'm Doctor Stroia of Făgăraș, the grandson of [Father Hanzu] from Cacova, Sibiu County.'

The doctor was sitting on a bed across the room from the spot reserved for me. As a veteran detainee, he followed the formal custom of introducing me to all the cell's inhabitants, starting with the men located next to me, a distinguished group of oil-magnates from Prahova Valley. [During the introduction] the entire room went silent.

'Doctor' I addressed Dr. Stroia after finishing a prayer. 'Could you provide me with the answers during the Holy Liturgy?'

'Certainly! You must come closer though, by the bunker beds on this side. Here, we're hidden from the peep-hole in the cell door.'

Thus took place the first Holy Liturgy, by all and for all, not in a whisper but in a quiet voice, from the bottom of our souls and in a bath of tears. In our new "Cathedral," I preached a few words of wisdom from the Gospel of the day. An ecumenical moment followed when the Catholic priests joined our Liturgy.

From that day on, we enjoyed a similar experience every morning, in addition to an Evangelical teaching, with explanations, questions and answers."

12 Mircea Păcurariu writes in *Sibiu Scholars of Past Times*, on page 511:
"Cacova [...] a beautiful village in Sibiu County, has gifted our country with a few individuals of great prestige: [...] like Dr. Stanciu Stroia (1904–1987), director of the Făgăraș [Regional] Hospital."

13 In *Liberty has the Face of God*, Victor Ioan Pica, another former anti-communist partisan, describes people who have sympathized with the rebel struggle and helped their cause. He writes in chapter 10 titled *The Forest is Brother with the Romanian*, on page 117, the following paragraph:
"In Făgăraș, a man the partisans trusted greatly was Doctor Stanciu Stroia. A true gentleman in every aspect of his conduct and a noble character, [...] he was a native of the Sibiu region and the son of a shepherd. Very competent in his profession [...] and of a high intellectual standard, he managed to gain the affection of every single peasant. His free time was often spent laboring in the fields, scythe and hoe in hand, alongside the farmers hired to cultivate his land.

With his carriage, pulled by an obedient and clever horse—a city sensation at the time, due to his ability to return home all by himself, safely keeping to the right side of the road—the doctor was busy running around town for business.

Nowadays, on the spot formerly occupied by the towering and hospitable house of Doctor Stroia, surrounded by its flower-filled gardens, lies a vacant terrain adjacent to a water dam. How many villagers walking by this meadow [...] know or remember the charitable figure that once graced this land?

'They took everything they could from me!' the doctor exclaimed upon his return from prison. 'But I refused to give them my soul!'

And he did not even deign to walk by his defiled house."

APPENDIX

The native *Romanian spelling* of place and personal names was preferentially chosen throughout the text (e.g., Basarabia versus Bessarabia, Dobrogea versus Dobruja) with the exception of popular terms, which are more recognizable in the English version (e.g., Bucharest instead of București or Transylvania rather than Transilvania).

A guide to *Romanian pronunciation*: ă is spoken like *a* in *a*bout, *a*way, or the *u* in h*u*rt; â and î are pronounced identically, approximately like *i* in f*i*ll or *o* in less*o*n (they have no true equivalent in the English language); ș is said like *sh* in *sh*ip or pu*sh*; ț is pronounced like *ts* in i*ts* or effor*ts,* and ci sounds like *chi* in *chi*n or *che* in *che*ap.

The *metric system* used by the author was preserved in the translation. The following conversion values are listed for the unfamiliar reader: 1 centimeter = 0.39 inch, 1 meter = 1.09 yard and 3.28 feet, 1 kilometer = 0.62 mile, 1 gram = 0.03 ounce, 1 kilogram = 2.20 pounds, 1 litre = 0.26 gallon, 1 hectare = 2.47 acres and 0° Celsius = 32° Fahrenheit.

ABOUT THE AUTHORS

Stanciu Stroia—Biographical Dates

- August 10, 1904—Born in Cacova, Transylvania, Romania.
- May 13, 1906—His father, Dumitru Stroia is murdered in Russia.
- 1926–1927—Elected president of the Cluj Medical Students' Association.
- April 1928—Graduates with honors from the University of Cluj Medical School.
- 1928—Publishes his doctoral dissertation *Radiotherapy in Basedow Disease*.
- October 28, 1928—Marries Valeria Grama, student at the Music Conservatory in Cluj.
- September 6, 1929—Son Zeno is born.
- 1928–1930—Serves as clinical assistant in internal medicine at the University of Cluj, under Professor Iuliu Hațieganu.
- 1932—First internal medicine specialist in Făgăraș and founder of the internal medicine department at Făgăraș Regional Hospital.
- June 12, 1933—Daughter Lucia (Tita) is born.
- 1945—Elected director of the Făgăraș Regional Hospital.
- 1945—Refuses to join the Romanian Communist Party.
- May 1949—Relieved of his functions as social services president and hospital director after labeled undesirable by the Communists.
- 1950–1951—Refuses to work as an informer and is the object of permanent surveillance by the Securitate.

- April 30, 1951—Arrested for "helping and not denouncing anti-Communist partisans."
- January 8, 1952—Sentenced to six years in prison for "favoring the crime of plotting against the Romanian state."
- 1953—His family is evicted from their private property, his estate is nationalized, his medical practice confiscated, and his house later demolished.
- December 1952—Transferred to Aiud Penitentiary via a triage in Jilava prison.
- 1953–1954—Falls ill with scurvy and is denied medical care.
- November 1956—His sentence is arbitrarily increased by another year.
- March-June 1957—Incarcerated at Făgăraș Castle.
- December 6, 1957—Released and threatened with re-arrest if he were to disclose his experience.
- March 23, 1958—His mother Iosefina Stroia passes away.
- 1958—Forbidden to practice medicine in Făgăraș; relocates to the under-served city of Ilia, Hunedoara County.
- June 1966—Granted political and judicial rehabilitation at his request.
- December 31, 1968—Retires from medical practice.
- 1969—Moves to Bucharest, close to his daughter and grandchildren, and spends the summers in Cacova, where he offers free medical consultations.
- October 14, 1975—Valeria Stroia, his wife of forty-seven years, passes away.
- 1971–1975—Out of his initiative, a mass grave of fallen World War I Romanian soldiers is restored on Merezi Hill.

- 1975–1978—With substantial personal funding, a monument honoring World War I and World War II village heroes is erected in Cacova.
- 1979—Begins writing his prison memories despite being monitored by the Securitate.
- 1982—Provides editorial contribution to the historical book titled: *The Battle of Sibiu-Cîineni: September 1916*.
- 1986—Finishes writing his memories.
- July 29, 1987—Passes away in Bucharest at the age of 83, seven months after the death of his son-in-law, Dr. Liviu Duşleag.
- December 22, 1989—A popular uprising ends the Communist dictatorship in Romania.

Dan L. Duşleag was born in 1966, in Bucharest, Romania, as Stanciu Stroia's only grandson. He refused to join the Communist party when pressured in 1984 and rejected the Securitate's efforts to recruit him as an informer in 1985. He was denied a passport and was forbidden from leaving the country as a consequence. An active participant in the December 1989 anti-Communist revolution and the ensuing student demonstrations ending in a violent crackdown, he became disillusioned with the slow progress of democratic reforms in Romania. A graduate of the University of Bucharest Medical School, he immigrated to the United States in 1990 and completed his pediatric training at the University of Chicago and the University of Illinois in 1998. He is a board-certified pediatrician and a clinical assistant professor at the Indiana University School of Medicine. Author of research studies in medical journals and a history enthusiast, this is his first venture into book publishing.

INDEX

The following is an index of names and places, political, historical, religious, medical, and general terminology. When a person's first name is missing in the text and is unidentifiable, the individual's title or position is noted next to the last name. Dr. Stanciu Stroia's immediate family members mentioned in the manuscript are listed under their first names.

A

Administrative punishment 176
Agnita 53
Aiud 12, 22, 26, 36, 38, 41, 46, 57, 63, 71, 72, 75, 76, 77, 99, 100, 101, 102, 104, 108, 110, 111, 119, 121, 122, 128, 135, 139, 140, 141, 142, 144, 150, 151, 152, 153, 154, 156, 162, 165, 168, 170, 171, 175, 176, 178, 180, 182, 215, 227, 230, 239, 247, 250, 251
Aiud railway station 152
Alaska Wing 119, 146
Alba County 102
Alba Iulia 64
Alexandrescu, Grigore 70
Alexandrescu, Lieutenant 42, 43
Alina (Dușleag, Alina) 188, 195
Allied Tehran Conference 5
Allies 191
Allies Control Commission 162, 163
Ambrus, Petre 78

America (see U.S., U.S.A., United States) 4, 12, 20, 161, 224, 241, 244
American/Americans 4, 5, 14, 16, 19, 144
Animal Farm 9, 243
Anti-Communism 16, 39
Anti-Communist 6, 11, 19, 32, 33, 35, 43, 75, 102, 106, 152, 156, 179, 221, 222, 223, 238, 239, 241, 248, 249, 250
Anti-intellectualism 12
Anti-Semitism 39
Anti-Soviet 62, 63, 121, 147, 239
Antonescu, Ion 3, 39
Apuseni Mountains 148
Arad 53, 107, 176, 235
Archpriests 137
Ardeal (see Transylvania) 53, 58
Argeș River 59
Army Corps, 7th 50
Army, German 52
Army, Polish 166
Army, Red 4, 5, 180

Army Reserves 59
Army, Romanian 26, 28, 33, 39, 54, 55, 115, 146, 194, 225, 236
Army, Soviet 52, 78
Asia 2, 54
Association of Former Political Detainees 17, 102, 249
Astra Petroleum Society 137, 162
Atanasiu, Victor 194, 244, 247
Attila 25
Augur 189, 191, 250
Aurel, Dan 193
Auschwitz 107
Ausgleich 25
Austria 25, 28, 101, 191
Austria-Hungary 25, 191
Austrian/Austrians 25, 63, 64, 101, 191
Austrian-Hungarian 64, 101, 191
Autocracy 19
Axis 3

B

Baia Sprie 128, 130
Băile Bazna 127, 128
Băița 79
Bakaiew, Colonel 164
Balaj, Cornel 50, 51, 145
Băldescu, Radu 54, 55
Balkans 2, 3, 5, 63, 242
Balthes, Melita 45
Banat 33, 54, 156, 191
Banat Mountains 33
Banat Swabians 54
Bandit 11, 155, 186

Bărăgan 176
Bârsan, Gheorghe 66, 143, 222
Basarabia 3, 4, 66, 78, 79, 110, 165, 216, 228, 230, 233
Beclean 146, 228, 234, 235, 236
Beligan, Grigore 183
Berlin 54
Bethlen, Count 103
Bethlen, Istvan 103
Bible 134
Bica, Gheorghe 68, 222
Black Sea 46, 51, 52, 103, 113, 155, 172, 223, 225, 227
Black Shirts 106
Blitzkrieg 166
Bogățean, Captain 132
Boițeanu, Ana 238, 239
Bolintinul din Vale 59, 60
Bolshevik 4
Bordeianu, Ion 78
Borzaș, Frosina and Joji 218
Borzești 223
Botoșani 227, 239
Bottom of hell 40
Bourgeois/Bourgeoisie 42, 48, 71, 121
Brașov (Kronstadt) 38, 41, 53, 54, 106, 162, 166, 170, 184, 190, 225, 226, 227, 228, 229, 230, 234, 235, 236, 247
Brebenaru, Gheorghe 218
British 5, 121
Brotea, Alexandru 145, 225
Bucharest 2, 35, 51, 57, 59, 64, 72, 79, 99, 102, 103, 108, 110, 116, 121,

135, 147, 176, 182, 188, 190, 192, 193, 194, 195, 222, 225, 238, 239, 241, 242, 243, 244, 249
Bucharest Architecture Institute 193
Bucharest Commercial Academy 222
Bucharest Polytechnic Institute 35, 79
Bucharest Theological Institute 135
Bucovina 3, 4, 191, 231
Budapest 25, 26, 28, 53, 103
Bulgaria 3
Butunoiu, Marius 193

C

Cacova 5, 13, 21, 22, 27, 29, 31, 41, 59, 114, 129, 135, 148, 171, 174, 181, 188, 189, 190, 192, 193, 194, 215, 219, 222, 235, 245, 249, 250, 251, 252
Cahul 79
Calciu-Dumitreasa, Gheorghe 196
Caleţeanu, General 55
Câmpulung-Moldovenesc 239
Cantacuzino Hospital 183
Cantacuzino Institute 147, 239
Capătă, Captain 218
Capitalist 6, 9
Caracal 53
Caragiale, Ion Luca 70
Carol I (see Karl I) 59, 99
Carol II 59, 60
Carpathian Mountains (see Transylvanian Alps) 26, 53
Casina Romana 68
Catholic 25, 137, 138, 252

Ceauşescu, Nicolae 10, 80
Central Military Hospital 59
Central Military Medical Laboratory 147
Central Military Museum 190, 193
Central Powers 191
Central Romania 13
Chains 105, 114, 116, 130, 153
Chihaia, Viola 218
Chişinău 103
Christ 136, 167
Christendom 2
Christian 27, 173, 190, 195
Christianity 2, 39
Christmas 26, 27, 100, 118, 173, 216
Churchill, Winston 4
Cincul Mare 68, 227
Cindrel Peak 26
Ciocănelea, Traian 167
Ciupea, Ioan 63, 169, 221, 226, 236, 245, 248, 249
Cluj (Klausenburg) 54
Cluj Medical Students' Society 63, 74
Clujul Medical 67
Codlea 223, 224
Codreanu, Corneliu Zelea 39
Codrescu, Andrei 13, 241, 242
Collectivization 5, 243
Communism 1, 6, 9, 10, 16, 17, 18, 19, 33, 39, 55, 178, 226, 242, 244
Communist 5, 6, 9, 10, 11, 12, 13, 15, 16, 17, 18, 19, 32, 33, 35, 43, 50, 52, 57, 60, 61, 62, 67, 71, 75, 76, 79, 102, 104, 106, 121, 136, 145, 152, 156, 160, 169, 179, 180, 181, 186, 193,

194, 215, 216, 221, 222, 223, 225, 226, 236, 238, 239, 241, 242, 248, 249, 250
Conditional Time Law 172
Constanța 52, 53, 163, 228, 230, 233, 235
Constante, Lena 13, 122, 145, 242
Cornea, Doina 222
Cornea, Gheorghe 66
Crainic, Nichifor 103
Craiova Treaty 3
Cristian, Nicolae 188
Cuza, Alexandru Ioan 59
Czitrom, Alice 181

D

Dâmboiu, Victor 145, 223, 225
Damocles Sword 186
Dan (Dușleag, Dan) 20, 129, 188, 189, 193, 195, 215
Danube 36, 54, 147,
Danube-Black Sea Canal 46, 51, 103, 113, 155, 223, 225, 227
Death canal (see Danube-Black Sea Canal) 155
Democracy 6, 18, 19, 169, 236
Democratic 13, 19, 33, 67, 132, 160, 222, 223
Detroit 222, 233
Deutsche Mark 138
Deva 171
Diaconescu, Constantin 12, 145, 147, 149
Division, 16th Mounted 59

Division, 18th Infantry 54, 55
Dobrogea 3, 4, 117, 120, 172
Doctor, Remus 114, 115, 222, 229
Don River 22
Donbas 144
Dordea, Mircea 223, 229
Dorobanțu, Captain 142
Drăghici, Alexandru 141
Drăguș 223, 228, 229, 230, 233, 234
Dridif 161, 217, 228, 231, 233, 235
Dual Monarchy 25
Duma, Major 156
Dutch 118

E

East 2, 61, 64, 216, 244, 248
Easter 27, 28, 29, 31, 56
Eastern European 2, 6, 10, 15, 152, 180
Eisenhower, Dwight 5
English 15, 133, 134, 241
Eremia, Ion 12, 145
Europe 2, 6, 12, 15, 238, 241, 242, 244
European 2, 3, 6, 10, 15, 60, 152, 180
Ex-minister(s) 75, 101, 103

F

Făgăraș 13, 31, 33, 34, 35, 36, 37, 42, 45, 46, 48, 55, 57, 58, 59, 62, 65, 66, 67, 70, 71, 72, 73, 74, 76, 77, 78, 102, 112, 117, 122, 143, 144, 159, 161, 162, 164, 166, 167, 168, 169, 171, 173, 175, 178, 180, 182, 183, 184, 215, 217, 218, 221, 222, 223, 225,

226, 227, 228, 229, 230, 231, 232, 233, 234, 235, 236, 238, 245, 247, 248, 249, 250, 251, 252
Făgăraş Castle 162, 167, 168, 169, 223, 231, 236, 238
Făgăraş County 37, 58, 59, 62, 66, 73, 76, 169, 221, 222, 223, 225, 249
Făgăraş Regional Hospital 13, 58, 67, 143, 144, 166, 169, 252, 255
Fascism 6
Fascist 3, 34, 39, 63
Feldioara 184, 226, 227, 229, 231
Ferdinand 60
Firlej, Antoni 166
Flacăra 193
Flanders 54
Forced Labor 46, 53, 54, 77, 103, 113, 128, 135, 144, 176, 225
France 166, 191, 230
French 16, 134, 141

G

Galaţi 99, 110, 223, 228, 231, 233, 235
Ganea, Gheorghe 182
Gangster 48
Gavrilă-Ogoranu, Ion 33, 37, 78, 245, 249
Genocide, Communist (see Red Holocaust) 16
German/Germans 3, 4, 5, 6, 26, 45, 47, 48, 51, 52, 53, 54, 55, 61, 62, 64, 78, 137, 138, 141, 142, 145, 164, 166, 189, 194, 222
German Migration 53
German-Soviet non-aggression pact 3

Germany 3, 4, 52, 54, 63, 138, 142, 166, 191
Ghelar 186
Gheorghe Lazăr high school 68
Gheorghiu-Dej, Gheorghe 11
Gherla 46, 99, 100, 225, 226, 229, 230, 231, 232, 234, 235, 238, 239
Giroşanu, Horea 193
God 9, 10, 15, 21, 27, 41, 60, 121, 128, 136, 151, 159, 170, 177, 179, 181, 195, 196, 224, 252
Godeanu, Gavrilă 189
Godeanu, Vasile 189
Goga, Octavian 64, 65
Goma, Paul 222
Good Samaritan 129
Grama, Letiţia 218
Grama, Vincenţiu 160
Grave cell 40, 43, 46
Great Britain 4, 5
Greavu, Lae 45, 222
Greece 172
Greek 137, 155, 239
Greek Catholic 137
Grind 46
Gruia, Gheorghe 192
Gulags 12, 238

H

Habsburg Empire 25, 54
Hanzu, Alexandru 28, 29
Hanzu, Ana 28
Hanzu, Ioan Jr. 138, 190, 191, 245, 251
Hanzu, Ioan Sr. 28

Hărşan, Aurel 219, 245
Haţieganu, Iuliu 69, 185, 245, 246, 250, 255
Heroes' Grave 189, 192, 250
Heroes' Monument 194, 250
Heroin 37
Hippocrates 155, 156
Hippocratic Oath 14, 155
Hitler, Adolf 3, 4, 54, 63
Hohenzollern-Sigmaringen 59
Genocide, Communist (see Red Holocaust) 16, 221
Holy Roman Empire 101
Hula Săcelului (see Săcel) 171
Hunedoara 50, 168, 185
Hungarian/Hungarians 25, 26, 28, 64, 101, 102, 103, 106, 152, 153, 176, 177, 190, 191, 222, 248
Hungarian Uprising 152
Hungary 3, 6, 25, 53, 63, 101, 152, 153, 154, 156, 157, 169, 191
Hunger 6, 12, 13, 102, 139, 145, 149, 150, 173
Hunger strike 149, 150, 173
Hunger swelling 145

I

Iacob, Teodor 192
Iancu de Hunedoara 168
Iaşi 61, 62, 150, 226, 227, 229, 231, 232, 233
Iaşi Medical School 61
Ilia 50, 51, 77, 107, 124, 138, 159, 171, 182, 183, 185, 186, 187, 188, 235

Ilia Polyclinic 50
Ilia Regional Tribunal 187
Imperialist 11, 121
Independence War against Turkey 64, 160, 178
Independenţa Factory 193
Informer/Informers 6, 32, 45, 47, 78, 107, 112, 114, 115, 116, 117, 122, 154, 159, 168
Internal Medicine 13, 58, 67, 68, 115, 116, 185, 186, 251
Ionescu, Alexandru 145, 239
Ionescu, Mircea 247
Iorga, Nicolae 39
Iriminoiu, Ghiţă 115, 116
Iron Cross 54
Iron Curtain 4
Iron Guard 39, 62, 63, 75, 99, 101, 102, 104, 107, 111, 122, 123, 155
Islam 2
Italian 16
Italy 3, 63
Ivan's Boot 5

J

Japan 3, 144
Jewish 16, 222
Jibou 182
Jilava 46, 55, 99, 100, 215, 223, 228, 230, 232, 239, 250

K

Karl I (see Carol I) 59

killinger, Manfred von 51
Kohler, Magistrate 132
Krebs 26

L

Lalu, Ioan 22
Lang, Professor 141
Latin 62, 68, 70, 126, 189
Latin maxim 62, 68, 70
Lead and copper mines 128
League of Nations 2
Legion of the Archangel Michael (see Iron Guard) 39
Lenin, Vladimir Ilyich 6, 114, 216
Leningrad 141, 142
Levi, Clara 218
Ligia (Corovei (b. Stroia), Ligia) 188, 195
Lisa 76, 227, 228, 229, 230, 232, 233, 234, 235, 236
Litan, Gaia 218
Liturgy 136, 251, 252
Liviu (Duşleag, Liviu) 159, 188, 195, 215, 219, 257
Los Angeles 223
Lower Rhine 54
Luca, Vasile 121
Lupaş, Toma 194

M

Macedonian/Macedonians 117, 120, 172, 174
Magazin Istoric 193
Magyar/Magyars 25, 53
Magyar Kingdom, 53
Magyarize, 25
Malinowsky, Marshal 164, 165
Man of Steel (see Stalin) 11
Maniu, Iuliu 131
Maramureş 128, 185
Mărăşeşti 194
Maria Theresa 101, 168
Marinescu, Floricel 10
Marinescu, Gheorghe 56
Marx, Karl 6
Mârza, Vasile 61
Mateiaş 225, 227
Mateiaş, Virgil 222, 231, 246
Mazilu, Nicolaie 34, 35, 37, 217, 222, 231
Mediaş 53
Mercea, Pavel 193
Merezi Hill 189, 190, 193, 194, 248
Mezei, Gheorghe 42, 43, 47
Michael the Brave 54, 168
Michael the Brave Order 54
Michael, King 3, 4, 5, 59, 60, 165, 216
Miclăuş, Coman 193
Milas, Achile 239
Military Academy, Bucharest 194
Military Arts Studio 193
Military Instruction Center 55
Ministry of Buildings and Facilities 161
Ministry of Health 65, 66, 185
Ministry of Internal Affairs 55, 71, 72, 75, 77, 99, 116, 141, 171, 176
Ministry of Labor 65, 187
Ministry of Military Affairs 194

Mircea the Old 58
Mitulescu, Nicolae 239
Moga, Aurel 68
Mogoş, Ioan 35, 37, 222
Moldova 61, 78, 185, 244
Molotov, Vyacheslav 3
Monarchy 1, 5, 25, 60, 106
Morse 71, 111, 133, 156
Moscow Percentage Agreement 4
Munteanu, Vasile 76, 222
Mureşanu, Andrei 178

N

National Liberal Party 1, 108, 222
National Museum of Transylvanian History 221
National Peasant Party 1, 131, 223
Nazi/Nazis 3, 52, 63, 142
Nedelcu, Ioan 218
Negoiu 74, 76, 77, 158
New York City 165
Niculescu, Agent 78
Nisipeanu, Florica 190
Nistru (Dniestr) 61
Nomenklaturists 6
Non-commissioned officer 52
North Korea 104
Northern Bucovina 3
Northern Romania 128, 148
Northern Transylvania 3, 63
Northwestern Europe 15

O

Oancea, Zosim 135, 136, 145, 222, 232, 246, 251
Oceacov 61, 63
Ocnele Mari 121, 122
Officers' School 55
Ohaba 76, 227, 228, 229, 231, 232, 234, 235
Oil (see petroleum) 2, 3, 4, 107, 137, 251
Oituz 194
Olt 65, 189, 192, 229
Oltenia 147
Olteţ 41, 45, 228, 230, 231, 232, 235
Oneşti 223
Opriţoiu, Petre 218
Oradea 53, 64, 153
Orăştie 52
Orhei 78, 79
Orthodox 27, 28, 39, 55, 135, 136, 167, 173, 187, 190, 195, 223, 225, 251
Orthodox Church 167, 187, 195
Orwell, George 9, 243
Ottoman 54, 64

P

Pădureni 37
Pann, Anton 178
Paramilitary 39, 106
Paratyphoid fever 163
Parhon Endocrinology Institute 182
Parhon, Constantin I. 61
Paris 2, 4, 63, 74, 166, 230
Paris of the Balkans 2

Paris, Peace Treaty of 4, 63
Paris, The Little 2
Partisans (see rebels) 32, 33, 35, 43, 56, 71, 73, 74, 76, 77, 157, 222, 223, 239, 249, 250, 252
Pascal, Maria 78, 80
Pătrășcanu, Lucrețiu 121
Pauker, Ana 121
Pavlovian 141
Pearl Harbor 3
People's Council 160
Pereni, Coriolan 217
Periprava 46, 135
Persona non grata 216
Petroleum (see oil) 2, 137, 162
Pica, Victor Ioan 222, 233, 246, 252
Piłsudski, Józef 166
Pitești 223
Ploiești 4, 148, 235
Poarta Albă 223
Poland 166
Policemen prison 236, 248
Polish 165, 166, 167
Political detainee(s) 13, 17, 76, 102, 132, 135, 143, 145, 172, 186, 221, 223, 236, 247, 249
Pop, Alexandru 70
Pop, Jean 222, 233
Popa, Coman 191
Popa, Ioan 192
Popescu-Doreanu, Nicolae 69, 218
Poplaca 154
Popular Republic 5, 52
Potts Disease 137

Prayer 136, 183, 217, 251
Presse Medicale 67, 141
Prime-secretary 186, 187
Prisoners' Act 106, 172
Prisons of an Orthodox Priest 136, 251
Pro-German 62
Pro-Hitler 54
Proletariat 6
Pronatalism 9
Pro-Russian 61
Prussian 59
Prut River 78
Purge 12, 16, 221, 223
Purice, Simfora 217

R

Rabin 218
Radio Free Europe 12, 238
Radiology 13, 116, 138, 147
Rafael, Elena 239
Râmnicu-Vâlcea 126
Rășinari 65
Rats 40, 41, 107
Răulea, Emilia 192, 193
Râușor 45, 112, 160, 161, 218, 222, 223, 226, 227, 228, 229, 231, 232, 233, 234
Rebels (see partisans) 33, 74, 76
Regional Medical Association 183
Rehabilitation 157, 187
Reproduction Control 9
Resettlement Program 80
Ribbentrop, Joachim von 3
Rieger Factory 24

Rizea, Elisabeta 239
Roentgen 160, 184
Roman Catholic 25, 137
Romania 1, 2, 3, 4, 5, 10, 12, 13, 16, 17, 26, 33, 46, 51, 52, 53, 59, 60, 62, 63, 64, 75, 102, 103, 108, 128, 131, 137, 147, 148, 166, 172, 178, 180, 189, 191, 195, 221, 223, 226, 241, 242, 243, 244, 245, 247, 250
Romanian/Romanians 1, 2, 3, 4, 5, 6, 9, 10, 11, 12, 13, 16, 19, 22, 25, 26, 28, 32, 33, 35, 38, 39, 52, 53, 54, 55, 58, 59, 60, 61, 62, 63, 64, 65, 68, 70, 74, 75, 78, 101, 103, 106, 108, 110, 115, 116, 121, 122, 134, 135, 138, 141, 142, 143, 145, 146, 147, 150, 152, 160, 162, 164, 165, 167, 176, 177, 178, 179, 180, 186, 189, 193, 194, 195, 215, 221, 222, 223, 225, 226, 236, 239, 242, 243, 244, 247, 248, 249, 250, 252
Romanian Academy 103, 250
Romanian Marseillaise 178
Romanian Medical Academy 68
Romans 68
Rome 137
Roosevelt, Franklin D. 4
Roşca, Ion 45, 46, 222
Roşiorii de Vede 42
Rostov 22, 23
Rudenko, Colonel 163
Rupea 225, 227, 229
Russia 22, 26, 27, 52, 142, 191
Russians 145, 162, 163, 164, 180, 242

Russification 5

S

Săcel (see Hula Săcelului) 48
Sadoveanu, Mihail 134
Saint Mary 27
Saint Nicholas 26, 173
Saint Ephraim 136
Saints Peter and Paul 27
Sălişte 25, 164, 194
Sâmbăta de Sus 175, 226, 227, 228, 229, 230, 231, 232, 233, 234
Santayana, George 18
Satu Mare (Sathmar) 54
Saxon/Saxons 47, 53, 54, 62, 127, 137, 144
Scrob, Gheorghe 148
Scurvy 26, 116, 129, 141, 144, 146, 149, 155, 169, 172, 182, 183, 185, 186
Second Vienna Award (see Vienna Dictate) 3, 63
Secret police (see Securitate) 11, 31, 77
Securitate (see secret police) 10, 11, 31, 32, 33, 34, 35, 37, 38, 40, 41, 42, 43, 44, 45, 48, 50, 55, 57, 70, 71, 72, 74, 76, 77, 79, 80, 110
Sedria orphanage 23
Semenic Mountains 156
Sevastopol 52, 54, 55
Siberia 216, 246
Sibiel 22, 135, 233
Sibiu (see Hermannstadt) 23, 24, 25, 26, 28, 29, 38, 39, 40, 41, 42, 46, 47, 48, 50, 52, 54, 56, 57, 65, 68, 74, 99,

135, 144, 152, 153, 154, 155, 156, 159, 164, 165, 170, 171, 175, 179, 180, 181, 188, 191, 193, 194, 215, 222, 223, 229, 230, 231, 232, 233, 234, 235, 244, 245, 247, 249, 250, 251, 252
Sibiu Courthouse 50, 57
Sibiu Garrison 193
Sibiu Independența Factory 193
Sibiu Military Tribunal 74, 152, 154, 156
Sibiu Penitentiary 40, 50, 52, 99
Siebenbürger 54
Sighișoara (Schässburg) 53, 54, 175, 176, 230
Simeria 171, 193
Șinca Nouă 227, 229, 232, 233, 235
Slavic 61, 165, 222
Snagov, Lake 51
Socol, Silviu 34, 35, 36, 37, 222, 234
Sonea, Octavian 146
Southeast Russia 22, 52
Southern Basarabia 79
Southern Romania 147
Soviet/Soviets 3, 4, 5, 6, 11, 12, 13, 32, 33, 51, 52, 54, 55, 62, 63, 69, 78, 79, 121, 132, 147, 152, 163, 164, 165, 180, 216, 221, 238, 239
Soviet Union 3, 4, 5, 11, 32, 54, 79, 180
Split 166
Stalin, Joseph 4, 5, 11, 13, 15, 56, 216, 242
Stalingrad 4
Stalinist 13, 17, 152
Stanciu, Lucian 76, 222

Ștefănescu, Agent 78
Stela (Stroia (b. Băcilă), Stela) 79, 181, 195
Stroia, Dumitru 22
Stroia, Ioan 222
Stroia, Iosefina 23, 27, 136, 256
Stroia, Mitică 26, 152
Stroia, Ștefan 28
Sturza, Lieutenant Colonel 59
Supreme Court 108
Swabians 54
Swiss 38
Switzerland 5

T

Tache, Lieutenant 38, 175
Tarciniu 126, 127, 128
Tartar 168
Techirghiol Resort 67
Teiuș 132, 179
Ten Commandments 40
Teodosiu, Captain 32
Țeposu Emil 235
Terrorists 11
The Battle of Sibiu-Cîineni 194, 247, 257
The Capital 67
The Communist Manifesto 67
The Ordeal 102
The Silent Escape 122, 242
The Sworn Brotherhood 36
Theology 45, 137
Third Reich 4, 53
Timișoara (Temeswar) 54
Timișoara Court of Appeal 126

Tiraspol 61
Tisa 28
Tissot 38
Tita (Duşleag (b. Stroia), Lucia) 79, 80, 158, 159, 163, 181, 188, 195, 255
Titulescu, Nicolae 2
Toderiţa 37, 226, 227, 229, 230, 232, 233, 235, 236
Transhumance 22
Transylvania (see Ardeal) 3, 4, 13, 22, 25, 53, 54, 58, 62, 63, 64, 65, 101, 102, 164, 173, 175, 176, 189, 190, 191, 222, 242, 243, 247, 250, 251
Transylvanian 53, 54, 103, 106, 111, 176, 221, 225
Transylvanian Alps (see Carpathian Mountains) 53
Transylvanian Saxons 53, 54
Tuberculosis 65, 66, 73, 109, 137, 138, 169
Turda 80, 234
Turkey 60, 64, 160, 178
Turkish Empire 53
Turkish invasions 2, 64, 168
Turtoi 139
Typhus Exanthematicus 61

U

U.S. (see America, United States, U.S.A.) 33, 121, 222
U.S.A. (see America, United States, U.S.) 228, 230, 233
Ucea 184, 227, 228, 230, 231, 233, 235, 236
Ujbea Mountain 24
Ukraine 78, 145
Ukrainian 56, 61, 164
United Nations 2
United States (see America, U.S., U.S.A.) 4, 223, 225, 257
University of Bucharest 116
University of Cluj 63, 79, 115, 117, 148, 165, 218, 249, 250
University of Leningrad 141
Uranium mines 144
Urdea, Bebe 218
Urdea-Slătinaru, Gheorghe, 222, 246
Utopia 6, 9

V

Văcăreşti 153, 228, 234, 235
Vâlcea Regiment 189
Valea Neagră 223
Valy (Stroia (b. Grama), Valeria) 14, 26, 135, 159, 160, 161, 188, 222, 255, 256
Vespers 136
Veştem 68
Vienna 3, 25, 28, 62, 63, 103
Vienna Dictate (see Second Vienna Award) 3, 62, 63, 103
Vinţul de Jos 171
Virgin Mary 224, 225
Viştea 76, 184, 226, 227, 229, 230, 231, 232, 234, 235, 236
Voice of America 12
Voinescu, Boldur 108

W

Wagner, Richard 111
Wake up, Romanian 178
Weil, Simone 16
West 2, 5, 52, 54, 64, 138, 165, 242
West Germany 52, 54, 138
Western/Westerner 2, 5, 6, 12, 15, 33, 54, 176
Wood, Neal 18, 244
World War I 1, 3, 5, 16, 26, 33, 54, 55, 59, 61, 63, 64, 65, 139, 144, 148, 163, 189, 191, 192, 193, 194, 216, 222, 223, 225, 243, 247
World War II 1, 3, 5, 16, 33, 54, 55, 59, 61, 63, 65, 144, 192, 193, 216, 222, 223, 243
Wranghel, General 166

Y

Yalta 247
Yugoslav 143
Yugoslavia 36, 51, 143, 166

Z

Zarca 101, 124, 131, 251
Zăvoi 27, 193, 250
Zeno (Stroia, Zeno) 14, 35, 79, 80, 181, 195, 219, 255

978-0-595-34639-4
0-595-34639-1